HEALTH AND WELLNESS
IN THE RENAISSANCE AND ENLIGHTENMENT

D0146922

HEALTH AND WELLNESS
IN THE RENAISSANCE AND ENLIGHTENMENT

JOSEPH P. BYRNE

Health and Wellness in Daily Life
Joseph P. Byrne, Series Editor

 GREENWOOD

AN IMPRINT OF ABC-CLIO, LLC
Santa Barbara, California • Denver, Colorado • Oxford, England

Library of Congress Cataloging-in-Publication Data

Byrne, Joseph Patrick.
    Health and wellness in the Renaissance and Enlightenment / Joseph P. Byrne.
       pages cm. — (Health and wellness in daily life)
    Includes bibliographical references and index.
    ISBN 978–0–313–38136–2 (hard copy : alk. paper) — ISBN 978–0–313–38137–9 (ebook) 1. Health—History. 2. Mental health—History. 3. Medicine—History—15th century. 4. Medicine—History—19th century. 5. Public health—History. I. Title.
RA776.5.B97   2013
610.9—dc23   2013007961

ISBN: 978–0–313–38136–2
EISBN: 978–0–313–38137–9

17 16 15 14 13   1 2 3 4 5

This book is also available on the World Wide Web as an eBook.
Visit www.abc-clio.com for details.

Greenwood
An Imprint of ABC-CLIO, LLC

ABC-CLIO, LLC
130 Cremona Drive, P.O. Box 1911
Santa Barbara, California 93116-1911

This book is printed on acid-free paper ∞

Manufactured in the United States of America

Contents

Series Foreword

Communities have few concerns that are as fundamental as the health of their members. The United States' current concern for societal provision of health care is as much a political, ethical, economic, and social matter as it is a technical or "medical" one. Reflection on the history of health and medicine may help us to place our contemporary concerns in context, but it also shows how far humanity has come in being able and willing to provide for the highest levels of health and health care possible. It is a reminder, too, of the possibilities the future presents. Our culture believes in progress, but it is also aware that unforeseen challenges will continue to appear. Health and medicine are cultural as well as biological constructs, and we live each day with the constraints and opportunities that follow.

This series of seven monographs explores the courses that human health and medicine have taken from antiquity to the present day. Though far from being complete in their coverage, these volumes map out continuities and changes over time in a set of health and medical fields. Each author has taken on the same outline in order to allow the student of health, medicine, and history to discover conditions, beliefs, practices, and changes within a given period, but also to trace the same concerns across time and place. With this in mind, each volume contains chapters on, for example, healers, children's health and healing, occupational and environmental threats, and epidemic disease. To the extent possible, we authors have striven to emphasize the ways in which these have affected people in their daily lives, rather than viewing them through the lenses of the healers or their profession. These are designed not for the specialist scholar but for the younger and general student, as well as for the general public. Our hope is that these volumes constitute a small and very useful library of the history of health and medicine.

As editor, I have striven to bring on board authors who are medical historians as well as fine teachers who have the ability to transmit their knowledge in writing with the same enthusiasm they bring into the classroom. As an author, I am sharing the discoveries, the joys, and not least the challenges and frustrations that all of us have encountered in producing this series.

Joseph P. Byrne
Honors Program
Belmont University

CHAPTER 1

Factors in Early Modern Health and Medicine

FACTORS IN INDIVIDUAL HEALTH AND WELL-BEING

The notion that all people are created equal is a fine political and legal standard, but in terms of health and wellness it could not be further from the truth. Within every human community, however large or small, are a wide variety of health conditions. Some are a matter of birth and family, others depend upon the course of one's life, and still others emerge from specific historical circumstances.

Birth and Family

"We choose our friends but not our family," the old saying goes. One's bloodline provided a set of genetic traits and dispositions. In the age before our modern knowledge of genetics and disease, and compensating drugs and therapies, an inherited predisposition to alcoholism, sickle-cell anemia, poor eyesight, cancer, or crippling depression could mark one for life. In addition, one's mother provided not only genes but the prenatal environment for the child: Did she smoke, consume alcohol, eat a healthy diet? How old was she? Was she beaten or forced to perform difficult work while pregnant? Where in the birth order was the particular child? How helpful were the midwife and assistants at the birth? In each of the five cultures—the Aztecs, Chinese, Europeans, Muslims and Caribbean slaves—this volume highlights

Figure 1.1 A wealthy Dutch family celebrates the birth of a child. Two gentlemen remain discretely hidden behind a screen, while the midwife presents the new family member. Hieronymous Janssens (1624–1693). (Christie's Images/Corbis)

pregnant women, new mothers, and most infants were provided special care. After all, they were the future of the family and society, whether an empire or a plantation worked by slaves.

The "accident of birth" also determined where and when one was born, and into what social class. At that time it was not that one set of environmental challenges and opportunities was "better" than another, but that they were different. Rural and urban environments presented different opportunities and hazards. In Europe, for example, health care professionals and institutions such as orphanages and hospitals were urban phenomena, but the air, water, and food were often unhealthy. Infants in well-off families were often sent to nurse in the countryside where conditions were recognized as being healthier.

Within a society a family's social and economic class determined opportunity. Higher status might mean one could avoid hard physical labor, have a richer and more varied diet, ride a horse rather than walk, avoid epidemics by fleeing, afford appropriate medical care when needed, live in a more safe and secure residence, and likely retain and pass along one's privileged status to one's children. For one born into the lower classes, early life might be marked by hard physical labor and hazards, poor living quarters, poor diet, hygiene, and health care options, greater exposure to disease, and few options in charting one's future.

Of course, one was also born male or female. Across cultures and classes, girls tended to be less valued than boys; abandonment and even infanticide were far more likely to have girls as their victims. In general, men had more and more varied options in life, greater access to education, and control of wealth and resources. The family identity usually passed through the males, while women left their birth family and "married into" their husband's family, often taking their husband's family name. Even today we speak of the woman's father "giving away the bride" at a wedding. A woman was above all valued for reproduction, but the children would not be hers or her birth family's but belong to the father and his birth family, sharing his name and social identity.

The Course of One's Life

The early modern girl growing into womanhood faced few choices, whatever her class. Since fathers usually determined the fates of their daughters, with relatively few exceptions women became wives and mothers at an early age. The European, Chinese, and Islamic cultures kept especially tight reins, as the unattached young woman with neither husband nor guardian was deemed likely to be or become a prostitute. While some became nuns or household servants, the sixteenth-century Reformation ended the first option in much of Europe and the second always left the woman vulnerable to being fired or molested. Most women married within their birth status group. Outside of war, epidemics, and other environmental disasters, the greatest threat to the health and even lives of women in all cultures was pregnancy and childbirth.

Men tended to have more options in life than women, including some level of mobility, both social and geographic: even poor peasants could become wealthier peasants by hard work and a good marriage. Depending on class, men had many more occupational choices and could reasonably choose to remain rural or move to the nearest big town. The man's accomplishments as a hunter, warrior, apprentice, artist, or student really determined his—and his family's—status in the community. The higher one's status the greater were his opportunities to avoid the community's hazards or have access to its resources, or to move beyond it to improve his position. But there was also the matter of individual choice. We know that even the wealthiest modern

Americans can choose to endanger their health by avoiding a good diet, exercise, and medical checkups, while embracing junk foods, drugs, alcohol, or tobacco. The same was true in the early modern community: the larger and less traditional the community, the greater the freedom to go against the societal norms.

For the adult male and his family, good health depended on his wealth and status, occupation, choice of residence, access to healthy foods and clean water, personal habits of eating, drinking, and hygiene, and access to and choices in health care.

The Vagaries of History

Everyone has always been subject to the occasional accident: being hit by lightning, falling from a ladder, setting oneself on fire, or eating poisonous mushrooms. Such things may happen to king or serf, mature adult or child, man or woman. But sometimes the broader forces of history impinge on people and directly affect their health and well-being.

Warriors or soldiers suddenly descend on a small community and disrupt every aspect of life. Women are molested, and protesting husbands and fathers beaten or killed. Food and animals are stolen; crops and residences are destroyed; and local holy men are murdered out of religious hatred. Typhus, dysentery, plague, and venereal disease are left behind as the predators move on.

During the Reformation, Protestant leaders closed down Catholic female monasteries and convents in areas such as England, Holland, and northern Germany where they held sway. Women who had dedicated their lives to divine service were now cut adrift. Some sought and found new places of residence among secure communities of nuns in Catholic areas. Many, however, found husbands and took on the joys and hazards of childbirth and family.

We have several autobiographies of Africans enslaved before 1800, and each recounts the horrors of suddenly shifting from lives of freedom safe within their communities to becoming first captives, then prisoners, and then slaves in a strange and far-off land.

In Peru's highlands, far from any of the dimly rumored white men whose sudden appearance along the coastlines was both exciting and troubling, a village begins to suffer from a divine curse. Red blotches and fever blanket bodies of the very old and very young, killing them very quickly. The healthy and vigorous succumb until few are left to tend the sick. The gods are angry, the shamans confused, and the community terrorized, or simply destroyed. The virus—perhaps measles or smallpox—had been carried into the place not by the strange white men down on the coast but by a friend who had been the latest in a chain of contacts.

A natural disaster? An accident? Yes, but the historic moment that brought the men of Portugal and Spain, in search of knowledge and riches, touched off a perhaps unprecedented demographic catastrophe in which each life was utterly transformed by death or survival. Historical trends and forces determined the health and well-being of millions in the early modern world.

THE EARLY MODERN WORLD

An Age of Empires

The chronological period from roughly 1500 to 1800 was an era of empires. The African Songhai Empire, which had controlled populations from the mouth of the Gambia River to Lake Chad, fell to Muslim troops sent from Ottoman-controlled Morocco in 1589, ending the last of the great empires of the Sahel. The ensuing social disruption and political power vacuum invited the rule of local warlords and even more successful exploitation by Arab and European slavers.

The Aztecs were one of many groups of natives living in what is today Mexico. By the fourteenth century, they had established themselves as rulers over an empire that spread from coast to coast and from modern Nicaragua to the northern desert. Led by fierce warriors who preferred to capture their enemies and sacrifice them to their gods, they shared the stone-based technology with their neighbors and readily borrowed their arts of civilized living. Their capital of Tenochtitlán was a magnificent city of canals and perhaps 80,000 residents in the highland Valley of Mexico, which the Spaniards compared favorably with Italy's Venice. Aztec doom came early in our period, when the Spanish conquistador Hernán Cortés and fewer than 600 soldiers brought their guns, horses, and deadly diseases to the Aztec world and quickly claimed it for the Spanish Crown. Henceforth the Aztec Empire was the Spanish colony of New Spain, or colonial Mexico.

China experienced most of its Late Imperial period of the Ming (1368–1644) and Qing (ching, 1644–1911) dynasties during these three centuries. The emperor, who was said to have the "mandate of Heaven," ruled according to ancient traditions and through a court and a classically educated bureaucracy of civil servants. Their capital was Beijing (Peking), a city purported to have had 672,000 residents in a country of 110 million. The era was one of widespread prosperity and relative peace, with a national population that doubled or perhaps tripled in size. Cities grew as commerce thrived and material wealth increased for rich and poor alike. There was an increase of social mobility, and as Charlotte Furth put it, "of urbanization, the spread of a money economy, of the loosening of status boundaries, [and] of cultural experiment."[1]

Yet in many ways, China turned in on itself. As with the classicism of the sixteenth-century European Renaissance, Chinese intellectuals, including men of medicine, were focused backward on their national traditions (Neo-Confucianism). Printing was revitalized among the Chinese, with more and higher-quality works appearing. Literacy and the distribution of books were far from universal, but both were spreading further than in previous centuries. The revival of traditional Chinese cultural values known as Neo-Confucianism emphasized the wisdom of the ancients as well as benevolence: doing good for the benefit of others and society. This could mean the sponsoring of useful—including medical—books and the provision of medical care for the needy.

Unlike Renaissance Europeans, however, the Chinese had little use for the bits of Western culture that washed up on their shores and made few attempts to reach out from their Middle Kingdom. Some 800 Christian missionaries from Europe entered China between 1552 and 1795, but the religion made little headway. Certain imported goods were more welcome, including peanuts, corn, sweet potatoes, cinchona (quinine), tobacco, and opium.

The Islamic World was dominated by three early modern empires: the Ottoman Turks, the Safavids of Iran, and the Mughals in India. Since each developed the use of firearms and cannon to a high degree, they are often called the "gunpowder states." The Turkish Ottoman Empire had conquered Byzantine Constantinople in 1453, bringing to a formal end the thousand-year-old Christian empire. They continued their conquests in the Balkans, seizing Hungary and reaching Vienna by the 1680s. During the 1510s the Turks expanded their hegemony along the Mediterranean from Syria south through Egypt to North Africa. By 1520 the sultans controlled major capitals and trade centers such as Istanbul (former Constantinople), their capital, with perhaps 200,000 people in 1500, Damascus, Cairo, and Alexandria. Their empire straddled three continents. They saw themselves as the heirs of the ancient Roman emperors and great medieval caliphs. As recent conquerors they had to neuter their enemies and flaunt their own form of Muslim benevolence. The lives of the common folks remained largely untouched, and the vibrant intellectual life of medieval Islam remained a matter of past glory.

From 1501 the Muslim Safavid dynasty ruled an empire that lay between Mughal India and the Ottomans. It included parts or all of modern Iran, Iraq, Azerbaijan, Armenia, Georgia, and Afghanistan. Such a broad empire required a firm center point, and the rulers called themselves shahs and identified with the great ancient Persian empires. To defend their long borders they needed at least to match their surrounding Ottoman and Mughal rivals. Under Shah Abbas, in the early seventeenth century the state reorganized its military. He followed the effective Ottoman model of combining infantry with firearms, cavalry, and artillery. The Safavids' major cities included the venerable caravan trading centers of Isfahan and Herat, and their culture was closer kin to that of the steppe and mountain tribal folk of south-central Asia than to the civilizations of India or the Mediterranean.[2] Even so, much of their intellectual culture remained influenced by the Greek heritage absorbed by Islam in the tenth and eleventh centuries, and this included medicine.

In India, from 1526 the Mongol dynasty of the Muslim Mughals blended their Central Asian steppe traditions with the ancient, sophisticated, and wealthy Hindu urban civilization. They created a culture with magnificent written and visual expressions—the Taj Mahal comes to mind. Since this text does not engage this region, however, we shall leave it here.

Europe from its Renaissance through its Enlightenment hosted the Habsburg Empire, Russian Empire, Portuguese Empire, Spanish Empire, Dutch Seaborne Empire, British Empire, and Napoleon's short-lived French Empire. Each was aggressive both commercially and militarily. The French and the Habsburg rulers of Spain and the Holy Roman Empire fought in Italy for control of the peninsula for six decades (1494–1555), and Louis XIV battled endlessly for domination of bits and pieces along his frontier. They developed firearms, artillery, and the techniques of using them effectively, which gave them the advantage against all adversaries but each other. In Europe, the period opened with the Spanish destroying the last Iberian Muslim state, Granada, in 1492 and subsequently sponsoring Columbus's fateful voyage. In 1494 the French army of King Charles VIII bullied its way through Italy to retake (unsuccessfully) Naples from the Spaniards. The era ended with Napoleon's opening bid for domination of the entire continent. The real gains were to be grabbed at the rest of the world's expense, however, and every empire except the Austrian Habsburgs seized a share of Asia, Oceania, Africa, or the Americas for its own. The globe shrank as European sailing ships mastered the oceans and Europeans made claims on much of the world.

From 1492 Europeans conquered and colonized most of the Western Hemisphere. Huge swathes were depopulated by disease, and entire cultures disappeared. The enormous and well-organized empires of the Aztec and Inca in Latin America crumbled before tiny Spanish armies and waves of disease. As a terrible balancing, the kingdoms along the West African coast sold some 12 million of their subjects and neighbors into European colonial transatlantic slavery. European ships also brought the riches of Southern and East Asia and Oceania to their homelands and other colonies. In exchange they brought Christianity and Western technology, including effective firearms, navigational aids, and some aspects of Western medicine. From a world historical perspective, the era from Columbus to the French Revolution is usually considered the early modern period, the threshold to our own.

Europe's Brave New World

Contact with the world by sailing ship initiated and sustained exchanges of plants, animals, people, technologies, and ideas. Some of these were commercially traded, some stolen, some imposed by force, and some exchanged purely by accident, as with infectious diseases. African kings traded people for European weapons of war, and European tables featured exotic chocolate from Mexico, coffee from South America, tea from China, and sugar from the Caribbean, while North American tobacco was smoked to get high and avoid plague.[3] Rapidly expanding European populations demanded more and cheaper goods, and the combination of trade in cotton and early industrial organization shifted colonial demands from luxuries to the simple pleasures of soft and easily laundered clothing.

Over the three early modern centuries, the population of Europe roughly doubled, despite the continuing cycles of bubonic plague. Due to both natural population growth and immigration Europe's cities, especially its capitals, expanded by several times. In the absence of census data there are many estimates: London went from perhaps 70,000 in 1500 to nearly a million in 1800, Paris from 200,000 to 550,000, and Rome from 50,000 to 150,000. Despite demands for labor, poverty increased in the resident and transient subcultures of Europe's cities. Meanwhile, educational opportunities were expanding and making literacy more common, a trend greatly aided by the invention of the printing press in the 1450s and by Protestantism's emphasis on reading the Bible. For various reasons—including war, religion, public health needs, and perhaps dreams of the old Roman

Empire—Europe's political leaders, from local guild leaders to the pope and emperor, were seeking actively to increase their power and authority at the expense of traditional competitors, such as the Church and nobility. Politically, it was the age of absolutism.

Intellectually, Europe in 1500 was in the midst of its Renaissance love affair with Greek and Roman antiquity. This reinforced the ancient, largely incorrect, yet revered traditions of Hippocrates, Aristotle, and Galen and their theories of health and medicine. The coincidence of global discovery and the religious, social, and political revolution known as the Reformation, however, challenged old certainties. The Catholic Church, Aristotle's geocentric universe, and Galenic medicine all came under attack, but they each proved quite resilient. By 1600 several differing denominations had revised Catholic teaching in many places, and the cultural trend was toward replacing religious opinion with natural or scientific truth. Personal experience, experimentation, and observation (empiricism) gained authority as men such as Galileo, Francis Bacon, and René Descartes outlined the proper techniques for gaining truth from empiricism (scientific method). By 1700 this new and cumulative study of nature (Scientific Revolution), including the human body, was in full swing. The backward-looking focus of the Renaissance had all but died out in favor of the intentional creation of a new, secular, and humane world based on knowledge and freed from superstition, ignorance, and human want. The ongoing advances in knowledge and technology seemed to promise Enlightenment and freedom where darkness had once shrouded humanity. During the French Revolution, the people of Paris turned Notre Dame cathedral into the Temple of Reason. Could there be a better symbol of the Enlightenment's aspirations?

SOCIETAL FACTORS IN HEALTH AND MEDICINE

An individual's genes, childhood, and adult status and choices all operated within a cultural framework of possibilities and options created by nature and history. Five aspects of early modern societies that were important to the nature of health and the provision of health care included cities and urbanization (city growth), standards of living, sanitation and hygiene, patterns of endemic and epidemic disease, and state provisions for medical education and health care.

Cities and Urbanization

Throughout the early modern world, cities of varying antiquity were growing in size and importance. By 1800 about 3 percent of the world's population lived in cities, but because of their wealth and concentration of functions they dominated the world around them. They provided political centers, goods and services, employment, religious ritual, protection, education, and social mobility. But as they grew, cities became more densely populated, dirtier, harder to feed, more poverty stricken, and disease ridden. In Europe, with plague slowly disappearing, newly common diseases included smallpox, tuberculosis, syphilis, and influenza; and imported cholera waited in the wings. Communicable diseases require certain densities of people to sustain themselves. Without a high concentration of potential victims, the germs eventually disappear as they kill their hosts, die away, or simply fail to find healthy new hosts. Cities provided these densities.

Early modern cities were also centers of animal life, and many illnesses came directly from animals. We know of swine and bird flu, of tick-borne spotted fever, of rabies, and of poisonous spiders and snakes. In 1700 wool workers contracted anthrax from sheep's wool; milkmaids cowpox from cows and cowherds ringworm from their cattle; caravan drivers scabies from camels and wranglers glanders from horses.[4] Like influenza, bubonic plague is a disease of animals (zoonosis) that "jumped" to humans when nearby rats died off and the fleas that carried the germs changed their diets to human blood.

Ship traffic brought many diseases into port cities and disseminated them from infected cities. A host of different pathogens and parasites could live in a ship's water supply, and in or on its rats, passengers, slaves, cargo, or crew. Once among a new population that neither understood nor was immune from the dangers, the pathogens and their carriers could thrive.

Standards of Living[5]

In any city the poor occupied more ramshackle quarters that could freeze during winter and swelter during summers. Human, animal, and food waste in large amounts attracted insects and scavengers and their diseases. Water and food supplies could be tainted or poisoned in the absence of sanitary water supplies and reliable food storage.[6] The poorest poor might well lack permanent housing and be reduced to a single garment, which would naturally be filthy and perhaps ridden with fleas. These were a particular problem in the cooler, northern climes. Even the presence of good food did not mean that the poor could partake of it, and poor nutrition weakened immune systems and invited opportunistic diseases. Poverty also meant that one lived with a greater physical threat from one's desperate peers, from fire and accident, and from many infectious diseases—all with little or no access to reasonable health care or necessary medicines. In such situations children and the elderly were at greatest risk. During epidemics, some cultures including Europeans provided aid to the poor, hiring public physicians or surgeons. But these were as much a means of social control as an act of humanity.

By definition the higher classes had access to the better and best residences, nutrition, material goods, and services, including medical care. Servants could maintain a certain level of cleanliness, and in some societies possession of rural properties could mean escape from the city's endemic or epidemic environmental hardships.

Nutrition

Healthy foods in the Christian and Islamic worlds meant those that were appropriately "hot," "cold," "moist," or "dry" according to Galen's teaching from the second century, or "hot" or "cold" according to ancient Chinese lights. Qualities or contents such as protein, fat, fiber, vitamins, carbohydrates, or calories had no meaning. Diet was largely a matter of opportunity and culture, and the vast majority of most people's diets came from carbohydrate-rich grains and tubers. Yet even staples could lead to serious deficiencies: corn (maize) could cause pellagra and a niacin deficit that could cause symptoms from diarrhea to dementia and death; too much unbalanced and unhusked rice could lead to beriberi, a vitamin B1 deficiency; and many bread grains could harbor ergot, a fungus that caused a very uncomfortable condition known as Saint Anthony's Fire. Too little vitamin C led to scurvy, a lack of vitamin A to night blindness, and a lack of iodine to goiter.[7]

In Africa cultural norms forbade the consumption of eggs, and tsetse flies kept many societies from herding cattle and using cows' milk. The starchy diets of taro, bananas, yams, rice, and millet were slim on vitamins and protein, resulting in chronic malnourishment even in years of plenty. Under Caribbean slavery the Africans' diets improved but little, with the addition of small amounts of meat and fish and some local vegetables grown in private gardens. On sugar plantations some surplus brown sugar and molasses came their way at harvest time.

But the ships that carried the gold and slaves also carried plants and seeds. Above all, plants from the Americas made their way to Europe, Africa, and China. Maize, squashes, sweet potatoes, multiple types of beans, tomatoes, and of course the potato enhanced diets around the world. This helped stabilize populations in Eastern Europe and allowed a population explosion in Ireland. Frederick the Great of

Prussia had his troops force peasants to plant them when a famine struck. About the same time France's Louis XVI tantalized his guests by hiding potato plants in a secret garden and by serving potato dishes fit for a king.[8]

Hygiene and Sanitation

By all accounts the Aztecs and Chinese were clean societies that valued personal hygiene and environmental sanitation. By contrast early modern Europeans were comfortable amid filth even in the greatest of palaces. Changing one's soiled clothes and laundering them, bathing, and maintaining oral hygiene came slowly to Europeans. Poorer folk had few garments and keeping them clean was not really an option, especially during the winter. Bathing was known, and bathhouses could be found in many parts of later medieval Europe, but the miasma theory of disease that was popularized with plague claimed that open pores allowed poisonous air into the body. By 1500 bathing was all but taboo, only to be revived with the withdrawal of plague by the eighteenth century. Of course a society that tolerated poor personal hygiene courted a host of personal problems from skin and eye diseases to infections and deadly parasites.

The accumulation or regular disposal of human waste materials, including food scraps, will either draw or keep at bay many types of disease-carrying pests. Toilets were only coming into fashion in Europe as our era closed, and were unknown elsewhere. In China waste collectors made regular nightly rounds and used the material to fertilize a city's nearby fields. This presented its own health problems, but it effectively removed the objectionable stuff from the population centers. Some European cities attempted something like this with "night soil men," but it was easier to dump waste into the gutters and urban streams that flowed into larger rivers that flushed it to the unfortunates downstream. Water supplies in many urban areas were filthy and no less so in downstream rural areas. One reason for the fads of boiled coffee and tea and the mixing of rum with water was that it seemed to make the fluid safe to drink.

Patterns of Epidemic and Endemic Disease

This chapter could feature long lists of diseases that were "always there" (endemic) in a particular locale, as the common cold is for us, and a somewhat shorter list of epidemic diseases that struck for short periods and killed large numbers of people. Endemic germs tended to make people sick but quickly recover, which allowed both the pathogen and the host to survive and thrive. Endemic diseases often became embedded in a region because the local population developed forms of resistance or immunity over long periods of time or as a result of natural exposure. Africans developed a form of iron-poor blood cells known as sickle cell, which made them naturally resistant to the most common form of African malaria. Childhood measles in Europe was fairly benign and conferred natural immunity, so after maturing people were safe from the more deadly adult version. When nonimmune adults came into a measles outbreak, or when measles carriers took the disease to a nonimmunized population, such as the Indians of South America, the result could be (and was) catastrophic.

Local environments also provided various insect vectors of disease such as fleas, flies, ticks, and mosquitoes; venomous animals such as scorpions, certain toads, black widow spiders, and black mamba snakes; large predatory animals such as tigers, bears, wolves, and people; internal parasites such as hookworms and Guinea worms; and soil-induced infectious agents such as tetanus and yaws-causing spirochetes. Control of the larger animals had been part of civilized life for centuries in most places, and poisonous snakes and reptiles were well known and avoided by locals. To neutralize most other challenges required the revolution in modern medicine and public health that took place after 1800. Even now we often have to react with antibiotics or antivenoms. Today we can look back and understand how diseases operated among early modern populations, but at the time nowhere on Earth did anyone make the connections we can in retrospect. People lived with their disease regimes, blaming cases on spirits or witches, or on God's displeasure, or on some natural but unknown causes. Insofar as early modern people reacted effectively to their threats, some progress could result. Quarantines helped stifle plague revisitations; draining swamps curbed malaria; and Africans' willingness to relocate away from still waters and avoid cattle reduced their exposure to tsetse flies. Even when they did not understand how or why such measures worked, they trusted their experience.

State and Educational Provisions for Health Care

In China the benevolent emperors supported the Medical Bureau and the publication of classics in traditional medicine. They expanded the medical content of civil service exams, ensuring that failed applicants would be well prepared to practice traditional medicine in their communities. They funded the public apothecaries that mixed drugs to exacting specifications and distributed them to those who needed them, and in the eighteenth century they provided public granaries to feed the hungry during droughts or famines.

In the Ottoman Empire the sultans established hospital-like bimaristans in their newly won empire. Their patronage stemmed from a sense of social duty, but equally from their Muslim desire to please God through good works and from their status as new conquerors to show their goodwill to the conquered. Older bimaristans continued to operate, and market officials continued to monitor the quality of food and drugs. While some medical innovation occurred at court, however, it tended not to flow outward into the broader society, as it did in China. In one area some limited progress was achieved, as some efforts were made to improve public sanitation and to limit plague's spread by grudging attempts at quarantine.

Because Europe remained divided into multiple independent states, it is difficult to generalize about governmental efforts, but a few points are in order. First, governments sought greater control over their people, and this meant the gathering of information (it was the birth of attempts at accurate censuses, bills of mortality, and the science of statistics). These tools were used for military drafting, taxing, monitoring of epidemics, and the very limited provision of aid to the needy. Second, governments increasingly valued their people's good health in the face of plague and other epidemics. They valued them as taxpayers, childbearers, workers, and soldiers. Healing trained soldiers to fight again, keeping mothers safe to have more children and increase the state's population, and preventing the wholesale slaughter of urban populations by disease led to state actions such as building military hospitals, licensing midwives, and imposing isolation and quarantine when epidemics struck. Third, states created few educational institutions but supported the idea that medical practitioners needed to be educated as well as licensed. Partially, this was at the prompting of the professionally educated or trained and organized physicians, apothecaries, and surgeons, who sought to protect their high status by maintaining a monopoly. This was a trend that continued throughout the early modern period.

Fourth, formally recognized European practitioners continued to be divided into university-educated physicians and apprenticed and trained surgeons and apothecaries. The early modern trend, however, was toward professionalization. Physicians were to undergo practical medical training in such areas as medicinal botany, anatomy, and physiology, and through clinical training in hospital wards with real patients. On the other hand, schools were opening up to provide educational opportunities to apothecaries, surgeons, and even midwives, to increase their knowledge and effectiveness. Fifth, this formalized education was increasingly informed by the advances in the sciences of the Scientific Revolution and Enlightenment. By the eighteenth century "empirical medicine" was not what the uneducated did[9] but was the standard informed by the scientific method: hypothesize, test, observe, record, repeat, and share. Yet many discoveries bore no fruit among the sick or injured, and some inventions, such as the microscope, were underused in advancing practical medicine.

Sixth, European medicine was gathering under its wing a number of human conditions that had previously not been considered "medical." This has happened in our day. When this author was a student, homosexuality was formally considered a mental illness and alcoholism was not. Today, the definitions have been reversed. Likewise, there was an important shift in defining some conditions. For example, lunatics went from being possessed by demons to being mentally ill, which radically changed the way they were treated. Similarly, giving birth came to be recognized as a medical procedure rather than just an act of nature. One can say that both labor and madness were medicalized by the culture and that the scope of medicine was thereby expanded.

Finally, no medical culture, however sophisticated, possessed an understanding of the foundations of most modern medicine. The discovery of fundamental physiological processes and, most importantly, of germs and their role in human health and medicine had to await the nineteenth century.

NOTES

1. Charlotte Furth, *A Flourishing Yin: Gender in China's Medical History, 960–1665* (Berkeley: University of California Press, 1999), 155.

2. Xinru Liu, *The Silk Road in World History* (New York: Oxford University Press, 2010).

3. See Jürgen Osterhammel and Niels Petersson, *Globalization: A Short History* (Princeton, NJ: Princeton University Press, 2005).

4. A. Mantovani et al., "A Historical Overview of Occupational Diseases Connected with Animals," in *Contributions to the History of Occupational and Environmental Prevention*, ed. Antonio Grieco (New York: Elsevier, 1999), 239–46.

5. See, for example, Robert C. Allen, Tommy Bengtsson, and Martin Dribe, eds., *Living Standards in the Past: New Perspectives on Well-Being in Asia and Europe* (New York: Oxford University Press, 2005).

6. See Mary K. Matossian, *Poisons of the Past: Molds, Epidemics, and History* (New Haven, CT: Yale University Press, 1989).

7. Roy Porter, ed., *Cambridge History of Medicine* (New York: Cambridge University Press, 2006), 39–41.

8. Bill Laws, *Spade, Skirret, and Parsnip: The Curious History of Vegetables* (Stroud, UK: Sutton, 2004), 7–9.

9. An "empiric" was one who practiced medicine with neither formal training or education, nor a license.

CHAPTER 2

Education and Training: Learned and Nonlearned

Though most sick and injured people have always been treated at home by experienced family members or neighbors, by 1500 societies had developed healing theories and practices that were controlled, utilized, and passed on by specially educated or trained specialists. Many cultures had a range of types of healers, including spiritual practitioners (diviners, priests, monks, magicians, witch doctors, shamans), internists (herbalists, physicians, apothecaries, empirics, folk healers, wisewomen), and those who manipulated the body from the outside (surgeons, barber-surgeons, dentists, midwives, bonesetters, acupuncturists, leeches). Literate societies such as the Europeans, Muslims, Indians, and Chinese usually drew a distinction between practitioners who were formally trained in theory and practice through written texts and, sometimes, schools, and those whose knowledge derived from oral traditions, experience, or apprenticeships. Nonliterate societies tended to be more accepting of varying approaches to healing, since in the end it was success that really mattered.

WESTERN TRADITIONS

The Western medical cultures of Europe and much of the Islamic world had long been dependent on the Greek and Greco-Roman traditions of Hippocrates and Galen. Lacking codified medical traditions of their own, medieval Muslims and Christians adopted the classics wholesale.

Arab and Persian scholars and commentators had their heyday between the ninth and eleventh centuries. Latin Christian medical thinkers absorbed much through translations of Islamic texts as well as bits of the originals two and three centuries later. Muslim medical students trained through reading of texts and practice gained in the bimaristans—which served as both hospitals and teaching facilities—that graced most large cities. European students gained formal knowledge of the Greek tradition through medical faculties associated with universities. Salerno, on the cusp of the Muslim, Byzantine Greek, and Latin worlds in southern Italy, hosted the first Christian medical school, and by 1500 dozens dotted Europe's landscape.[1]

European Medical Education

The early modern medical curriculum, whether European or Muslim, featured the ancient ideas of Galen[2] and Hippocrates. Despite developments in medical education between 1500 and 1800, the core of Western medical theory remained the body's four humors and the attempt to maintain their balance. Each person's body contained four humors, usually visualized as fluids: blood, phlegm, yellow bile, and black bile. Each of these corresponded to or was associated with a vast range of phenomena from planets to personality types and bodily organs. In addition, there were four qualities—hot, cold, wet, dry—that were also associated with the humors and organs, as well as all foods and beverages, herbs and drugs, and one's age, sex, diet, level and type of exercise, and other physical attributes or conditions. A person's "complexion" was a mixture of the balancing of humors and the appropriate balancing of qualities. This was a factor of diet, activity, passion, and other generally controllable variables. Under normal circumstances, the trained physician understood how to use foods, drink, medicines, exercise, and procedures such as drawing blood to maintain or restore good health, all of which were articulated by Hippocrates and Galen.

The sixteenth century saw the spread of printing (from 1454) and the humanist interest in original classical texts. New, printed editions of Hippocrates and Galen replaced older, Muslim-influenced commentaries and editions, and reinforced the Greeks' influence among scholars and doctors alike. Command of ancient theory in Greek and Latin lay at the root of distinction between the formally educated physician and the other "illiterate" practitioners. While surgeons and apothecaries may have understood humoral theory in order to follow physicians' orders, they had been trained as apprentices and belonged to craft guilds that ranked with carpenters and painters. Like theologians and lawyers, university-trained physicians did not work with their hands, unless to study a flask of urine or feel a pulse. They were strictly internists who prescribed the diet, exercise, and medicines that their theory dictated. Their guilds tended to rank with those of judges, international merchants, and bankers, and their fees reflected their acquired status. Most commoners could never afford a physician's service, which is why many towns hired physicians to serve as salaried civic doctors, with the stipulation that they serve all comers.

In 1500 medical schools relied almost exclusively on classical medical texts and those derived from them. Education was largely theoretical, with experience being acquired after graduation, often as civic physicians. Anatomy as a formal subject of study was in its infancy, with educational dissections being few and far between. Since surgeons literally handled the human body, there seemed little need for it. Most physicians knew few of the qualities of healing herbs (simples) or their compounds beyond their being "hot" or "wet."

The cultural phenomena we label the Renaissance, Scientific Revolution, and Enlightenment had some effect on medical education. By 1600 the earliest anatomy and dissection theaters had been built for student physicians, and the Netherlander Andreas Vesalius had pioneered both dissection and demonstration of the corpse by the physician and the use of high-quality anatomical illustrations. Botanical gardens were established around medical schools for teaching purposes, especially important as European discovery and colonization revealed new plants with clear medicinal value. Perhaps most important was the innovation of students accompanying the professor on his hospital rounds, widely adopted only in the eighteenth century. This integration of the hospital with the classroom would prove to be a major step in Western medical education.

The differences between the model medical curricula in 1500 and 1800 demonstrate some of the changes the era implemented. At a typical Italian medical school in 1500, after spending several years studying the liberal arts and philosophy, the medical student spent four or five years studying Latin translations of Arabic and Greek texts including Hippocrates and Galen. Astrology was considered a necessary medical subject (mandatory in Bologna from 1405) but anatomy was not. By 1800 the model of medical education had shifted northward. German medical schools did not share a common curriculum, but the dozen or so students enrolled in a typical program spent three years studying anatomy and physiology, chemistry, and botany in year one; pathology (diseases) and materia medica (medicinal plants and drugs) in year two; and therapy, clinical practice, prescription writing, and in some obstetrics, surgery, and forensic (legal) pathology. Lectures dominated years one and two, and experiential learning the third. Similar trends reached through the Netherlands (especially Leiden) to Edinburgh, Scotland, whose highly influential medical school was founded in 1726. Its standard three-year curriculum consisted of anatomy, chemistry, surgery, botany, materia medica, midwifery (obstetrics), medical "theory and practice," and clinical medicine. Everything except the largely Galenic "theory" portion was new to our period, having been pioneered and established during the intervening years. The biggest differences may have been the recent inclusion of surgery and midwifery, which had been the monopoly of guild surgeons and midwives, and botany and materia medica, which had long been the purview of non-university-trained apothecaries. By the later eighteenth century, much broader expertise was expected of the university-trained physician. This was significant insofar as Edinburgh directly influenced English medical education and early American medical schools in Philadelphia and New York. Edinburgh's success may also be gauged by the fact that it graduated 219 students from the West Indies alone between 1744 and 1830.[3]

Challenges to the Galenic model of humoralism were not unknown, though they had little effect on early modern formal education in the short run. The most important was that presented by the sixteenth-century German physician and alchemist known as Paracelsus. Among the first generation of Protestants, he associated the established medicine with paganism and Catholicism and sought to "reform" medicine as Martin Luther had done Christianity. He and his followers shifted emphasis away from the four humors and organic treatments to inorganic chemicals that he believed dictated health and illness. Though his conclusions were as misguided and false as those of mainstream medicine, his challenge developed into iatro- (medical) chemistry. Many wealthy clients and patrons supported Paracelsians, and their research helped open up important windows into human physiology even if their treatments and remedies proved futile. The fact that chemistry appeared on Edinburgh's curriculum is a testament to his long-range impact.

Medical Preparation in the Ottoman and Safavid Empires

The Islamic world dominated by the Ottoman Turks blended many cultures. As in Europe and elsewhere many types of healers circulated, with roots in Arabic, Persian, Turkic, North African, and Islamic religious traditions. Homeschooling, tutors, apprenticeships, self-study, and courses taught at bimaristans or mosques all provided levels of practical medical knowledge for a wide range of practitioners, both male and female. Only at Istanbul's Süleymaniye complex was there a recognized school of medicine, and little about its operation has been uncovered. Formal medical education of males in Islamic countries seems to have been associated primarily with the bimaristan, a health and religious facility provided with royal or noble patronage. Galenic theory and hands-on training appear to have characterized education in these institutions in the same way that the education of religious scholars took place in mosques. Most learning still appears to have been based upon self-study rather than formal instruction, and some bimaristans included extensive medical libraries. A position on the staff of these facilities placed one at the top of the medical ladder and reflected years of practical experience in junior positions.[4]

Such a system hardly encouraged experimentation or innovation, and little occurred across our period. People learning to become medical practitioners of whatever type accepted the classical texts and formal or informal practical experiences offered as they came. In the Islamic world the closest thing to professors of medicine were more bureaucrats than healers, especially under the Ottomans. The once rich Muslim intellectual and scientific tradition that had produced the great medical authors and texts studied by Muslims, Christians, and Jews alike had largely dried up. In medicine this accompanied the rise of what was called Medicine of the Prophet (Muhammad). Alongside the empirical and Galenic approaches to medicine was this body of teachings attributed to Muhammad and interpreted by religious rather than secular medical specialists. To criticize or compete with this system of explanation and practice when invoked was considered an offense against Islam. The relative dynamism of the post-Reformation West drew Ottoman Christian students in small numbers, and the little change that occurred between 1500 and 1800 was generally attributable to borrowings from Europe.

Medical preparation in the area dominated by Safavid Persia was even less innovative and organized. Their rulers expended very little in support of the bimaristans and their educational roles, and no more in overseeing how practitioners were trained or functioned. As in the Turkish Empire dissections, and therefore detailed and accurate anatomy and physiology, were all but unknown. Medicine amounted to the application of Galenic principles and folk healing. While this could and did often prove effective in daily life, it nonetheless demonstrates the intellectual stagnation under Safavid rule. Since they were

Figure 2.1 Eighteenth-century copy of a Safavid Persian anatomical illustration of a pregnant woman. The original was in *Tibb al-Akbar* (Akbar's Medicine) finished in 1701 by Muhammad Akbar. It is a Persian translation of the 13th-century Arabic *Causes and Symptoms* by Najib al-Din al-Samarqandi. Note the rather crude level of detail and depiction of anatomy, which reflects the Safavid culture's relative disinterest in the subject. (National Library of Medicine)

geographically detached from Europe, the practical advances absorbed by the Turks, for example in public health, were lost on the Persians. What seems to have had an impact arrived via missionaries and some merchants, especially from England after 1600.[5]

Patients, Suffering, and Care in the West

Insofar as the Islamic tradition centered physician education at the bimaristan, it de-emphasized the wall between theory and actual patient care. European medical students were only beginning to benefit from this hands-on teaching method—working with real patients—in the eighteenth century. To those preparing to practice, patients remained largely abstract entities little understood physiologically or psychologically. Aside from drawing patients' attention to such health factors as diet, exercise, and air quality or providing some useful pills or syrups to induce vomiting or stanch diarrhea, Western physicians had little that was effective to offer the suffering. Internal medicine, whether humoral or iatrochemical, was founded on misunderstandings of the human body and its functioning. Until the seventeenth century experimentation was limited, though experienced physicians often noted which remedies or techniques worked and which did not. Although many important biological discoveries emerged from the Scientific Revolution, including the fact that the blood circulates through the vessels, being pumped by the muscular heart, they had little impact on medical education or practice. Though the microscope was in use for nearly two centuries, and scientists speculated about "animalcules" or other microscopic disease-causing agents, germs were identified and germ theory became fruitful only midway through the 1800s. The learned explanation of epidemics such as bubonic plague—poisonous air (miasma)—did not change between Galen's time and the building of the first automobile despite centuries of direct experience with the disease. Some treatments, such as mercury for syphilis and bleeding for just about everything, were at least as bad as the ailment.

Some strides were made, however, though rarely by the medical world's heavy hitters. A diplomat's wife introduced inoculation for smallpox (with the virus) from Istanbul to Europe early in the eighteenth century, and country doctor Edward Jenner showed success with vaccinations of cowpox material at century's end. The vitamin deficiency disease known as scurvy, which slaughtered long-distance sailors, was conquered in 1795 by introducing lime juice into shipboard diets, but only after nearly 50 years of recommendations by British naval surgeon James Lind.[6]

For the most part, however, early modern medical theory and education had little effect on people's general health and comfort. Physicians retained their high status, though prayer remained a powerful prophylactic and remedy among Christians and Muslims alike well into the modern era. Inexpensive and popular vernacular books of medical recipes and remedies circulated in Europe from the beginning of the seventeenth century, enabling common folk to have confidence in treating themselves and their own. Some of these were written by well-known practitioners, such as Nicholas Culpeper, who mischievously shared the profession's London pharmacopoeia, or official catalogue of medicinal plants and drugs, with the public at large.[7] Others came from literate women who sought to help others who needed it but could not afford a physician.

EARLY MODERN MEXICANS

In 1500 the Aztec people and state dominated the Central American region today known as Mexico. Theirs was a cumulative culture that benefited from earlier Olmec, Toltec, and other societies, and raised their own to a very high level. They had a well-ordered political organization ruled over by a king and clear traditions, and held together by a fierce army of warriors. In 1519 Spanish conquistadors entered Mexico and began the disintegration of the Aztec state and the imposition of colonial government and the Christian religion that would characterize Mexico well past 1800. Aztec medical theory and practice was the norm until missionaries and royal bureaucrats introduced European medicine from the 1520s. While native medicine remained active in many places, where the Spanish held sway their medical personnel, institutions, and practices dominated, though they were not averse to adopting elements of Aztec practice, especially the use of medicinal plants.[8]

Aztec Theory and Practice

For the Aztec, the world was alive and all things had impacts on all other things. Human life, including health and illness, was governed in part by the stars and sky deities, and those of the earth and its interior. In all things there was a duality at work, which was best when balanced: hot/cold, male/female, up/down, order/chaos, creation/destruction. The gods were dualistic, in that they were both creators and destroyers, givers of health and of sickness and death. Health was the proper balance of the various dualities and forces of the body (*tonocayo*), and illness was imbalance. Aztecs imagined three bodily forces: *yolia*, located in the heart, was responsible for vitality, knowledge, and personality, and that spiritual force that survives death; *ihiyotl*, centered in the liver, was the power of respiration that could be polluted by immoral personal actions whose emanations needed to be cleansed with baths or sweat baths; and *tonalli*, located in the head, provided the body's correct (or incorrect) temperature, tending to wander away from the body during irrational states such as sex, sleep, extreme fear, drunkenness, or a haircut.

As in most societies, typical illnesses and accidents were treated by the sufferer or in the home, usually by women, along practical lines learned from experience. Diet, physical activities, accidents, and natural poisons were at the root of many maladies, but so were gods, spirits, witchcraft, and complex natural forces. When one's condition was serious the *tíctl*, or healer, was called in. These apprentice-trained men and women were part priest and part doctor, recognizing the unity of the spiritual and physical worlds. They diagnosed conditions, at least in part by the body's temperature—indicating the condition of *tonalli*— and recommended courses of action. Diagnosis might also include divination and hallucinogen-induced trances to determine spiritual causes. They combined the skills of herbalists, surgeons, diviners, and magicians.

The few Spanish-mediated texts—original native works in the Nahuatl language were destroyed by the conquerors—discussing medicine also mention specialists. Further training in the Aztec temples in astrology and other arts enhanced one's supernatural abilities and reputations, earning him the title of priest-healer, *tepoxtlatl*. Other practitioners that served ailing Aztecs included their equivalents of surgeons, women midwives, bonesetters, specialists on the eyes and teeth, and blood letters (the last to be expected given the important place of human sacrifice in Aztec religion). Therapies ranged from such psychosomatic practices as appearing to pull an ailment-inducing object from the sufferer's body (by *techichinani* specialists), offering prayers and sacrifices to malicious gods such as Tlaloc (the gods who induce suffering can relieve it), bleeding to balance the body's temperature, and providing medicinal plants and their blends to be taken internally or used externally.

Colonial Mexican Medicine

European medicine and practitioners entered Mexico with the conquistadors, missionaries, and royal bureaucrats that oversaw Spanish colonization. The first physician to arrive was Diego Pedraza in 1525, the same year that Spanish Mexico City appointed Mexico's first civic barber-surgeon. Smallpox and other infectious diseases ravaged the native population, inflicting a crushing demographic and psychic blow. Spanish sources report a native willingness to adopt the newcomers'

medicine, perhaps because they associated the murderous diseases
with it (who hurts can also heal) or because they noted the failure of
their own. In 1570 a Mexican press published the first medical book in
the hemisphere, and by 1578 Spaniards had established the New
World's first medical school in Mexico City.

Of course transplanted Spanish medicine followed the Galenic
model, and education in the New World paralleled that of the Old.
There was a twist, however, in that Spain's kings Charles I and Philip
II insisted that colonists seek out anything medically useful from the
new conquests. This especially applied to plants used by the natives:
one of the earliest colonial medical books included 60 native remedies.
This openness ended in the 1570s, perhaps with the university's
founding.

Placating the rain gods with human sacrifices necessarily came to an
end, as did the native practice of male circumcision with amazingly
sharp obsidian knives. The latter was associated by the Spanish
Catholics with Judaism and fell afoul of the religious authorities.
Bathing, which the Aztecs embraced, was denounced by orthodox
Galenism as a means of opening pores and letting "corrupted" air into
the body. Other "superstitious" practices such as divination were likewise rooted out. The Spanish licensed physicians through the *protomedicato*, the Mexican medical office. As important as qualifying skills
was religious "purity of blood," which kept formal preparation and
practice out of the hands of Jews, Muslims, blacks, or non-Christian
natives.

The limited number of physicians opened the door to the *curandero*,
an unlicensed practitioner who tended to blend native and European
medicine with strains of African medical culture. Following the Aztec
model the *curandero* was often from a family of medical folk or apprenticed with a recognized healer. Most avoided any overt religious rituals
or overtones to their practice, though Spanish authorities often found
them objectionable. The early modern Church, colonial authorities,
and patrons continued to impose European medicine on Mexico
through the provision of hospitals, infirmaries, and other elements of
the Western system, marginalizing but never eliminating the native
healing traditions.

AFRICAN SLAVES IN THE CARIBBEAN

After imported infectious diseases savaged Native American populations during the early 1500s, Spanish and Portuguese slave traders
began the transportation of millions of West Africans to the Caribbean

islands and the Atlantic coasts of North and South America. They were expected to accept their new status and perform whatever labor was needed for the dominant agricultural or mining concerns among which their owners placed them. Over time, generations of enslaved blacks populated the Caribbean islands, but until the slave trade was finally abolished, fresh infusions of native Africans continually renewed the island populations. As in Mexico, Europeans in the Caribbean controlled productive land and its exploitation, having brought with them culture, technologies, and medicine. In a very uneven way across the West Indies—colonized by Spaniards, French, Dutch, and English planters and their African slaves—European and African medical traditions and practices either clashed or blended as slaves struggled to maintain their health in an unforgiving climate, performing physically draining tasks in the midst of indigenous and imported diseases and the psychic drain of their dehumanizing condition.[9]

African Traditions

Like the Aztecs, West Africans viewed the visible and invisible forces of nature, natural and divine, as simple aspects of the same unified world. An ultimate divinity oversaw all, but less powerful spiritual entities influenced or controlled the natural world inhabited by people. The spirits of dead ancestors also had powers to influence the natural order, perhaps using reward and punishment to enforce moral codes of the tribal societies. When a person fell ill, the first level of explanation was basic cause and effect: he fell from a tree and the fall broke his leg. When such a relationship was unclear, or the curious sought to know why he fell from the tree, spirits and ancestors filled in the blanks. Diseases and other painful conditions were readily attributed to spirits, and there was a fine line between the physical practitioner and the spiritual one. It seems that typically the physician was both priest and magician. Understanding the spiritual causes behind suffering, or divination, was the highest skill or gift, because the proper explanation led to proper remedies and success. Spirit possession—allowing a divinity or ancestor's spirit to enter one's consciousness—was one especially dramatic technique of divinatory diagnosis.

Medicine in early modern West Africa, then, was as much about pleasing angry ancestors or bribing mischievous gods as it was about setting a broken leg or curing stomach cramps. It was about ritual as much as herb lore, charms and amulets as much as cutting out bladder stones. Healing spirits needed to be invoked and the malevolent ones appeased. Human health was essentially part of a continuum of natural success, from earth's fertility to a child's birth, and the same societal specialists sought to understand the divine patterns. Of course, diviners could use their knowledge of the spiritual to harm as well as help, to expose people to malevolent powers as well as to protect them. Less potentially dangerous folks handled the less alarming medical emergencies, from childbirth to abscessed teeth and battle wounds. Some in each community had command of local plant lore, providing internal means of resolving many health issues.

Slave Medicine in the Caribbean

There was a wide range of white planter attitudes and behaviors toward black slaves and their health. Down to the eighteenth century it was not unusual to work labor to death, literally, investing as little as possible in medical personnel, service, facilities, and supplies. Some

Figure 2.2 Illustration from 1796 depicting Graman Quacy, who was enslaved as a child in the area of present-day Ghana. Quacy became a freedman in Dutch-controlled Surinam and gained international renown as a healer and botanist. He created a bitter medicinal tea made from the plant *quassia*, which killed intestinal parasites. His European-style clothing and especially his feathered hat denote his high social status. (National Library of Medicine)

owners relied on their own family members to tend sick or disabled slaves. Pressures from enlightened intellectuals and abolitionists had an impact on French and British plantations in particular, however, especially as the threat against the slave trade made the prospects of simply "buying more" less and less likely. Most planters had access to white physicians and surgeons who varied widely in training, experience, and competence. Humane planters provided some type of infirmary facilities and both regular and emergency practitioner visits as needed. As the prospect of abolition loomed, midwifery and infant care took on a new importance. In the British West Indies, a medical manual for slaves (John Grainger's *An Essay on the More Common West Indian Diseases*, London, 1764) lagged behind the first for whites by 85 years. Grainger dealt with the universal conditions of worms, fevers, diarrhea, tetanus, dropsy, cholera, throat sores, and hepatitis, and the predominantly black conditions of leprosy, yaws, night blindness, Guinea worm, hernias, burns, and ulcers.

Slaves who had long been resident or had grown up in captivity understood the owner's medicine as a means of preserving or restoring their health. For new arrivals, however, the strange inattention to the gods and spirits made much white medicine a very alien thing, even when it proved successful. Language barriers aside, the white healers were far too reminiscent of the slave traders, inspectors, sailors, and brutal overseers to be trusted very far.

Both the shortage of competent white medical personnel and native distrust of white healers led to the employment of enslaved medical personnel in both French and British Caribbean colonies. Large French plantations featured crude slave hospitals overseen by enslaved black women known as *hospitalières*, who were aided by less respected *infirmières*. These women relied largely on European-style healing and the use of native plants as materia medica. They had high status among the slaves and were generally privileged by whites for their position and skills. Karol Weaver's study of eighteenth-century French Saint Domingue found that *hospitalières* could be domineering and insufferable or noted as excellent caregivers and administrators. There was little in the way of preparation for such a position, though it is likely that *hospitalières* tended to come from among the *infirmières*.[10]

Eighteenth-century English island colonies had similarly varied provisions for sick and injured slaves. Larger and wealthier plantations featured well-built infirmaries staffed with slave personnel, including a "doctor" or "doctors," assistants, nurses, an attendant for children, a cook, a midwife, and an attendant for those with yaws. A study of 10 plantations owned by John Tharpe in 1805 lists 51 black medical personnel for 3,000 slaves. Thirty-four were women, 23 were African-born, and only 6 of the 51 were declared "able" to do field work; the rest suffered from some disability, from missing a leg to being "insane." Those who could not work healed.[11]

Among the slaves who worked in the fields there were self-designated healers of the older African type. In French colonies *kaperlatas* were practitioners of both spiritual and natural medicine who had high status among the slaves. They sold and traded familiar drugs, amulets, charms, and rituals, and were believed to be possessed of traditional powers to interact with the spirit world. As blacks empowered by their own people, they were naturally subversive leaders who represented the freedom of the Old World, and some helped foment rebellions that expressed the slaves' desire for self-determination.[12]

THE CHINESE

Practitioners

As in other early modern societies, China's late Ming and early Qing (ching) dynasty leaders supported a wide range of healers. When a person suffered an illness, his or her choice of practitioner was dictated in part by availability and cost, by the sufferer's worldview, by the nature of the malady, and by the reputations of available and affordable healers.[13]

China's religious traditions, especially Daoism and Buddhism, provided spiritual practitioners who specialized in protecting people from, and ridding people of, the onslaughts of angry ancestors, malicious ghosts, and demons. In both China and Japan, various anthropomorphic "disease gods" explained widespread epidemic outbreaks of measles, smallpox, and other infectious diseases. These entities inflicted ill health and disease on good people and bad alike, which explained why the good suffer. The stricken person wore amulets or talismans and had prayers, spells, rituals, and even exorcisms performed to placate or neutralize the troublesome spirits. This was no mere peasant superstition, as even well-educated medical professionals admitted the powers of spiritual forces, especially in adverse mental conditions. Other healers, perhaps the most common, relied on folklore and their own experience at using herbs and other common substances as remedies. The Chinese did not discriminate between men and women whose knowledge and techniques were rooted in long traditions. Where priests and monks learned their healing crafts in temples, these empirics usually came from families recognized for their practical medical skills, or had studied the craft as informal apprentices. Other popular, itinerant, or illiterate practitioners with special skills included midwives, bonesetters, magicians, acupuncturists, and specialists on body parts such as skin, teeth, and eyes.

China also had a long history of formal medical theory and practice. This was established in an expanding set of classic texts. The first was the *Yellow Emperor's Classic Canon of Internal Medicine*,[14] supposedly by the ruler and physician Huang Ti from the third millennium BCE. The heavily edited and commentated book is known from what was probably a second- or third-century-CE text. Ambitious men of the upper class studied these as a standard part of their preparation for careers as local or imperial government bureaucrats. Many who could not pass the rigorous examination for metropolitan civil service (the *jinshi* degree, for which an estimated 1 in 3,000 passed) established medical practices as scholar-gentleman physicians (*ruyi*). The Imperial Household in Beijing also sponsored a formal medical academy (Great Medical Office) educating 300 students at a time, whose curriculum shrank across our period as its integrity shriveled. These scholar-physicians, whether self-educated via the classics or formally at the academy, were solidly in the Confucian tradition of acquired expertise and social benevolence through public service. China's medical elite, they were generally unavailable to the common sufferer and made their fortunes and reputations by treating the wealthy. They formed a true profession based on their shared body of knowledge (the classics) and Confucian values (which underwent a revival in the seventeenth and eighteenth centuries), and status and privilege conferred by society.[15] Theirs was a growing profession fueled by economic prosperity, growing affluence, and competition for business. The profession was also formally supported by the Chinese state through its ritual temple worship of Huang Ti and two other early medical authors—the Three Emperors—as divinities, a move probably meant to undermine the status of Daoist and Buddhist religious healers.

The Dao, Yin and Yang, and the Five Elements

Formal or learned Chinese medicine was intimately linked to the place of human beings in the cosmos. As with Chinese religions and most philosophies, medical theory explained the universe as a living and moral entity. Humans were enveloped and interpenetrated by the natural forces of the cosmos. Human action and development were meant to be in synch with the flow of the universe: this defined good health. The Dao, or Way, was the Chinese expression of the proper conduct that kept one both physically healthy and morally good. The doctor, priest, and philosopher all sought to keep people on the Dao. The famed philosopher Confucius (551–479 BCE) taught the application of balance and moderation as the foundation of the individual good life as of the good state. The health of each was at heart a matter of correct choices, of human action and self-discipline. Harm followed immorality.

In the human body, the principles or forces that needed to be maintained in balance were labeled "yin" and "yang." Yin was associated with earth, night, water, cold, damp, dark, contraction; female, wife, the earth being fertilized, the body's interior; constructive, conservative, positive action; lowliness, disease, evil, and death. Yang was essentially the opposite of each yin characteristic: sun, day, dryness, heat, light, expansion; male, husband, the heavens fertilizing the earth with rain and sunlight, the body's exterior; aggressive, destructive, negative action; nobility, health, good, and life. Winter and fall were yin, and spring, summer, and late summer were yang. Human organs were either yin or yang, and the two forces coursed through the body with blood and air through imagined ducts or conduits. Habits, food, and other factors could rob the body of yin or yang, or replenish it. Bad health resulted from an imbalance. The mind, body, and spirit were all interconnected through the force of qi (chee), which was directly affected by the yin/yang balance. Maintaining proper qi was the key to Chinese medicine.

Further, the Five Phases or elements —earth, fire, water, metal, and wood—of which everything physical is constructed, including man, were connected to or associated with a long list of phenomena, including the seasons, planets, numbers, directions, flavors, odors, colors, emotions, the body's tissues and organs, and climate (wind, heat, humidity, cold, dryness). Spiritual "resources" as well as bodily fluids were associated with specific yin organs: liver with tears and soul; spleen with saliva and ideas; heart with sweat and spirit; kidneys with spittle and the will; and lungs with mucus and animal spirit. Of course, each organ is also associated with yin or yang. This whole system of yin/yang, seasons, elements, and concordances or correspondences was of ancient origin and found its first full articulation in the *Yellow Emperor's Classic Canon of Internal Medicine*.

Despite the dominance of Huang Ti's *Canon*, Chinese medical tradition and practice had long developed variations and schools that privileged one or another of the tradition's many complex variables. Treatments for the same disease might vary widely with the physician's understanding of the underlying cause of the ailment, be it the seasons, winds, diet, or demons. We have little evidence on how

Figure 2.3 A visual guide to the points along the stomach meridian into which an acupuncturist would insert his needles. In traditional Chinese medicine, the life force, *qi,* was channeled through meridians to organs. Hollow organs such as the stomach were associated with *yang.* Illustration from Wen-chih Ch'en's *Yang K'o Hsuan sui,* 1628. (National Library of Medicine)

patients chose among physicians, other than the importance of reputation, but if a large swath of the educated Chinese had both studied medicine—as part of their general education—and provided the learned physicians with their clientele, it is likely that the physician's "school" often mattered.

NOTES

1. An excellent introduction is Mary Lindemann, *Medicine and Society in Early Modern Europe*, 2nd ed. (New York: Cambridge University Press, 2010).

2. On the postclassical history of Galen's impact see Vivian Nutton, "The Fortunes of Galen," in *The Cambridge Companion to Galen*, ed. R. J. Hankinson (New York: Cambridge University Press, 2008), 355–90.

3. On German schools see Thomas H. Broman, *The Transformation of German Academic Medicine, 1750–1820* (New York: Cambridge University Press, 1996); curriculum on Edinburgh from Richard Sheridan, *Doctors and Slaves: A Medical and Demographic History of Slavery in the British West Indies, 1680–1834* (New York: Cambridge University Press, 1985), 60.

4. Miri Shefer-Mossensohn, *Ottoman Medicine: Healing and Medical Institutions, 1500–1700* (Albany: State University of New York Press, 2009), 141–43.

5. Cyril Elgood, *Safavid Medical Practice: The Practice of Medicine, Surgery, and Gynecology in Persia between 1500 and 1750* (London: Luzac & Co., 1970), 1–12, 121–28.

6. On Jenner see Jennifer Lee Carrell, *The Speckled Monster: A Historical Tale of Battling Smallpox* (New York: Dutton, 2003), and Edward Jenner, *Vaccination against Smallpox* (Amherst, NY: Prometheus, 1996); on Lind see David Harvie, *Limeys: The Conquest of Scurvy* (Stroud, UK: Sutton, 2002).

7. See Benjamin Wooley, *Heal Thyself: Nicholas Culpeper and the Seventeenth-Century Struggle to Bring Medicine to the People* (New York: HarperCollins, 2004).

8. For further information on the Mexican tradition see Suzanne Austin Alchon, *A Pest in the Land: New World Epidemics in a Global Perspective* (Albuquerque: University of New Mexico Press, 2003); Noble David Cook, *Born to Die: Disease and New World Conquest, 1492–1650* (New York: Cambridge University Press, 1998); Sherry Fields, *Pestilence and Headcolds: Encountering Illness in Colonial Mexico* (New York: Columbia University Press, 2008); Robert McCaa, "Spanish and Nahuatl Views on Smallpox and Demographic Catastrophe in Mexico," *Journal of Interdisciplinary History* 25 (1995): 397–431; Clara Sue Kidwell, "Aztec and European Medicine in the New World, 1521–1600," in *The Anthropology of Medicine: From Culture to Method*, ed. Lola Romanucci-Ross, Daniel E. Moerman, and Laurence R. Tancredi (Westport, CT: Bergin and Garver, 1997), 19–30; Bernard R. Ortiz de Montellano, *Aztec Medicine, Health, and Nutrition* (New Brunswick, NJ: Rutgers University Press, 1990), all of which provided information for this section.

9. Sheridan, *Doctors and Slaves*; Mark Harrison, *Medicine in an Age of Commerce and Empire: Britain and Its Tropical Colonies, 1660–1830* (New York: Oxford University Press, 2010); Robert Voeks, "African Medicine and Magic," *Geographical Reviews* 83 (1993): 66–79.

10. Karol K. Weaver, *Medical Revolutionaries: The Enslaved Healers of Eighteenth-Century Saint Domingue* (Chicago: University of Illinois Press, 2006), 48–55.

11. Sheridan, *Doctors and Slaves*, 89–94.

12. Weaver, *Medical Revolutionaries*, 3–5, 10, 113–119.

13. The literature on Chinese medicine is quickly expanding. This section relies primarily on Charlotte Furth, *A Flourishing Yin: Gender in China's Medical History, 960–1665* (Berkeley: University of California Press, 1999); Chen Ping, ed., *History and Development of Traditional Medicine* (Beijing: Science Press, 1999); Paul U. Unschuld, *Medicine in China: A History of Ideas*, 2nd ed. (Berkeley: University of California Press, 2010); and Chao Yuan-Ling, *Medicine and Society in Late Imperial China* (New York: Peter Lang, 2009).

14. Ilza Veith, *The Yellow Emperor's Classic of Internal Medicine* (Berkeley: University of California Press, 2002).

15. On the debate over the importance and application of traditional Chinese medical ethics during the early modern period see Paul U. Unschuld, *Medical Ethics in Imperial China: A Study in Historical Anthropology* (Berkeley: University of California Press, 1979), 56–106.

CHAPTER 3

Religion and Medicine

For most of human history, healing the human body was understood as being ultimately in the hands of God, gods, or other entities that transcended mere mortals. In many cultures, the shaman, witch doctor, or priest remained a major healing figure throughout the early modern period. Jesus and other religious figures healed miraculously when they walked the earth, and control over bodies and their sicknesses was considered a sign of power over life itself. Humans contacted these entities—spirits, jinn, ancestors, ghosts, gods, demons, saints, or the Almighty himself—through religious ritual, and did so because their faith and culture told them to do so. By 1500 many cultures had blended spiritual healing with remedies or rituals that were medicinal in nature. In the West, European cultures were in the process of segregating the body and spirit, the medical and religious: to the detriment of religion but the benefit of the sufferer. When European cultures took their medicine across the globe, they sometimes imposed Western religions and Western medicine on those they met.

The following short studies examine ways in which medicine and religion intersected within and between cultures across the globe between 1500 and 1800. They are meant to be indicative of certain patterns of human response and are by no means exhaustive of a rich and variegated topic.

THE EXPANDING CHRISTIAN WORLD

Roman Catholic Saints and Western Medicine

Healing bodily ills was long the stock-in-trade of Christian saints, or holy people, since Saint Peter's shadow was said to have cured the lame. Early stories of saints often featured miracles of healing—even resuscitating the dead—that were meant to be signs of God's favor with them. Christians did not believe the healing power was the holy person's but that God worked miracles through her as a benefit and a sign. Once deceased, the holy person properly came to be called saint and his or her ability to display God's favor through medical miracles remained.

From the early 1500s the Christian Church experienced the split known as the Reformation. Factions that "broke away" from the Catholic Church—Lutherans and Radicals in Germany and Scandinavia; Calvinists in Switzerland, France, Scotland, and the Netherlands; Anglicans and others in England—discarded many traditional Christian beliefs and practices, including those associated with helpful saints. In response, the Catholic Church reemphasized the roles

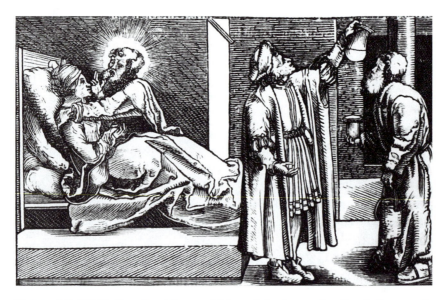

Figure 3.1 While the physician and his assistant examine the dying man's urine, a stereotypical medical activity, the patient is miraculously cured by the haloed saint who appears by his bedside. Copy of a woodcut attributed to Holbein, from the German translation of Boethius' 6th-century *Consolation of Philosophy*, 1537. (Lacroix, Paul. *Science and Literature in the Middle Age*, 1878)

of the saints as sources of help from and advocacy before God. Certain saints had long been associated with specific diseases, such as Saints Job and Lazarus with leprosy, or more recently Sebastian and Roche with plague. Some were generalists, such as the ancient Roman physicians Saints Cosmas and Damian; others were believed to help with childbirth or broken bones or smallpox. Still other saints had local or regional reputations, such as plague saints Rosalia in Palermo, Sicily; Archbishop Carlo Borromeo in Milan and Vienna; and Saint Januarius (San Gennaro) in Naples. Jesus's mother Mary was a universal advocate on whom any faithful Christian could call for help. She was often depicted spreading her cloak around her devotees protecting them from disease or other threats.

The line between the saint as advocate asking for God's help and the saint as powerful in his or her own right was often very thin. When a Catholic prayed to a saint for help, he probably did not make a clear distinction in his own mind between the two. Either way, if the supplicant survived, he might thank the saint by depositing a thank-you gift of a small statuette or painting in a local church or shrine. These served as testimonials to the saint's aid, bidding others to depend upon it. Wealthy thankful individuals might decorate whole chapels with frescoes of the helpful saint's life, or large portraits to be placed above altars. When a community wanted to give thanks for salvation from an epidemic, they might build special churches such as Venice's Santa Maria della Salute or Vienna's Karlskirche. Epidemics tended to spawn these expressions, since the belief was that ultimately God sent pestilence (as in the Old Testament) and the saint had convinced Him to direct His wrath away from the person, family, or community.

Canonization and Medicine

In 1588, Pope Sixtus V in the bull *Immensa aeterni Dei*, as part of the Catholic Reformation, regularized the process of canonization by which the central church recognized the holiness of its heroes. To be declared a saint by the Catholic Church, one had to have been true to Church teaching, heroically practice Christian virtues, and have a number of miracles clearly attributed to him or her after death. A formal proceeding, which included the "devil's advocate" who did his best to disprove the supporting evidence, now carefully gathered and examined sworn testimony to miracles. Much of this material has survived and has been recently studied by Jacalyn Duffin.[1]

Duffin found that between 1588 and 1800, 91 percent of the miracles attributed to candidates were healing miracles. This compares with

96 percent (486/506) during similar twentieth-century proceedings. The people who were cured were not just members of religious orders (only about 9% were), nor were they all gullible peasants. Of those whose status is known, nobility rank first, from kings on down. The impoverished are also well represented, but so are members of physicians' families. Those who testified to the miracles were also often doctors, and by 1800 if a physician had not intervened in the medical case, then the claim would be tossed out.

The Church's demands grew stiffer over time. The purported miracle had to be completely unexpected, unnatural, not due to medical care or procedures, ideally spontaneous, permanent, and clearly the result of the person or those around him calling upon (invoking) the candidate for sainthood. Duffin found various manners of invocation surrounding the basic prayer, from pilgrimages to having holy relics placed on the sick person. Miraculous healings spanned the range of human illnesses, with fevers and malaria predominant, followed by orthopedic conditions, neurological problems (especially vision), cancers (tumors), and a long list of other conditions. There were even 20 cases of resurrections, most of infants or children.

The Catholic Church in 1588 was still reeling from the Protestant split and sought to rationalize one of its most mystical practices. The process and its effect was powerful in its day and remains of note today, as in the cases of Pope John Paul II and of Mother Teresa—herself a powerful caregiver in life.

These traditions and beliefs spread to Portuguese, Spanish, and French outposts and colonies around the world. Their professional missionaries—Franciscans, Dominicans, and Jesuits—saw to it that they were preached for the salvation of the souls of Indians, Africans, Native Americans, Pacific Islanders, Japanese, Chinese, and many others. Where the European newcomers laid down roots, as in South America, Catholic beliefs and practices sometimes replaced and sometimes blended with those of native cultures. In many of these, healing saints and healing deities often melded, residing beneath the Church's radar but emerging in times of need.

Witches and Sorcerers

If the early modern Catholic Church was willing to side with rationality and the growing medicalization of society regarding canonizations, it was equally willing to remain downright superstitious for two centuries regarding men and women suspected of consorting with demons or the devil himself. Often the diabolical effect was sickness, plague, or even death of innocent victims of demonic arts. But Catholics were far from alone in their opposition to the devil and his minions. One only need remember Salem, Massachusetts, and its Puritan judges in 1692. Christians had a particular fear of witches since the Bible clearly commanded "suffer not a witch to live." Their conception of evil and harm was embodied in the figure of Satan, an entity clearly opposed to God. The linkages of witches and Satan in the popular and even learned imaginations tarred even the most innocently accused woman or man.

Part of the problem was with the healing abilities of many of the people labeled by their communities as witches. Just as the midwife knew both how to birth a baby and how to kill it through abortion or infanticide, so a community healer could, it was commonly believed, injure, maim, or even kill. If prompted by the devil, then harm was as likely as health. This paranoia was fueled when the ministrations of the "old lady in the woods" backfired, in fact causing injury. In an age that believed God sent plague and saints could heal from beyond the grave, it was perfectly logical that old ladies would consort with demons and slaughter farm animals or sour all the community's milk.

By the eighteenth century, both Catholic and Protestant authorities came to recognize that much of the witch craze had been irrational and misdirected. Not that people did not consort with Satan, nor that certain individuals did not have the power to injure. Such cases came to be seen as very rare, however, and fear of witches was branded as the hysterical superstition it usually was. Both sacred and secular societies in the West were adopting the Enlightenment era's rationalism with its disdain for the unscientific. As contemporary medicine made great strides in explaining many ailments, the "old lady in the woods" as causative agent disappeared with celestial conjunctions and the evil eye.

Protestant Religiosity

The Reformation redirected popular Protestant religiosity away from what Reformers considered superstitious reliance on saints toward God and the Bible. Though denominations and individuals differed in specifics, it is safe to say that Protestants believed that their health and welfare were ultimately in God's hands. The best way to preserve or improve both was through adherence to His will as found in the Bible. As prayer and fasting are both mentioned in Scripture, Protestant persons, congregations, and entire nations (England, Denmark, Brandenburg-Prussia) accepted these forms of individual and group penitence in the face of sickness, and especially epidemics.

When plague broke out in seventeenth-century England, both Anglican and Puritan leaders urged prayer and fasting, even publishing prayers and directions for leading families in a godly direction. The practice was carried to the New World and informed colonial civic life in New England as well as the British West Indies.

Dutch Calvinists held the same beliefs, though they seem to have been less insistent in carrying these with them to their far-flung holdings. In rejecting Catholicism, all Protestants rejected its ordained and sacred clergy, especially its professional missionaries. The result was that where Catholic colonization directly reached out to evangelize the natives—whether Japanese shoguns or Mayan farmers—Protestant efforts were only as effective as their spirit-driven congregants. This began to change with the rise of Methodism in the eighteenth century and other English evangelizing movements in the nineteenth, especially in Africa.

AFRICANS AT HOME AND ENSLAVED

West African Medicine: Body and Spirits

The peoples of early modern West Africa by no means constituted a single cultural unit. Their environments, languages, beliefs, practices, and shared experiences differed widely. They did, however, share certain fundamental beliefs about the natural world, the realm of spirits, and the intersections of the two. "Intersections" is probably the incorrect term, since for African societies there was no distinction between one and the other. Spirits—whether gods or ancestors—operated as truly and significantly among living people as did any natural phenomena. Their impacts could be positive or negative, just as those of an animal, plant, or the weather could be either.

Sickness or other physical ailments were often conceived of as the result of spirits' anger, vengeance, whim, dissatisfaction, or service to a malevolent devotee. Conversely, gods or ancestors who imposed sickness could also protect one from it, cure it, or lead a healer to identify (diagnose) the problem and apply the proper remedy. Some gods were thought to control certain diseases. The powerful earth god Sakpata was believed to impose, cure, and protect people from smallpox. Others, like the largely destructive Legba, were associated with a wide range of maladies: "Legba has many *gbo* for headache, for colic, for dysentery, for leprosy, for eye trouble, for rheumatism, and for all other kinds of illness."[2] *Gbo* were physical objects associated with avoiding sickness or healing, including talismans, amulets, and other ritual items. Keeping such entities satisfied meant good health or quick

Figure 3.2 Modern rendition of a traditional West African figurine representing Sakpata, the Yoruba god of smallpox. Adorned with layers of meaningful organic objects (*gbo*), such as shells and monkey skulls, these types of carvings have traditionally been created for protection from maladies such as smallpox. The blotches of blue and white represent the characteristic red marks on the skin. (Centers for Disease Control)

recovery, and West African healers were as much priests or shamans as practitioners of medicine in the European sense.[3]

Gods or ancestor spirits required acknowledgment and sacrifice, rewarding the cooperative and punishing the others. Prayers, songs, dances, and other rituals blended together into a spirit-pleasing display, while sacrifices might include food, alcohol, live animals, or blood. Human sacrifices were not unknown, though unlike among the Aztecs, they were apparently rare. Best known were those of powerful expansionist rulers, such as Agaja of Dahomey, who was said to have killed 200,000 as sacrifices to the war divinities.[4] Due attention to Sakpata, Legba, or other appropriate deities allowed healer-priests to work with them, diagnosing and appropriately prescribing treatments. Ancestors and gods might speak to healers, revealing the cause or course of a disease and its remedies. More dramatic was spirit possession. The spirit was drawn down into the healer or other devotee by dance or another ritual, often aided by hallucinogens or other mind-altering substances. Enveloped in a trance, the devotee provided a mouthpiece for the helpful divinity. This technique was also employed when an unsolved murder required divine help to identify the responsible party.

Enslaved Africans in the Caribbean

The millions of West Africans transplanted to the Western Hemisphere during the early modern period brought their cultures with them. Without the ability to record their beliefs, and under the assault of masters and resident black slaves to conform to the norms of their new home and employment, the recently enslaved appear to have lost at least some of the key elements of their belief systems. Specific entities associated with the homeland may have come to be understood as regional or local in their scope and power rather than universal. Mixing with slaves of various origins, recent arrivals would have been exposed to differing names of divinities, and perhaps new spiritual pantheons. Christianity, too, had an influence, depending on the attitudes of the slaveholders and their religious backgrounds (Spanish or French Catholic, English or Dutch Protestant). But even if the spiritual landscape had changed, the role of spirits in imposing, protecting from, and remedying illness could not have.

Recent studies have demonstrated that slave masters of European descent imposed European medicine on slaves who were injured or fell ill.[5] More difficult to demonstrate is the hold spirit medicine continued to have on enslaved blacks. Of course, spiritual medicine required the special priest-healers, who had very high status in Africa. Such powerful figures and potential leaders of revolt were undesirable from the white slavers' viewpoint, and would have been culled out if known. As Karol Weaver shows, however, such healers and leaders did emerge in some African slave communities. It was through the success of their healing practices that their reputations were made.

Afro-Caribbean slaves also adapted elements of Catholicism in their new homes, a process that remains rather dim to modern observers.

Savvy priest-healers realized the power of syncretic religion, which blended Catholic beliefs and practices with those of West Africa. Healing or helpful saints retained their place among Catholics long after Protestant churches abandoned them, and for many slaves they replaced African tribal entities. Catholic prayer and other rituals, often led by strangely dressed celebrants and illuminated by candles, had an appeal to people who had lost their own spiritual guides. Catholic sacramentals—objects associated with prayer or other rituals—such as scapulars, rosaries, holy water and oil, and statues of Jesus and saints came to be seen as *gbo* and were adopted as tools with healing power. When wielded by enslaved priest-healers, they were sources of power taken from those who had physical power over them.

RELIGION AND MEDICINE AMONG THE AZTECS

Precolonial Religion and Medicine

Like many premodern peoples, including those of West Africa, the Aztecs of what is today Mexico had powerful beliefs concerning the intervention of gods and lesser spirits in human affairs. This included health and illness; the veil between medicine and religion was very thin. Aztec deities had the same dualistic powers to help or hurt that the African gods possessed. For example, the major rain god Tláloc could enrich the earth and its peoples by providing abundant fresh water. Conversely, he could withhold his gift and cause drought, or inundate the land, killing crops, animals, and people with his flood. Lesser divinities governed elements of nature including geographic and weather features, such as mountains and winds, and could use their powers to help or destroy the people. Still others controlled specific diseases, inflicting, protecting from, or remedying as they saw fit.

Most of the Aztec pantheon had some role to play in human health.[6] The sun god Tonatiuh was necessary for life itself; too little or too much of his gift and famine struck the people. Tláloc governed the rains but was also associated with human, animal, and crop fertility, tuberculosis, and other respiratory illnesses. The famous Quetzalcóatl, for whom the Aztecs mistook the conqueror Cortés due to his fair skin and beard, was noted as a teacher of medicinal herbal lore, as were the goddesses Tzapotlatena and Tonantzin. Xiptótec was the patron of healers and held sway over abscesses, scabies, (later) smallpox, and some other skin diseases, while Nanáhuatl handled more severe ones such as elephantiasis and leprosy. The war god Huitzilopochtli could determine life and death on the battlefield, while the goddess Tlazoltéotl determined whether mothers in labor and their infants lived or died. Xoaltecuhtli was responsible for the mind, and Amímitl for one's bowels and dysentery.

Aztec religion discerned a very strict moral code that the gods and spirits expected humans to obey. While the deities could be whimsical in their infliction of sickness or other misfortunes, these were usually the result of human misbehavior and divine punishment. Sorcerers could also call upon gods to cause pain or suffering, and gods could punish wicked parents by making their children suffer. The key was to redress the moral imbalance through prayers and rituals. The most dramatic ritual was human sacrifice, during some of which the beating hearts were cut out of victims' bodies. The most famous of these took place in 1486 at the dedication of the new temple in the Aztec capital, in which 70,000 people were said to have been sacrificed. At times of military defeat, drought, famine, or disease, the world seemed clearly out of balance, and the cosmos itself, not merely some petulant divinity, needed to be reset.

The scholar Bernard Ortiz de Montellano[7] sees the Aztec worldview as essentially fatalistic. The norm of life on Earth is suffering, and the gods are the agents of that suffering through the instruments of misfortune, accident, and sickness. There are no guarantees in life—even the good suffer—but people must strive to obey the laws of nature and acknowledge the gods. An apt metaphor was living on the razor's edge of a mountaintop, with a deep crevasse on either side. As with the Greeks, balance (survival) meant moderation in all things and a stoical outlook on life. When that failed, the sorcerers ("owl men"), shamans, and priests went to work divining the causes—especially which deity or deities bore responsibility—and prescribing or carrying out the appropriate remedies. Allowing oneself to be possessed by a spirit and reading the message in a handful of corn kernels tossed on a table were among the forms of diagnosis or prognosis by divination. If it was determined that a spirit had caused the disease, then healers oversaw spiritual remedies ranging from confession of sin to sacrifices or the eating of ritual cakes. Spirits might also inhabit medicinal plants, whose natural healing virtues were thus increased. In each case the healer was the bridge between the patient and the divine disease, "the Lord of transformations."[8]

Colonial Mexico

During most of the early modern period, the world of the Aztecs was dominated by the Roman Catholic Spaniards and their descendants. In villages and regions where the Spanish presence was light, the local people continued their beliefs and practices. Even so, spiritual healers were always subject to persecution by the religious authorities such as the Inquisition. Where the Catholic presence was stronger and the expectation that all subjects of the Spanish king would be Catholic, the natives found much that was familiar in the new rulers' medicine. The Catholic emphasis on saints, sacramentals, and religious rituals coupled with a rather fatalistic outlook, a Galenic medical emphasis on moderation and balance (of humors), and a positive interest in native healing practices and medicinal plants made acceptance of European religion and medicine rather easier than it might otherwise have been.[9]

Positive, healing saints replaced the dualistic gods; a new set of prayers and rituals took the place of the old ones; and the Indians saw transformative power embedded in miraculous paintings, amulets, and the Catholic priesthood. The same missionaries who led the religious liturgies and processions often also baptized the newly born, cared for the sick, and blessed the dying. Spanish culture could not abide the continuation of human sacrifices, but the new and healthful religion emphasized the healing power of the sacrifice of Jesus Christ (so powerfully portrayed through the crucifix) and of many of the Christian martyrs to whom Catholics prayed. Even the Catholic belief in the literal presence of divine Jesus in the Eucharistic bread that was consumed by believers paralleled native beliefs of spirit possessions and cures effected by eating ritual cakes—"god cakes"—in which one of the healing deities was thought to be present.

The replacement or blending of spiritual healing traditions produced the *curanderos*, who often served the far-flung native villages and rural communities. These healers utilized native and imported medical techniques and remedies as well as both Aztec and Catholic spiritual practices. Mexican Catholic authorities distrusted these practitioners because they feared that the *curanderos* derived healing power from the devil, a fear reinforced by the healers' retention of Aztec practices and the Church's inability to oversee the Catholic elements in their practice, such as prayers and sacramentals.[10]

MING AND QING CHINA

Chinese Medicine: Worshipping the Ancestor Physicians

In traditional China, physicians were considered social equals of artists and other craftsmen, despite their role as healers. This status, however, was augmented by the Chinese practice of ancestor worship. Before the early modern period temples dedicated to the Three Emperors (*sanhuang miao*), ancients considered by many to be the founders of medicine, drew worshippers to sacrifices of pigs and sheep overseen by physician-priests. Temples held images of the three, with their four assistants, and 28 famed physicians. The Yüan dynasty (1274–1368) emperors and their bureaucrats mandated and patronized these temples as a way of emphasizing their connection with the divine but also as a way of maintaining an authoritative presence among physicians and their patients. This was useful, since the Chinese state played no clear role in examining, licensing, or otherwise controlling doctors or medical practice.[11]

Ming dynasty rulers (1368–1644) shifted this support, as they concentrated attention on themselves and their capital. By 1500 the craft of medicine was firmly associated with the Three Emperors, but state officials sought to have their worship concentrated in the capital and under their control. Three kneelings, nine bows, and three sacrifices (cow, sheep, pig) for each emperor constituted orthodox worship. Local temples, however, languished or disappeared without state support. The Qing dynastic rulers (1644–1912) continued the pattern of reduced support for provincial temples, while centralizing worship in the capital.

Local worship also shifted, as both urban and rural people developed and expanded the cults of local medical ancestors and of the Medicine King (*yaowang*). The identity of this figure changed with time and place, but by the sixteenth century it was usually Sun Simiao (581–682) a physician still worshipped today. Patronage from local social leaders replaced state support for medical cults, signaling a new level of popular acceptance of medicine as more than a mere craft. Chinese elites, whether the emperor or wealthy local merchants, built and funded these places of worship because they shared the core Confucian virtue of benevolence. Elite physicians, itinerant healers, herb peddlers, and others associated with medicine hung about these *yaowang miao* (temples) awaiting and seeing patients, further associating their work with divine aid of ancestor-gods. Secondary temples and shrines dedicated to healing and healers also popped up with local support due to people's demand for them. None of this was entirely new, and much reflected venerable local village and urban practice and belief.

Chinese Medicine: Demons and Spirits

Very early Chinese medicine also had a dominant role for malevolent spiritual forces as causes of all sorts of human illnesses. Despite the development of a rational system of medical theory and practice based upon it, spiritual forces of "evil" continued to play a significant role throughout the early modern (Ming-Qing) period. Among the people, concern for demonic influences and effects probably remained the norm long after 1800. As late as the eighteenth century, spell casting was a formal academic medical specialty (though it was removed), and exorcists in both cities and villages had plenty of business. Every classically trained or learned physician had to know the principles and procedures of defeating evil, if only to placate certain clients. Virtually every Ming-Qing Chinese medical text has a place for spiritual cures, even if, as physician Chang Chieh-pin wrote around 1624, "demons are created in one's mind."[12] An eighteenth-century edition of the works of physician Hsü Ling-t'ai approvingly includes his opinion: "Whenever illnesses were caused by demons and spirits, the uneducated claim that demons and spirits truly possess the ability to bring misfortunes to man. Educated persons, however, maintain that although the specific characteristics of some illnesses may give the impression, demons and spirits in reality do not exist. Both of these views are false."[13]

Ancestors' ghosts, those of unjustly killed people, and nature spirits had potential to assault one in a lonely place, usually at night. Possession through the nose or mouth could result in unconsciousness; other ailments could be imposed through natural channels. Since the Chinese did not separate the spiritual and physical aspects of reality or medicine, there was no effective barrier against malevolent activity. Confucianism, however, did provide a prophylactic: one protected oneself from spiritual malevolence through virtuous living. Just as bad behavior could lead to naturally occurring disease, so it opened doors to demons.

Despite its ubiquity, there was no standardized theory or practice by which to deal with spiritually caused sickness. No doubt the itinerant or village healer or exorcist had local or familial traditions upon which to draw. Talismans and amulets might keep forces at bay, and noise, smoke, and potions using peach leaves and twigs might expel them when one was possessed. Learned authors recommended that their readers use both spiritual and natural treatments if there were any question . . . just in case.

NOTES

1. Jacalyn Duffin, *Medical Miracles: Doctors, Saints and Healing in the Modern World* (New York: Cambridge University Press, 2009).

2. James H. Sweet, *Domingos Álvares, African Healing, and the Intellectual History of the Atlantic World* (Chapel Hill: University of North Carolina Press, 2011), 125.

3. See Robert Voeks, "African Medicine and Magic," *Geographical Reviews* 83 (1993): 66–79.

4. Sweet, *Domingos Álvares*, 137.

5. A good example is Mark Harrison, *Medicine in an Age of Commerce and Empire: Britain and Its Tropical Colonies, 1660–1830* (New York: Oxford University Press, 2010).

6. On the various gods see Gordon Schendel, *Medicine in Mexico: From Aztec Herbs to Betatrons* (Austin: University of Texas Press, 1968), 16–31.

7. Bernard R. Ortiz de Montellano, *Aztec Medicine, Health, and Nutrition* (New Brunswick, NJ: Rutgers University Press, 1990).

8. Schendel, *Medicine in Mexico*, 167.

9. For example see Robert McCaa, "Spanish and Nahuatl Views on Smallpox and Demographic Catastrophe in Mexico," *Journal of Interdisciplinary History* 25 (1995): 397–431.

10. See Sherry Fields, *Pestilence and Headcolds: Encountering Illness in Colonial Mexico* (New York: Columbia University Press, 2008); Noble David Cook and W. George Lovell, eds., *"Secret Judgments of God": Old World Disease in Colonial Spanish America* (Norman: University of Oklahoma Press, 1992).

11. Yüan-ling Chao, *Medicine and Society in Late Imperial China* (New York: Peter Lang, 2007); for this and what follows, see chap. 2.

12. Paul Unschuld, *Medicine in China: A History of Ideas*, 2nd ed. (Berkeley: University of California Press, 1985), 329.

13. Ibid., 337.

CHAPTER 4

Women's Health and Medicine

Woman's health issues differed from those of men almost exclusively in the realm of reproduction. Despite male domination of learned medicine in China and the West in 1500, across cultures healing women in need and aiding in childbirth generally fell to other women. Aztec women practitioners, however, lost out to Spanish males, and by the eighteenth century, across Europe and China the medical specialties we may loosely label gynecology and obstetrics (*obstetrix* = midwife) were falling under the purview of educated professional males.

THE AZTECS

Women played powerful roles in maintaining the health of the Aztec population. Life came into the world through the instrumentation of their bodies, and their bodies nourished each new and young life. Bringing death, whether through warfare or bloody sacrifices to the gods, was a male occupation. Women healers (spiritual healers, herbalists, wound tenders, etc.), therefore, were considered to be on a par with males, sharing practical training and preparation in the temples for both spiritual and medical treatments.

Figure 4.1 An Aztec midwife administers herbs to a woman after childbirth. One of the 2,000 native-produced illustrations from the 16th-century *Florentine Codex* by Bernardino de Sahagún, who died in 1590. All images from the Codex are available at the World Digital Library: http://www.wdl.org/en/item/10096/. (Biblioteca Medicea-Laurenziana, Florence, Italy/The Bridgeman Art Library)

Pregnancy and Birth before the Spanish

The midwife or *tepalechuiani* (one who helps) was considered a specialized *tíctl* (healer), with the same social rank as a male healer. When doing her duty of overseeing a pregnancy and childbirth, she prayed to the healing goddess Yoaltíctl for protection as well as to the goddess of water, Chalchiuhtlicue, at the point of birth. The midwife knew which prayers, herbs, and sexual positions helped induce pregnancy as well as methods of contraception and, when desperate, abortion. Special care went to the first-time mother and her family, and the midwife taught all to see that the young mother, usually a teenager, ate properly and avoided strong emotions and strenuous work. Other, less obvious, activities were also to be avoided: viewing a lunar eclipse (believed to cause harelip in the child), chewing gum or tar (cleft palate), sleeping during the day (long eyelids), eating tamales from the bottom of the pot (could bring on a difficult labor), and viewing a hanging (could cause the umbilical cord to strangle the child).[1]

During labor and birth the Aztec midwife had full authority: the mother was "in your hands, in your lap, on your back."[2] The Aztecs respected cleanliness and kept the mother and birthing area relatively sanitary. The mother also received a steam bath to help induce labor and relieve stress. In his 1552 herbal, the native Martín de la Cruz provided the ingredients for washes to clean and lubricate the birth canal, and a solution to be injected "into the womb" to reduce labor pains.[3] Cacao, which was considered good for inducing menstruation and conception, was also recommended for aiding labor, as was an extract of possum tails. Once the mother's water broke, the midwife positioned the baby from the outside as the mother squatted to give birth. In the case of a successful birth, the midwife cut the umbilical cord, washed the infant, and prayed "Goddess, be pleased that his [or her] life may be purified; that the water may carry away all stain, for the child puts him [or her]self in your hands, oh Chalchiuhtlicue, mother and sister of the gods." The midwife formally named the child (whether the parents had a say is uncertain). Herbs and poultices helped induce lactation, and further steam baths helped clean and relax the mother.

In the case of an unsuccessful birth, the midwife retained control and did all she could to save the mother's life. The midwife was equipped with a very sharp obsidian knife and tongs to dismember and remove a dead infant, and knew how to use them. If the mother died giving birth to her first child, she was hailed as a *mochihuaquetzqui*, a valiant woman, and she was carried by a procession of midwives to a special temple for burial. She was considered as if a soldier fallen in battle, and some parts of her body were considered relics and worn as amulets.

Colonial Mexico

With conquest by the Spanish in the mid-1500s, the roles and status of Aztec female *tíctli* declined. Male priests and physicians replaced female practitioners, and midwives fell in status to the subordinate place their sisters held in European society. As in Europe, pregnancy and childbirth only became medical issues when something went wrong, and the male surgeons and physicians stood by to handle any emergencies. From the spiritual side, priests and friars replaced the spiritual healers, both male and female, and prayers to the gods were replaced with those to the Trinity or saints, such as Anne, who oversaw childbirth. Midwives who retained their pre-Christian religious practices or who showed too much skill with herbs risked the label witch and investigation by the Inquisition. In general, Aztec women declined in status not only by virtue of their having been conquered but by their very sex.[4]

CARIBBEAN SLAVES

In many West African cultures, traditional healing lore and skills were passed from mother to daughter. Though male healers with special powers were necessary for serious medical cases, women healers tackled most common conditions of both men and women. Women were especially important for monitoring pregnancies, facilitating births, performing clitorectomies, and tracking children's growth and development, including the young woman's emergence into adulthood. Healing was far less an occupational specialty than a fundamental skill like cooking or making clothing.[5]

In the world of the slave ship and plantation, the woman retained her role as healer and caregiver, though certain women rose to prominence for their skills. Some slave women tended the masters' children or other servants, and plantation mistresses sometimes chose to treat male and female slaves to the best of their abilities with European medicine. Of course, white male physicians and surgeons circulated through the slaves' world as needed, but women generally took on the full range of medical duties, as midwives, nurses, and herbalists, but also as doctors, surgeons, and spiritual healers. Unfortunately, little is known of them or their service.

Early on, Caribbean planters of all nationalities imported primarily males, and the few female slaves were valuable for both their healing skills and their fertility. After a while the low cost of importing slaves made keeping pregnant female slaves and supporting a nursery of slave children uneconomical, so "breeding" was discouraged. With the spread of abolitionism and restrictions on the slave trade in the eighteenth century, pronatalism returned and female slaves were prized again for their fertility. In the British Sugar Islands, the Consolidated Slave Act of 1792 provided rewards for live births. When births were welcome pregnant slaves were often protected by law or regulations from hard labor or brutal treatment, but even then miscarriages were common as were deaths from clumsy midwives and infection. Perennial problems of overwork, overheating, poor nutrition and living conditions, careless and inept health care, diseases, and sexual predation by both black and white males made pregnant or nursing young mothers terribly vulnerable.[6]

THE CHINESE

Women Healers

By 1500 the Chinese had had a long and continuous tradition of learned medicine that recognized almost exclusively the well-read male physician as a legitimate healer. Writing was a carefully guarded and shared skill that few women healers possessed, so rather little is known about them from their own words. Of named Chinese medical practitioners only 1 in 200 (0.50%) is female. Of some 12,000 known premodern Chinese medical texts, women wrote only 3. The earliest was by the sixteenth-century physician's daughter Tan Yunxian, *Sayings of a Female Doctor*. Part biography and part case book, *Sayings* explains that Tan read the standard medical classics in her father's library and learned women's medicine from her grandmother. Most who sought her out were women, and she applied a variety of treatments, from diet recommendations to medicines, acupuncture, and moxibustion.[7]

Yet women healers always played a wide variety of very important roles in Chinese society. Like Tan, many were educated in healing by other female healers or their husbands or fathers, or they educated themselves informally. Their patients tended to be children and other women, but they also served as smallpox inoculators, pulse takers, herbalists and medicine sellers, religious healers, diviners, and caretakers for chronic sufferers. Wives of notables often tended the medical needs of servants, local peasants, and the poor. Midwives and "wise-women" routinely advised and treated women for gynecological and obstetric problems, and Buddhist and Daoist nuns were noted for both their physical and spiritual healing treatments. Emperors of the Ming dynasty forbade male practitioners access to the women's rooms at court, relying on skilled women to tend to their wives and daughters. Yet the corps of learned physicians uniformly denigrated women healers for their lack of proper education and theoretical understanding, ignorance of proper practice, imitation of "genuine" physicians, and often lower-class origins.

Fuke, or Medicine for Women

Learned Chinese medicine had long treated the human body as male, with the female variations relegated to the knowledge and skills of women healers. In 651 CE the influential Sun Miao wrote that "illnesses of women are ten times harder to treat than those of men"; "they are unable to control their emotions by themselves, therefore the roots of their disorders are deep and it is difficult to cure them"; and "women's cravings and desires exceed their husbands' and they contract illnesses at twice the rate of men."[8] Four centuries later the Imperial Medical Service formally recognized *chanke*—medicine for childbearing—and this was broadened into the medical field of medicine for women, or *fuke*. From the learned male's standpoint, however, basic biological principles (*li*) were more important than variations, so learned medicine in the sixteenth and seventeenth centuries downplayed the distinctiveness of *fuke* as a field of medicine (*yi*). At the same time, the later Ming dynasty witnessed the rise in demand for printed medical texts, including those on *fuke*.

A work such as Xue Ji's sixteenth-century *Revised Good Prescriptions for Women* collected much that was traditional from previous centuries but moved the theoretical emphasis away from blaming most women's medical problems on pulses and "cardinal channels" to the blood, its storage in the liver, and depletion through the menses and childbirth. In *To Benefit Yin* (1620), Wu Zhiwang and his colleagues attacked the simplicity of Xue's work while preserving much traditional theory and practice dating back to the *Yellow Emperor's Canon*.[9] But *To Benefit Yin*'s popularity (34 known editions to 1911) was its acceptance of the complexity of *fuke*, given the structure of Chinese medical knowledge, and genuine attempt to clarify its subject through organization and careful definition. As medical professionals sought to establish themselves on ever-firmer foundations of theory and book learning, more and more works on *fuke* appeared. These tended to reflect the greater emphasis on organic—as opposed to spiritual or even environmental—causes and appropriate treatments championed by Wu. Out went "baleful ghosts," sky spirits, unclear yin influences, and generic "wind" and "cold." Medicine sought to demystify the female body and to recommend treatments that fit the organic nature of both its structure and its illnesses. This accompanied a broader cultural shift toward emphasizing the reproductive nature and function of women. In 1757 Hsü Ta-ch'un could write in his *Forgotten Traditions of Ancient Chinese Medicine*, "There is no difference between illnesses affecting females and those affecting males except for illnesses related to the monthly period, to pregnancy, and delivery."[10] Insofar as learned medicine could claim to understand and be able successfully to direct the care of pregnant or ailing women, it spread its professional control over the other half of China's population.

Midwives and *Fuke*, Pregnancy, and Birth

Through the eighteenth century more treatises on *fuke* appeared—for example *Treatise on Easy Childbirth* by Ye Feng in 1715 (182 editions), *Childbirth Treasury* by Ni Zhiwei in 1728, Yan Chunxi's 1730 *Essential Teachings on Childbearing*, in 1742 the great compendium *The Golden Mirror*, and by the monks of the Bamboo Grove Buddhist monastery the *Secret Book for Female Tranquility* in 1786—as male physicians continued to mark their new territory. But unlike the similar situation in

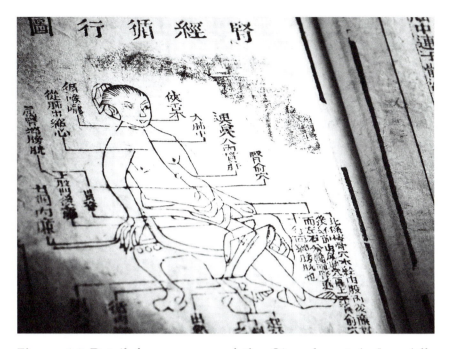

Figure 4.2 Detail from a page of the Qing dynasty's *Imperially Commissioned Golden Mirror of the Orthodox Lineage of Medicine* (1742). This specially produced collection of traditional and contemporary medical information included commentaries, clinical materials, and illustrations such as this in order to be useful to a wide audience. It was also notable in part for its inclusion of sections devoted to women's health, a field of increasing interest in the mid-18th century. (Photos.com)

contemporary Europe, Chinese physicians did not stoop to participate in child birthing. As before, they prescribed drugs and pronounced sage advice on prenatal care but left the birthing room to the women. Midwives remained despised even when vital, Ye Feng declaring them "frequently stupid and ignorant of the proper principles."[11] Their status fell as families invested in the new literature, which most midwives could not read, and physician-authors warned against employing "ignorant old women" to perform such an important function. In some ways the new literature was meant to replace the midwives' prenatal direction and advice.

Yet advice on contraception, conception, and prenatal care remained traditional, as did the birthing procedures and options by most accounts. Blood was the yin manifestation of the life force qi (chee) that joined with the male sperm to produce the fetus. Infertility might stem from insufficient quantity or quality of blood, or interference in the womb by wind or cold (or demons or ghosts, though belief in these was waning). Careful inspection of the menses before an attempt at conception could alert one to future problems. Some blamed inappropriate temperatures inside or outside the womb or moistness/dryness inside, blocked blood vessels, insufficient penetration by the penis, weak sperm, or orgasms that were not simultaneous. To increase the likelihood of a male child the male orgasm needed to be the stronger, the left or yang side of the womb had to host the fetus, and the day of conception needed to be a yang-dominant day, or the odd numbered days after the end of a menstrual period.[12]

Prenatal care remained standard in principle from the seventh through the nineteenth centuries: a balance of rest, movement, and diet to regulate the qi of both mother and child; maintenance of emotional stability; and protection of the womb from physical trauma. The Chinese taught that failure in any area could mean a corrupted fetus, an overly long pregnancy (they believed the norm to be 10 months; more than that probably meant a stillbirth), and premature birth or miscarriage. Though the medical literature of the eighteenth century often ignored or taught against concern for ghosts, ancestors, demons, gods, or magic rituals, no doubt most families adhered to traditions with the acquiescence of the "ignorant old" midwife. Ye Feng swept aside the spiritual traditions, but he also embraced the idea that childbirth was an act of creation in harmony with the universe, and the norm should be relatively pain free and safe for mother and child. He objected to any interventions—painkillers, stimulants, forced labor, or manipulation of the child in the womb or in descent—that were supposed to ease or shorten labor. His disdain for midwives centered on their insistence on such unnatural interference.

Of course the experienced midwife was invaluable if complications occurred during or after the baby presented. If the umbilical cord was strangling the child, if the child was dead and needed to be dismembered and extracted, if the afterbirth had not been ejected, or if the mother hemorrhaged, the midwife's expertise and demeanor could mean life or death. But just as the physician (if and when available) oversaw the prenatal mother, so he monitored the postpartum mother for damage to the genital area, for dangerous hormonal changes, for active lactation and the ability to feed the infant, for the replenishment of qi lost in labor, and for signs of infection or fever.[13]

THE EUROPEANS

Women as Medical Practitioners and Nurses

The existence of a small but learned and male-dominated medical profession in early modern Europe meant that the vast majority of medical problems were tended to by someone other than a physician. The tradition of the nurturing and caring woman anchored in the home ensured that mothers and grandmothers, sisters, wives, and daughters, took care of ailing family members and servants, and neighbors watched sick neighbors. In rural areas medical professionals were few; men and women relied largely on female healers from herbalists and wisewomen to midwives, faith healers, and charitable aristocratic wives who learned medical recipes and procedures from a growing list of vernacular medical self-help books authored by men and women.

In cities, guilds of physicians, apothecaries, and surgeons, as well as male civic authorities, ensured that recognized or even licensed female practitioners were few and far between. Lack of access to education meant women were generally excluded from becoming physicians. Skilled wives or daughters of apothecaries or surgeons might be acceptable substitutes, especially during emergencies such as plague or war. But two societal trends worked against the ambitious female healer. One was the growing concern for the protection of the male professions from encroachment by each other, by nonprofessional empirics or quacks, and by women. The second was the fear of witches and witchcraft, claims of which often tainted female healers both rural and urban. If the patient lived, it was thanks to the healer's pact with Satan; if he died, it was murder at Satan's behest. Though rare before 1500, witch hunts had claimed perhaps 200,000 lives—men as well as women—across Europe by 1700.

The term "nursing" stems from the same root as "nourish" (as in wet nursing), and links the occupation of caregiving (as opposed to healing) to the woman's supposed place and function in the home. When hospitals, orphanages, pest houses, and other institutions required caregivers the male administrators usually turned to women. Before the Reformation most such facilities were Catholic and staffed by monks, friars, or nuns. The French began consolidating and secularizing their hospitals in the late 1400s, and Protestant states, including England, replaced religious with civic administrators and staff. Female nurses changed diapers and bandages, laundered and changed bed linens, fed and medicated the sick, comforted the dying, and laid out the dead for burial. Since male professionals visited weekly or as needed, the female staff had to handle all care in their absence. It was hard and dirty work, and in Protestant countries with low pay and status, turn-over was common. In Catholic countries such as Italy, Spain, and Austria, nuns continued their service, providing spiritual as well as medical care and comfort. Some orders of nursing nuns predated 1500, but several were founded in the sixteenth and seventeenth centuries by pious and humane women, such as the Ursulines (1535) and Sisters of Saint Joseph (1650). The Sisters of Charity, founded by Saint Vincent de Paul, whose members served in madhouses, orphanages, hospitals, and even prisons, were not nuns but single and even married women who felt called to serve.[14]

Midwives

Though giving birth may not have been a "medical condition," it is and was often accompanied by hazards to both the mother and child. Both classical and Christian traditions considered women as humans who differed from the male anatomical and physiological norm, and formal medicine left much that was "gynecological" and almost all that was "obstetrical" to women healers, most often midwives. Women aiding other women in childbirth was traditionally a cross-cultural norm. In Europe, males were welcome in the birthing room only if an emergency occurred requiring a physician, surgeon, or priest. The local midwife was the expert on matters of reproduction from fertility to birth, and most physicians and surgeons were content to allow them to advise and practice both prenatally and during labor.

Most midwives had raised families of their own and had served neighbors and family during births. They learned much from older women, from their own experience assisting older midwives, and increasingly from vernacular manuals. For example in Germany Eucharius Roesselin published his *Rosegarden* (1513); it was translated into French in 1539 and English in 1540 as *The Birth of Mankind*. In Spain Damián Carbón penned his *Book of the Midwives' Art* in1541; and in 1608 Frenchwoman Louise Bourgeois wrote her *Diverse Observations*, the first work by a midwife. Because giving birth was considered both an act of creation and a foul and polluting act, the Catholic Church began administering moral oaths to midwives, first in Regensburg in 1452. A midwife knew how to administer contraceptives and abortifacients, gave legal testimony on stillborn and abandoned infants and young women's virginity, and literally held the mother's and child's lives in her hand, and so had to be of high moral character as well as technically skilled. Yet even by the eighteenth century an errant German midwife could be denigrated by a court document as handling "a laboring woman with little skill and less concern, and instead of trying to raise her spirits with good words, prattles on with silly talk, smokes too much, and drinks brandy."[15] As early as 1512 England licensed midwives; in 1556 a French edict required that midwives be registered; and in 1560 statutes controlled Parisian midwives. The latter stipulated who could be a candidate, her examination by two midwives and two master surgeons, and her oath and moral requirements (baptize a dying infant, shun abortion, report illegitimate babies, help the poor without charge).

One trend across the early modern period was that midwives be registered, licensed, and, eventually, formally educated. The Anglican Church licensed midwives in England, and in France medical practitioners, the Church, and the state all did so. In Venice they were licensed by the state, but in most of Italy by local priests. In Germany and the Netherlands, municipal authorities licensed midwives, and in Spain local physicians or the *protomedicato* (official medical office) did so. Another trend was toward a greater understanding of the female reproductive system, though this had a minimal impact on the knowledge and practice of female midwives. This intellectual advance accompanied a trend toward professionalization among midwives. By the eighteenth century this varied from place to place: increasing literacy meant a greater demand and greater supply of manuals and textbooks; some demanded (and some got) greater access to anatomical dissections and formal training, while others pushed for associations or guilds. At the same time, however, the male professions resisted the competition from women, and male midwives coming out of the surgeons' ranks began competing with the women. For many women (and their husbands) this was unacceptable, in part thanks to the thought of large male hands manipulating the emerging baby and its tender environment. For some, however, male midwives represented the cutting edge of proper science, combining theoretical knowledge as well as obstetrical training. They also used some new tools adapted to the purpose, such as forceps from about 1750.

Some women, such as Madame Angelique du Coudray in France, responded by providing across France formalized training of appropriate women, including the use of life-size models of the mother's birth canal. Du Coudray had been chosen by Louis XVI for the task, a reminder of the state's interest in healthy births. In Italy Bologna opened one school in 1753, and between 1757 and 1779 another 13 midwifery schools appeared. Spain's first opened in Madrid in 1787. By 1751 William Smellie of London had trained some 900 male midwives in two-week courses that tended to have practicing physicians and surgeons as students. Women's health care had to have improved somewhat by this embracing of obstetrics by the surgeon's profession, though this led to the further denigration of women midwives as ignorant and unskilled.[16]

Contraception, Conception, and Abortion

Early modern European midwives, and many other women, knew how to avoid pregnancy or at least lessen its probability. This was possible by prolonging lactation by nursing, or by coitus interruptus (male's pulling out), by inserting a semen-absorbing sponge in the vagina, or by otherwise blocking the entrance with an impermeable membrane (as a female condom does today). Herbalists, apothecaries, and midwives knew of the supposed contraceptive properties of certain plants, but these, like black hellebore, were also powerful abortifacients and had to be used very carefully. Ignorant and rural Europeans often relied on talismans, chants, and rituals. Then as now, the Catholic Church condemned the intentional termination of any pregnancy, and civil laws often provided the death penalty for those involved in abortions. Nonetheless, woman empirics, wisewomen, and male charlatans peddled abortifacients, even advertising under the euphemism "restoratives."

When conceiving was the issue, the same range of practitioners suggested a vast variety of sexual positions, types of foreplay, control of orgasms, astrological timing, poultices, potions, rituals, prayers, diet and exercise regimens, and talismans. Galenic humoralism, astrology, pagan folk beliefs, Roman Catholicism, and family lore all contributed to the mix. To produce a "dry" male child the French Dr. Joubert recommended conceiving right after the mother's period before the menses collected and produced a "moist" uterine atmosphere. He further suggested the "dry" male would benefit from conception during dry weather and while the mother consumed a "dry and cold" diet. The Italian Dr. Michele Savonarola wrote that the boy-desiring mother should lie on her right side, since it was supposedly warmer. Ideas like these spread through vernacular editions and translations of manuals, and from the literate to their friends and patients. Women were rarely dissected through the sixteenth century, so physicians had very little experience with women's reproductive anatomy: to the extent that many believed there were up to seven chambers in the uterus, with the central one that in which hermaphrodite babies were gestated.

Pregnant European women received what prenatal care they could. In cities physicians, apothecaries, and midwives could provide advice and reliefs for discomforts and monitor the baby's development. To prevent miscarriages practitioners prescribed all manner of prayers, amulets, jewels, ointments, and, more helpfully, strict regimens of healthful diets, soothing herbs, emotional stability, and plenty of rest. In rural areas a male professional would have been rather rare and would have been useful only in the event of problems such as fainting or unexpected vaginal discharges of blood or other matter. The pregnant woman would have relied on family, friends, the local pastor, and the midwife.[17]

Giving Birth, Nursing, and the Wet Nurse

The word "midwife" in English derives from the German phrase *mit weib*, "with the wife or woman." The most important task of both mother and midwife was to bring forth a healthy baby. In most European cultures the midwife prepared the birthing room, bringing her tools and drugs, and ensuring warmth, water, towels, and some modicum of comfort. Other women may have been present to encourage the struggling mother or to pray if matters went awry. Men's presence was a matter of culture. As labor began amulets and precious stones were laid on the mother's belly; her vaginal area was lubricated and massaged; and she was given an enema (often ipecacuah) to clear out her intestines and stimulants such as coffee or cocoa or an opiate such as laudanum.

The position the mother took to give birth was also a matter of custom, though over time it seems mothers were given multiple options. During the eighteenth century, as males took greater roles in birthing, the German birthing chair with its restrictive stirrups became widely popular, as did a special "lucinary bed" complete with stirrups, a reclining back, and a seat at the foot for the midwife.

As the baby descended the birth canal, it was best if the mother's effort alone could give it help. Urgent cries of "push!" in every European language accompanied the infant as it rotated in the canal and eventually emerged. When the baby was ill-positioned, however, the midwife earned her pay. Before the invention of the forceps in mid-eighteenth-century England (apparently), and for long after, the skilled hands of the midwife gently but firmly assessed the situation and did what they could. If she proved helpless, the surgeon was called in to do what he could. Assuming the baby was emerging intact, he still might have the umbilical cord wrapped around his throat, choking, and need further manipulation.

Through all of this ran the constant threat of serious wounding: the baby could be damaged or deprived of air; the mother could be badly bruised or slashed accidentally by one of the midwife's tools or left with hemorrhaging from a torn uterus. The constant threat was a vast variety of infections, from bacteria natural to the mother's interior, to those on the midwife's hands or tools, to those on bystanders or in the air or the dirt floor of the hut. In institutions where births were carried out, such as eighteenth-century lying-in hospitals, puerperal (from *puer*, boy) fever—a type of blood poisoning—could run rampant among recuperating mothers, in a week or so killing from 10 to 100 percent. The problem, of course, was lack of cleanliness in everyone and at every stage of the birth-giving process. For the woman, each birth was a gamble with death. Lindsay Wilson states that 1 of every 10 babies was stillborn (or killed during birth) and that 1 of every 80 births resulted in the death of either mother or child. One of every 10 adult women died in childbirth in eighteenth-century France. Another study showed that in England around 1650, there were 160 maternal deaths for every 10,000 births, dropping to 105 during the early eighteenth century and 75 as 1800 approached.[18]

For most women between 1500 and 1800, there was no question whether the new mother would suckle her own child. Women of the middling and upper class, however, could forbear nursing and hire a wet nurse, who had recently had a child of her own and was still lactating. The fathers were usually the ones who vetted and hired wet nurses, and decided whether the child and nurse would live at her home—often in the cleaner country air—or in the urban family home. Like midwives, wet nurses needed reputations for morality and responsibility. This was especially important if the child were to be left with her but only little less so if she joined the infant's family for a couple of years. The practice of wet nursing had had critics among churchmen and others for centuries, and enlightened society began to turn against the practice in the later eighteenth century. This was spurred in part by the opening pages of Jean-Jacques Rousseau's *Émile* in which he decries the practice as unnatural.[19]

Hysteria[20]

Sixteenth- and seventeenth-century Galenic physicians accepted the Aristotelian notion that women were by nature humorally cold and moist. Being thus physically and intellectually weaker than males, they were subject to a wider range of both physical and emotional illnesses than males. The uterus or womb served not only to host the fetus during pregnancy but to collect menstrual fluid, considered a poison, and other corrupted humors and noxious bodily fluids. These swelled the sack-like structure, causing it to move about the abdomen. It also released "vapors" that somehow rose to a woman's head and triggered abnormal behaviors. The resulting mental or emotional sickness took the name hysteria from the Greek word *hystera*—uterus—and it could range from mild to very serious. Symptoms included swollen abdomen, tightness of the throat and breathing problems, paralysis, loss of sensation, and uncontrolled contortions of the body. Menstruation and female orgasms released the substances that built up, but chaste women were supposedly deprived of orgasms and many women suffered problems with their menstrual cycles, for example due to poor diets or back-breaking work. Thus did early modern European medicine view what it labeled hysteria.[21]

Midwives, who often handled women's medical problems, had their personal remedies, including manipulating the uterus to stimulate menstruation or an orgasm, or tightly strapping or lacing the lower abdomen to keep the wandering womb in place. Male physicians sought the same basic goals, without the manual part: fumigation of the uterus with foul or fragrant odors, herbal douches, exercise, purgings, drugs, and diets that avoided moist foods. Some modern herbalists still recommend the harsh purgative herb black hellebore for "hysteria," promoting menstruation, and as an abortifacient.[22] Of course, if a demon, witch, or curse were to have brought on the condition, other measures were necessary, from exorcism to burning the offending witch. "Hysterical" symptoms of apparent loss of control appeared as what many believed possession by a spiritual force might look like. Exactly this way of thinking fueled the witch craze of the sixteenth and seventeenth centuries.

In turn, just such superstitions and ignorance provoked many later-seventeenth-century scientific revolutionaries, especially in England, to shine the light of reason on "women's problems." Prominent physicians felt that ailing women should no longer be left to "quacking jugglers and old women" but deserved the benefits of science. Dr. Nathaniel Highmore, admittedly using analogy rather than scientific observation, declared that hysteria stemmed not from the uterus but from the blockage and sudden release of blood into the lungs, which created the familiar suffocating effect and other hysterical symptoms. It was a problem of the blood's accumulation and "fermentation"—a trendy process—so he duly bled his hysterical patients. In the 1670s Dr. Thomas Willis also retained traditional Galenic therapies for what he labeled the "so-called uterine disease": bleeding at the neck, purging, and a regimen of diet, rest, and exercise. As a scientist, though, Willis shifted attention away from the womb and blood vessels to supposed blockages in the nerves. Along with others, he understood nerves to be tiny tubes through which "animal spirits" circulated through the body and back to the brain. Since everyone had nerves and a brain, hysteria was not a female problem at all. It was a "convulsive disorder," and thus similar in his mind to scurvy, asthma, and epilepsy. He went so far as to autopsy a woman who died during a bout of hysteria, and found no abnormalities in her uterus.

Willis's writings led to the demise of the exclusively female nature of hysteria during the eighteenth century. Spanish physician Martín Martínez disproved the roving uterus in 1728; the Italian Giovanni Battista Morgagni advanced the alternative theory of nerve blockage two decades later; and even Pope Benedict XIV, a science enthusiast, embraced the new model. But women had to remain both special and inferior to men, even enlightened men. In defining hysteria, science had begun replacing Galenic humoralism with a more mechanical model of the brain and conductive nerves, but the medium by which sense information was conducted to the brain and signals to the body's limbs and organs were conducted from the brain remained poorly understood and defined. Just as Isaac Newton labeled the famous force that attracted the apple to the earth "gravity"—heaviness—so Willis and others called the supposed medium "spirits": sometimes "animal" and sometimes "vital" spirits. Following John Locke's famous statement that we learn only by our sensory experiences, the theory was that through the flow of spirits the brain accumulated information and the person learned and became smarter. In males the flow was stronger and thus the male was both more intelligent and, by virtue of the greater flow to the limbs, had greater physical strength than the female. They believed women's less robust nervous system, smaller brains, and naturally weaker control over their emotions made them more susceptible to what were now labeled nervous disorders, though men were subject, too. Delicate women were associated with the aristocracy, and so were many types of nervous disorder; hence they became rather fashionable. Since no one had a clue as to how to treat weakened or blocked nerves and spirits, physicians retained Galenic guidelines of good living but added some of the many new patent drugs that claimed to strengthen female "vitals."[23]

The Cutting Edge: Mesmerism

From about 1750 Europe, and especially France, experienced an epidemic of "nervous disorders," or so practitioners proclaimed. In 1782/83 the English Royal Society of Medicine sponsored an essay contest whose entries explained why "nervous disorders are very widespread, and have never been more common in the two sexes."[24] The pressures of court or bourgeois life, childbearing and rearing, greater luxury and little exercise, repressed sexual urges, and other sexual anxieties topped the largely female-centric list. By the 1770s "vitalism" was in decline, however, as research in electricity and magnetism fascinated the fickle philosophical crowd, especially in Paris. But it was in Vienna that Franz Mesmer first demonstrated that the nervous "spirits" were actually a magnetic *fluidum* that could be externally manipulated by magnets or even his own biological magnetism. His cure of Franzl Osterlin made him famous, but his botching of the treatment of Maria Theresa von Paradies's blindness drove him to Paris. Here he broadened the claimed value of his treatments—handholding, hugging "magnetic" trees, demagnetizing baths—to cure pains of all sorts. Mesmerism was officially debunked in 1784, but Mesmer retained many faithful supporters, especially among women.[25]

NOTES

1. Bernard R. Ortiz de Montellano, *Aztec Medicine, Health, and Nutrition* (New Brunswick, NJ: Rutgers University Press, 1990), 142.

2. Sherry Fields, *Pestilence and Headcolds: Encountering Illness in Colonial Mexico* (New York: Columbia University Press, 2008), 47.

3. William Gates, *An Aztec Herbal: The Classic Codex of 1552* (Mineola, NY: Dover, 1939/2000), 108–9.

4. Clara Sue Kidwell, "Aztec and European Medicine in the New World, 1521–1600," in *The Anthropology of Medicine: From Culture to Method*, ed. Lola Romanacci-Ross, Daniel E. Moerman, and Laurence R. Tancredi (Westport, CT: Greenwood Press, 1997), 19–30.

5. Richard Sheridan, *Doctors and Slaves: A Medical and Demographic History of Slavery in the British West Indies, 1680–1834* (New York: Cambridge University Press, 1985), 74–75.

6. Mark Harrison, *Medicine in an Age of Commerce and Empire: Britain and Its Tropical Colonies, 1660–1830* (New York: Oxford University Press, 2010); Sheridan, *Doctors and Slaves.*

7. Yi-Li Wu, *Reproducing Women: Medicine, Metaphor, and Childbirth in Late Imperial China* (Berkeley: University of California Press, 2010), 21; also see Charlotte Furth, *A Flourishing Yin: Gender in China's Medical History, 960–1665* (Berkeley: University of California Press, 1999).

8. Wu, *Reproducing Women*, 42–43.

9. See the edition of Ilza Veith, trans., *The Yellow Emperor's Classic of Internal Medicine* (Berkeley: University of California Press, 2002).

10. Paul U. Unschuld, *Forgotten Treasures of Ancient Chinese Medicine: The I-hsüeh Yüan Liu Lun of 1757, by Hsü Ta-ch'un* (Brookline, MA: Paradigm, 1998).

11. Wu, *Reproducing Women*, 185.

12. Ibid., 94–120.

13. See also Volker Scheid, *Currents of Tradition in Chinese Medicine, 1626–2006* (Seattle, WA: Eastland Press, 2007); and Chao Yuan-Ling, *Medicine and Society in Late Imperial China* (New York: Peter Lang, 2009).

14. The literature on European female practitioners is large and growing; see the recent work by Leigh Whaley, *Women and the Practice of Medical Care in Early Modern Europe, 1400–1800* (New York: Palgrave Macmillan, 2011).

15. Mary Lindemann, *Health and Healing in Eighteenth-Century Germany* (Baltimore: Johns Hopkins University Press, 1996), 211.

16. Monica Green, *Making Women's Medicine Masculine: The Rise of Male Authority in Pre-modern Gynaecology* (New York: Oxford University Press, 2008).

17. Jacques Gélis, *History of Childbirth: Fertility, Pregnancy, and Birth in Early Modern Europe*, trans. Rosemary Morris (Cambridge: Polity Press, 1991).

18. Lindsay Wilson, *Women and Medicine in the French Enlightenment: The Debate over* Maladies des Femmes (Baltimore: Johns Hopkins University Press, 1993), 140.

19. Kirk D. Read, *Birthing Bodies in Early Modern France* (Burlington, VT: Ashgate, 2011).

20. On mental illness more generally, see chap. 9 in this book; and R. L. Martensen, *The Brain Takes Shape: An Early History* (New York: Oxford University Press, 2004).

21. See Andrew Scull, *The Disturbing History of Hysteria* (New York: Oxford University Press, 2009); for the late sixteenth and early seventeenth centuries, see Kaara L. Peterson, *Popular Medicine, Hysterical Disease, and Social Controversy in Shakespeare's England* (Burlington, VT: Ashgate, 2010).

22. John Riddle, *Dioscorides on Pharmacy and Medicine* (Austin: University of Texas Press, 1985), 124.

23. Anne C. Vila, *Enlightenment and Pathology: Sensibility in the Literature and Medicine of Eighteenth-Century France* (Baltimore: Johns Hopkins University Press, 1998).

24. Wilson, *Women and Medicine*, 127.

25. Thomas Dormandy, *The Worst of Evils: The Fight against Pain* (New Haven, CT: Yale University Press, 2006), 139–50.

CHAPTER 5

Infants and Children

Until recently, social historians and other scholars of early modern European family life often depicted parents as choosing to remain emotionally distant from their children. Their reasoning was that since childhood death rates were so high—for example, around 1700, 50 percent of London children died by age 12—parents did not want to get emotionally attached. Evidence included the practice of sending newborns out to nurse, frequency of abandonment and even infanticide, and the lack of a clear "culture of childhood" supported by families. More recent historians of childhood have redrawn the picture, portraying European culture as being truly invested in children, especially by the era of the Enlightenment. One view is that the nuclear family—as distinct from the extended family or clan—was invented during the seventeenth century by the urban middle class. Along with that was the invention or recognition of childhood as a distinct period of a person's life.[1] The facts of early modern childhood have not changed, but they have been reinterpreted and added to. In this chapter we survey the facts of childhood in various places rather than its interpretative history.

The emerging notion that children were not merely "little adults" but people in a unique phase of life had some important consequences. The early eighteenth century seems to have been a turning point. In Europe, the term "pediatrics" was coined to indicate the medical side of childhood and labeled a new framework for understanding and addressing the problems of childhood. New educational theories by John Locke and Jean-Jacques Rousseau emphasized the psychology of early learning and the importance of experience. From the states' point of view, children were valuable as the next generation and thus a resource to be nurtured and protected. At the same time, the industrialization taking place in Britain and elsewhere made claims on the small bodies, small hands, and nimble fingers that the young could bring to the new factories. With the assault on the vile practice of the slave trade plantation, owners prized Afro-Caribbean slave children as never before, since they alone would be the next generation of labor. The late eighteenth century even saw the emergence of maternity facilities and nurseries for slaves' children in the British West Indies.[2]

THEY ARE BORN: NEONATAL AND INFANT HEALTH

The Trauma of Birth

The child's entry into the world was natural but traumatic and hazardous. In many cultures the experienced midwife handled most issues, but she was supported by the surgeon or healer who waited in the wings to rescue the child and/or mother in an emergency. The child in the womb could have had any of many weakening conditions stemming from genetic inheritance or the mother's behavior or accidents. The trip from the womb to the world had its threats. He might not be situated correctly for the voyage and have to be repositioned manually; he might be tangled in the umbilical cord; he might not rotate as needed during descent; and he might contract dangerous germs from the birth canal itself or the midwife's unsanitary hands. The midwife might poke or pull the small body with too much force, crippling him for life. Once emerged, the light blow or spank might not get the lungs breathing properly; the cutting and tying of the umbilical cord could introduce infection or accidentally puncture the infant. Bacteria could cause diarrhea and accompanying dehydration. Though usually treated carefully, one would imagine, the light, air, sounds and other unfamiliar sensations assaulted the newborn as he was held upside down to drain the throat and ear canals, then washed and wrapped tightly. For mother, child, and midwife the successful live birth was a true triumph, however natural, for many passages into the world ended in tragedy.[3]

Infant Care and Nursing

Many early modern communities debated the rationale and wisdom of having newborn nurse with someone other than his or her birth

Figure 5.1 In this engraving of a work by Cornelis Troost (1697–1750), a wealthy Dutch woman rests in bed after childbirth, while the seated wet nurse prepares to feed the newborn infant. (National Library of Medicine)

mother. Poor families had no real options, and mothers breastfed their own if at all possible. Wealthier mothers, however, could become pregnant again sooner if they did not breastfeed, a choice often dictated by the male head of the household. Women who had been badly weakened or infected during labor or in its aftermath might choose not to nurse, and men who had fathered babies with unmarried servants or other women also often chose to send the baby away. Hiring a wet nurse, however, could mean either having her stay in the family's residence or sending the child to the wet nurse's home. Generally the fathers made the contracts, and generally with the nurse's husband. Reliable statistics are difficult to come by, and historians Rudolph Bell and Stephen Ozment warn against overestimating the practice in Italy and Germany respectively. On the other hand, Barbara Dunlap estimates that in later-eighteenth-century Paris, of some 20,000 babies born each year only around 3 percent were breastfed by their own mothers, and 92 percent were sent to the countryside to be fed by a stranger. In his *Èmile* (1762) French philosopher Jean-Jacques Rousseau, who fathered several children and sent them all to foundling homes, strongly advised breastfeeding by mothers as a healthier practice that bonded the two. In a modern study of British infants for the same period, deaths were shown to be 30 percent lower among those who were breastfed by their mothers.[4]

Of course, the healthfulness of the milk was in many ways dependent on the diet of the mother. In situations of slavery, poverty, or social disruption, or where vitamin-rich diets were simply not available, a nursing child might suffer nutritional deprivation. Tuscan mothers generally nursed for two years, and West Indian slaves for three when allowed. Slave children often suffered from beriberi, scurvy, pellagra, rickets, and other diet deficiency conditions thanks to the poor diets generally afforded by their owners.

Threats to Infant Health

The Shadow World

The shadow world presented a hazard only slowly disposed of across our period. Demons, ghosts, elves, fairies, demi-gods, breath-sucking cats, gnomes, jinn, witches, and a host of other religious or folk entities were invoked to explain sudden deaths, emotional traumas, emergent skin deformities, and other abnormalities that very young minds or flesh suffered. Aztec families feared that "emanations" (*ihiyotl* or "garbage air") from adults who broke sexual norms—homosexuals, adulterers, prostitutes—adversely affected the state of nearby infants' *tonalli* or animating life force. Invading Spaniards brought the notion of the evil eye (*mal de ojo*), a parallel threat from unhealthy adults or witches, whose glance could cause a variety of maladies. In both cases infants were protected by objects colored red, including coral necklaces, and cured with magical rituals involving eggs and herbs.[5] By the late eighteenth century, most cultures had eliminated these forces from medical considerations or at least reduced their perceived role.

Disease

Ming Chinese physicians considered smallpox to be the single greatest threat to a newborn's health. Smallpox was endemic in China and was linked directly to a notion called fetal poison. By the seventeenth century, many believed that the sex act creating the infant was polluting to both child and mother, and neonatal diseases, including smallpox, were the result. A paste of the child's roasted and dried umbilical cord and purgative pills of licorice and cinnabar became popular oral prophylactics against these diseases. Neonatal smallpox and other skin-manifesting conditions came to be seen as generated from within the baby's body as the poisons engendered in the sex act rose to the surface to escape. Rather than life threatening, they came to be seen as necessary to cleanse the body for a healthy childhood. These insights were collected by a new breed of physician who took interest in the ills of both women and children, a trend that later had important effects on both gynecology and pediatrics in China.[6]

The infant also faced a wide range of other diseases. Infant syphilis was encountered and discussed in Europe as early as the 1490s. Mothers could pass this on in the womb or it might be encountered in the birth canal. Doctors and laymen alike blamed it on the wet nurses when possible, and on the mother's own milk when used. Nine or 10 days after birth the infant might develop tetanus of the navel from exposure of the tender area to dirt and the germs. An estimated 25 percent who contracted this died. Measles, mumps, rubella, scarlet fever, flu, whooping cough, chicken pox, tuberculosis, various rashes, and other so-called childhood diseases plagued many in a given community, and any might turn deadly if the conditions were right and especially during an epidemic.

Those born in late-fifteenth and early sixteenth-century Latin America were swept away in huge numbers by the many infectious diseases introduced by European and later African newcomers. When in some cases the germs destroyed adults more readily than children, the loss of their caretakers left infants helpless even when unaffected themselves.

Infanticide

Infanticide is the intentional killing of an infant. It might have been accomplished simply by leaving the child exposed to the elements and wild animals, or by physical abuse of almost any kind. If it appeared that the murdered child was stolen or killed by accident, the murderer might even receive sympathy from the community. Sudden infant death that occurred in the parents' bed, whereby the infant died naturally or was crushed or smothered by one or both parents, could be a natural tragedy, an accident, or a tragic act of desperation. Both Jewish and Church authorities often imposed spiritual penalties on parents regardless of its determined cause: even an accident was attributed to God's punishment for the parents' sins. Among Catholics, infanticide was usually punished with excommunication. Infanticide was most commonly associated with situations of rape or incest, adultery, or some clear physical disability or mental defect on the child's part.[7]

A related phenomenon was infant sacrifice, practiced, for example, among the pre-Christian Inca of Peru. According to Spanish observers, Incan culture apparently considered infants and children to be "natural resources" possessed more by the community than their families. These "commodities" were among the finest of sacrifices made to the gods at communal turning points such as coronations, wars, and, ironically, epidemics. Among the Aztecs, the young were annually sacrificed to the god of rain, Tlaloc. For some reason the deity preferred those with hairlines sporting twin forelocks or widow's peaks.[8]

Accidents

Birth itself was fraught with harm from accidents, and after birth the child faced a long list of threats from accidents. Tightly wrapping swaddling clothes were often applied immediately to the newborn to protect her from the elements but also as a way of immobilizing her. Yet cradles could be overturned; children roll off of high furniture; animals wound, kill, or carry off infants. They could be smothered or choked, wounded by knives or other sharp household objects, burned by household fires or lamps, scalded by hot water, drown in tubs or ponds, or be injured by larger animals such as horses or wild boars. Toddlers, of course, could get into all sorts of danger moving about within the house or beyond into streets, yards, or fields. Threats came from rabid or poisonous animals, and from smoke, dust, worms, and other parasites and environmental factors. Children have always been prone to put things in their mouths, and given the unsanitary conditions so many lived in poisoning had to have occurred. They were also prone to choking on small objects and harm from oral experimentation with sharp or pointed objects.

In poorer families children often tended those younger than themselves, and the results could be tragic. Neglect was far more likely where no servant or family member was dedicated to caring for the very young. Of course caregivers were just as capable of being neglectful, and even a mother suffering from postpartum depression might give her little one little or no attention.

HAZARDS TO OLDER CHILDREN'S HEALTH AND LIVES

That infants were a special type of person and patient was obvious to all. Older children who could walk around and speak meaningfully, on the other hand, at some point became adults. At what point, however, was unclear and a matter of culture or debate. Very often children were treated medically as they were usually treated socially: as little adults. But their small bodies simply could not undergo purging or bleedings, and adult dosages of medicines seemed clearly inappropriate. When ill, children often had a difficult time describing their pains or even articulating where on their bodies the unnatural feeling was occurring. Doctors could and did check pulse, urine, stool, and temperature (hot, cold, normal), but their diagnoses were necessarily limited.

Disease

Medical treatises on what came to be called pediatrics (child medicine) were not new to early modern Europe, whether for the professional or, increasingly, the layman. Mothers and female custodians of children were always their first line of defense when illness struck. In his sixteenth-century *The Godmother*, the Italian Brother Mercurio discussed 37 childhood diseases in 28 chapters. He divided them into "internal" and "external" problems, though his logic is not always clear. The internal were fevers, chicken pox, bodily swelling, suppurations, epilepsy, convulsions, paralysis and torpor, nightmares, sleeplessness, running nose, congested nose, coughs, breathing problems, earaches, strep throat, mouth sores, teething, hiccups, vomiting, bedwetting, retained urine, stone, constipation, diarrhea, intestinal blockage, body aches, and worms. His external problems included cradle cap, lice, water on the brain, inflamed eyes, crossed eyes, cracked lips, scrofula, umbilical or navel problems, and distended colon. Importantly, he taught that none of these necessarily required a physician, and he provided practical and reasonable treatments for each. Near the end of the seventeenth century, English statistician John Graunt made the following list of diseases common to four and five-year olds: the fungal throat condition known as thrush; convulsions; the potentially bone deforming vitamin D deficiency known as rickets; worms; problems with one's teeth, and especially teething; chrysomes; and of course measles and smallpox.[9]

Accidents

Older children were more capable of avoiding many of the hazards to the very young. Being much more mobile, however, they were capable of getting into far more trouble. Around the house they were expected to work as if little adults, and this could lead to all sorts of accidents since their strength, coordination, and judgment were not as well developed as those of adolescents or adults. Falls from windows, stairs, or roofs, into wells or pits, down steep slopes, or from carts or horses could break bones or cause death. Scalding, burns, injuries from falling objects, cuts from knives, glass, or other household objects, kicks from horses or other farm animals, and bites from rabid dogs or other feral animals were also serious threats. The fear of being lost in a forest haunts many traditional stories and was no doubt a very real possibility.

Work-Related Hazards

In many urban settings boys were expected to work outside of the family from an early age. The guild and apprentice system in Europe, for example, allowed boys as young as six or seven to be placed by their families with masters who would train them in an occupation over the next decade or more. Youngsters had value by performing certain simple but important tasks in almost any setting. Known as shop boys they might be tasked with running errands, cleaning up, preparing materials, repairing machines, tending fires, fetching water, and a host of other jobs that differed by the occupation and as they grew older and more capable and experienced. They worked around men whose tolerance for childish misbehavior was probably typically low. They worked around dangerous machines such as printing presses and mill gears and by the eighteenth century in factories with steam-driven machines that were unforgiving of error. Children were used to clean chimneys from inside and squeeze into tight spaces to do the dangerous jobs grown men could not perform. Girls might help mothers who were laundresses, making themselves subject to the same problems the adults were and to the risk of falling into rivers and drowning. Even in the countryside children were used to tend sheep or other animals and risked both the disease of anthrax and predator attacks— especially wolves. Girls who were sent out as servants ran the risk of sexual assault, and boys beatings or other abuse from employers, masters, or other members of their households.

Violence

Defenseless children in the early modern world were also threatened by violence from other corners. At home, naturally abusive, drunken, or mentally ill parents or other older family members preyed on children as they do today. Corporal punishment by parents was expected among all levels of society, and there could be a fine line between severe discipline and violence. In Aztec Mexico physical discipline

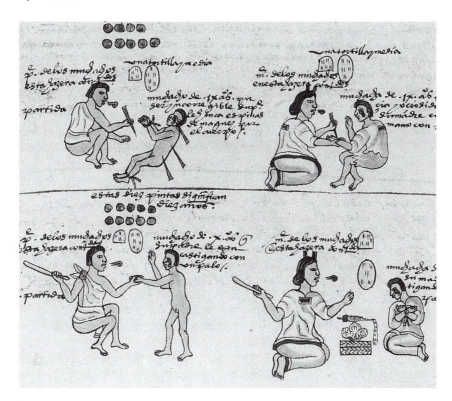

Figure 5.2 Scenes from Section 3 of the mid-16th-century *Codex Mendoza*, which was produced by Aztec artists. This image from folio 60r depicts punishment of young children aged 11 to 14 for a variety of behaviors, from deceitfulness to poor spinning. The work was created for Spain's King Charles I; Section 3 contained information and images about daily life among the natives, who were now his subjects. (The Art Archive/Bodleian Library Oxford)

was considered appropriate from age 10, and could include beatings and forced inhalation of burning chili smoke, the equivalent of modern pepper spray.[10] Among older girls there was always the threat of rape or molestation by older siblings or half-siblings or stepfathers; and stepmothers were stereotypically mean to and abusive of their stepdaughters. Bullying by older siblings or others could go too far and cause serious injuries. Because adult males tended to be given the benefit of the legal doubt in most early modern cultures, there was little recourse for those victimized in the household if the fathers did not intervene.

Outside the home, childnapping was known to most cultures, especially where domestic slavery was practiced. Of course, the very practice of chattel slavery was abusive and children felt its sting as did their parents. In West Africa native slavers seized athletic young boys to sell to the white slave traders, as in the famous case of Olaudah Equiano, who later gained his freedom and wrote of his enslavement and in favor of abolition.[11] Among older children pederast males preyed on boys, and girls could be stolen away or run away to lives of prostitution. Children also suffered from the ravages of war and other human-made disasters. Along with their parents or other care-givers, they were subject to being wounded, starved, stricken by disease, or physically abused. As violence swept through their world, they were often left orphaned and uncared for.[12]

EUROPEAN INSTITUTIONS OF CHILD CARE

The Islamic Ottoman Empire had no orphanages or foundling hospitals. In fact there was little provision for child patients in the bimaristans or other health facilities. The Muslim sense of family responsibility to its youngest members was very strong.[13] Europe was different.

Children who lost or were abandoned by their families suffered a number of emotional and mental problems in addition to the possibility of being physically abused. All things equal, the younger one was the less psychic damage was likely to be inflicted. Confusion, grief, sorrow, sadness, despair, and even guilt could accompany the change. These emotional states might be manifested in unacceptable behaviors including bedwetting, violent acting out, apathy and lack of affect, nightmares, disobedience, or eating disorders. In an age when children were to "be seen and not heard" and "spared not the rod," adult caregivers felt justified using corporal punishment to curb unacceptable behavior.

The Orphanage and Foundling Hospital

Christian charity had always pointed to the widow, the disabled, and the orphan as being worthy of support. Most children who lost both of their parents were taken in by other family members, neighbors, or, if old enough, guild masters who would raise them as apprentices. Both age and sex were important factors, since older children could earn their keep, and boys could be fostered or apprenticed out more readily than girls. On a farm both girls and boys could be put to work as early as age five or six. Younger children or infants were a matter of pure expense, and even uncles would be reluctant to take them in. During times of famine, war, or epidemic, orphans proliferated and support systems often disappeared altogether. Monks and especially nuns had traditionally cared for those otherwise left to their fate, and in Catholic countries many still did.

In the later Middle Ages, and especially after the Black Death, wealthy Christians provided and staffed homes for orphans and abandoned infants in larger cities. Some of these were run by the Church, but increasingly civic authorities or secular boards managed them. One of the most famous was the Ospedale degli Innocenti in Florence. It was established in the last will (1410) of the local merchant Francesco Datini, himself orphaned in 1348 by the Black Death. He arranged to have one of Florence's chief guilds administer his gift, since he did not trust Florentine Church authorities. The Ospedale still stands: having been designed by the great Brunelleschi, it was one of the earliest masterpieces of Renaissance architecture. It operated beside the hospitals of

Figure 5.3 Detail of a fresco in Florence's Ospedale degli Innocenti by late 16th-century painter Bernardino Poccetti. A little girl reads to the benefactors of the institution, while wet nurses feed swaddled infants, and boys standing in stiff lines recite their lessons. It is the picture of order and health, an idealized view of life in such a facility. (The Yorck Project/ DIRECTMEDIA Publishing GmbH)

San Gallo and La Scala, which also cared for children. In the seventeenth century Amsterdam hosted 11 orphanages, providing shelter to some 3,400 children. One was specifically for the children of citizens and one for those of poor residents. Mennonites ran three, Catholics had two, and Lutherans, Huguenots, and members of the Dutch Reformed Church administered one each. City regulations required that each child brought in first be thoroughly washed and deloused.[14] French cities had their Charités for orphans staffed by nuns and often attached to the Maison Dieu charity hospital. In Paris the Trouvés foundling hospital recorded having received 7,600 new charges in 1771 alone. Many of these died in the hospital, but city records also claimed that many Parisian newborns were simply left to die in the streets and fell prey to animals that roamed them.[15]

However well meaning the personnel that staffed these institutions, death rates, especially among infants, were horrific. In Renaissance Florence upwards of 7 in 10 died before their first birthday. In seventeenth- and eighteenth-century Paris and London, figures ranged from a third to 90 percent. Disease, neglect, accidents, sickness, and poor nutrition increased the death rolls, which were even greater during times of famine, epidemic, or war. Though practices differed, wet nurses were generally chosen to feed the youngest, and often this meant farming them out to the countryside with its hazards and uncertainties. Such wet nurses were probably paid little, resulting in many cases of children starving, being fed cows' milk, being neglected, or dying.

The poor, young mother leaving her infant in a basket at the door of a church or convent was not just a cliché; it was a reality for thousands. Unlike the orphan, the foundling was abandoned by his or her mother, or by a father who lost his wife to the birth or other cause. Though of course the baby did not understand, society tended to blame the mother for her action. Often the mother was unmarried; and whether the infant was a love child, a side effect of a life of prostitution, or a product of rape, society viewed the mother as having been irresponsible. The children, too, tended to be tainted by social disdain, marked as having had immoral, uncaring, or even cursed parents. With perhaps 70,000 residents, Florence's women abandoned an average of 200 infants each year from 1450 to 1500. During the terrible years of the 1530s, the average more than doubled to 540 per annum. During this time 22 percent of babies baptized in the city were abandoned.[16]

Like those in orphanages, children in foundling homes lived in conditions varying from tender and loving to brutal. Mortality was high and few lived to reach adulthood. Parents, mothers especially, could and did return to reclaim their infants. Some even gave birth, left the child with a facility, and then served as his wet nurse, gaining a small stipend for doing what she would have done for nothing. Such an arrangement served all parties involved, since the mother probably took much greater care of the child than if left to the staff and wet nurse.

Outside of cities parish authorities often tended those left with them, arranging for appropriate care, feeding, and sometimes even education. In Catholic communities some religious brotherhoods or confraternities and even formal orders of the Church, such as the Order of the Holy Spirit, were dedicated to infant care and placement. Where such organizations were lacking, desperate mothers or uncaring fathers resorted to infanticide or sale of the child into slavery or servitude.[17]

In European colonies foundling homes were among the first institutions established by both religious and political authorities. Out-of-wedlock births among white men and women who were lower-class natives or slaves often resulted in the offspring's abandonment. As late as 1700, King Philip V of Spain received reports of newborns in Havana, Cuba, being tossed into the sea, smothered by parents, and left in streets to be eaten by dogs. In 1711 Casa Joseph opened to receive foundlings, the vast majority of whom were newborns. Yet this was no panacea, as in its early years 75 percent of its charges died within six months of being admitted. Though conditions and survival rates improved (only 12% died in 1733), Casa Joseph had to close in 1755 due to misadministration.[18]

Lying-In Hospitals

The health of the mother was a major factor in the health of the child. When births took place under unsafe conditions, the infant often died, as did the mother. In Enlightenment Europe patrons or communities began founding lying-in hospitals—often associated with foundling hospitals. These were facilities in which a pregnant woman—whether married or not was a community norm—lacking any other resources could give birth with relative safety. Pregnant prostitutes, servant girls, errant daughters, runaways, and poor but married women had the help of one or more midwives or midwives in training, as well as a surgeon or even physician on call. The child was thereby protected from abortion or infanticide, at least until the mother was released, and had the benefit of trained personnel if needed. If necessary, the hospital arranged for the infant to be left with a foundling home. In Paris's later-eighteenth-century Hôtel Dieu charity hospital, 80 percent of pregnant women admitted were single and 90 percent of women who gave birth left their children behind to be cared for. Such facilities were not merely a matter of humanitarianism or Christian charity but of the state's concern for the survival of the next generation to bear babies, pay taxes, and fill the ranks of soldiers. Among the Aztecs before Cortés, newborn boys were given a small shield and a bow with four arrowheads as a symbol of their future profession as warriors. Infant mortality among the Aztecs was estimated at between 30 and 40 percent.[19]

Dispensaries

Poor urban mothers may have had their babies in lying-in hospitals, but if they kept their babies they faced myriad health issues for which they had no preparation or resources. Religious houses in Catholic countries, civic physicians, poorhouses, and other charitable organizations helped when they could, but if a mother were single or of known low repute, the odds of help were slim. In 1769 physician George Armstrong created a new type of facility in London to help poor mothers and their sick infants. His dispensary was merely a point of distribution for advice and free medicines. There were no strings attached or questions asked. Of course it is safe to say that the mothers who sought the help provided lived with their child or children in squalid conditions or filth, disease, and poverty. All too many of the children aided failed to live to pass it forward.[20]

NOTES

1. Rudolph Bell, *How to Do It: Guides to Good Living for Renaissance Italians* (Chicago: University of Chicago Press, 1999), 135.

2. Richard Sheridan, *Doctors and Slaves: A Medical and Demographic History of Slavery in the British West Indies, 1680–1834* (New York: Cambridge University Press, 1985), *passim.*

3. Some material from Jacques Gélis, *History of Childbirth: Fertility, Pregnancy, and Birth in Early Modern Europe*, trans. Rosemary Morris (Cambridge: Polity Press, 1991).

4. Bell, *How to Do It*, 135–36; Barbara Dunlap, "The Problems of Syphilitic Children in Eighteenth-Century France and England," in *The Secret Malady: Venereal Disease in Eighteenth-Century Britain and France*, ed. Linda Evi Meriens (Lexington: University Press of Kentucky, 1997), 114–27.

5. Bernard R. Ortiz de Montellano, *Aztec Medicine, Health, and Nutrition* (New Brunswick, NJ: Rutgers University Press, 1990), 223–25.

6. Charlotte Furth, *A Flourishing Yin: Gender in China's Medical History, 960–1665* (Berkeley: University of California Press, 1999), 178–82.

7. Shulamith Shahar, *Childhood in the Middle Ages* (New York: Routledge, 1992), 126–39.

8. Carolyn Dean, "Sketches of Childhood," in *Minor Omissions: Children in Latin American History and Society*, ed. Tobias Hecht (Madison: University of Wisconsin Press, 2002), 44; Ortiz de Montellano, *Aztec Medicine*, 195.

9. Katherine Knight, *How Shakespeare Cleaned His Teeth and Cromwell Treated His Warts: Secrets of the Seventeenth-Century Medicine Cabinet* (Stroud, UK: Tempus, 2006), 117–19; Bell, *How to Do It*, 141–51.

10. Sonya Lipsett-Rivera, "Model Children and Models for Children in Early Mexico," in *Minor Omissions: Children in Latin American History and Society*, ed. Tobias Hecht (Madison: University of Wisconsin Press, 2002), 66.

11. Olaudah Equiano, *The Life of Olaudah Equiano* (Mineola, NY: Dover Books, 1995).

12. See Laurence Brockliss and Heather Montgomery, eds., *Childhood and Violence in the Western Tradition* (Woodbridge, CT: Oxbow Books, 2010); and A. Lynn Martin, *Alcohol, Violence, and Disorder in Traditional Europe* (Kirksville, MO: Truman State University Press, 2009).

13. Miri Shefer-Mossensohn, *Ottoman Medicine: Healing and Medical Institutions, 1500–1700* (Albany: State University of New York Press, 2009), 132–34.

14. Philip Gavitt, *Charity and Children in Renaissance Florence: The Ospedale degli Innocenti, 1410–1536* (Ann Arbor: University of Michigan Press, 1991), chap. 1; Derek Phillips, *Well-Being in Amsterdam's Golden Age* (Amsterdam: Pallas, 2008), 169–83.

15. Reported in Linda L. Barnes, *Needles, Herbs, Gods, and Ghosts: China, Healing, and the West to 1848* (Cambridge, MA: Harvard University Press, 2005), 142.

16. Philip Gavitt, *Gender, Honor, and Charity in Late Renaissance Florence* (New York: Cambridge University Press, 2011), 30–31.

17. Shahar, *Childhood*, 122–25.

18. Ondina E. González, "Down and Out in Havana: Foundlings in Eighteenth-Century Cuba," in Hecht, *Minor Omissions*, 102–13.

19. Jacques Soustelle, *Daily Life of the Aztecs* (London: Phoenix Press, 1961/2002), 164.

20. Robert Kilpatrick, " 'Living in the Light': Dispensaries, Philanthropy, and Medical Reform in Late Eighteenth-Century London," in *The Medical Enlightenment of the Eighteenth Century*, ed. Andrew Cunningham and Roger French (New York: Cambridge University Press, 1990), 254–55.

CHAPTER 6

Infectious Diseases

Infectious diseases are those that are transmitted from someone or something that already has the disease's pathogens to someone who does not. No one "catches" a broken leg, a toothache, or diabetes from someone who already has the ailment, but one does "catch" a cold, plague, measles, typhus, malaria, or gonorrhea from an already infected source or carrier. Such diseases remained major causes of debilitation and death throughout the world and throughout the early modern period.

BACKGROUND

Pathogens and Epidemics

A carrier—which might be a fly, flea, louse, mosquito, tick, food, water source, or human—contacts a victim by sneezing or coughing, touching, biting, stinging, defecating on, injecting, or being consumed. The carrier thus passes the virus, bacterium, fungus, protozoon, or other pathogen into the new host's bloodstream, lymphatic system, lungs, digestive system, or other organs. If the victim is healthy, her immune system may isolate and destroy the invaders; she may already have immunity because of a previous infection by the same or related pathogen. If she is not healthy, and the pathogen is strong and numerous, it will overcome her body's defenses by outwitting or defeating them.

Some pathogens will do enough damage to kill their new host; others weaken her, leaving her unable to stave off subsequent, unrelated—opportunistic—pathogens. Still others, such as certain "childhood diseases," do minor damage and confer immunity by causing the body to create effective and long-lasting defenses.

Because these pathogens are passed through some sort of contact (even if only by breath), we call them contagious. In general, to thrive these need large numbers of people living in close proximity, so that the chain of contacts can be maintained and the organism can continue to survive and replicate. Where population densities are low, the pathogen runs out of victims and eventually changes or disappears. Where conditions are right, the carriers can contact many people. The chain begins and is sustained by new and susceptible victims. When many people are affected over a fairly short period of time we speak of an epidemic; when a great many people are affected over a very broad geographic area and relatively long period of time the outbreak is often labeled a pandemic. Prior to modern transportation, pandemics were rare because pathogens could be transported only at the speed of sail, river current, horse, or human legs.[1]

Even so, during the early modern period contagious diseases probably killed more people than any other factor. This was especially true where pathogens landed in "virgin soil," among populations that had never experienced the disease before. This biological "naiveté" meant that there was no natural immunity in the population and no known defenses or healing processes. After contact with Europeans and Africans, natives of North and South America were slaughtered by such diseases, as were many native Pacific and most Caribbean islanders. In turn, European sailors, slavers, soldiers, missionaries, and colonists died by the thousands of unfamiliar tropical diseases in Africa, the Americas, and the Caribbean. The early modern period saw the world shrink through European "discovery," trade, conquest, and colonization. Huge numbers of Africans were transplanted as slaves into the Western Hemisphere, bringing their own pathogens that found new victims among natives and Europeans alike.[2]

Limitations of Early Modern Medicine

Apart from gradual but inevitable mixing of populations and pathogen pools, the period was marked by a deadly ignorance of human physiology, microbiology, and medicine. No culture on Earth understood the medical model of the human body we take for granted today. Only fringe thinkers envisioned tiny "animalcules" causing horrific death tolls of plague or smallpox. Though inoculation as a means of protection against smallpox was known in Africa and other Islamic regions, and was adopted by Europeans in the eighteenth century, no one understood why and how it worked. And so it remained an isolated tool.[3]

The remainder of this chapter is a discussion of several among many major early modern infectious diseases, from plague to syphilis. They are organized by means and factors of transmission rather than by pathogen types or symptoms or another classification scheme that might be equally valid. People encountered these diseases in daily life or during epidemics through specific—if misunderstood—means.

THE CONTINUING SAGA: FLEAS, RATS, AND PLAGUE

The early modern period encompasses the second half of the Second Plague Pandemic (1347–1840s). Though sources are unclear about China, Europe and much of the Islamic world suffered recurring epidemics of bubonic and possibly pneumonic and septicemic plague. Though the medieval Black Death, the initial onslaught of the disease in the West from 1347 to 1352, killed perhaps 40 percent of the population and left few places unscathed, subsequent outbreaks were localized and usually much less deadly.[4]

Plague and the Early Second Pandemic

Plague is an animal disease (zoonosis) caused by the bacterium *Yersinia pestis*. It lives in bloodstreams of a wide variety of rodents and other small mammals, and is transmitted when fleas suck infected blood from one host and then deposit bacteria when feeding on a second host. If the colony of rodents dies off, its fleas seek new hosts on which to feed. If the new hosts are human and fleas are many, an outbreak of plague can occur. Inside the human, the bacteria multiply rapidly and many are collected in the lymphatic system. When accumulated in the lymph nodes of the groin and neck, the load of bacteria, pus, and other detritus causes nodes to swell into "buboes," a distinctive sign of bubonic plague. If collection is efficient and nodes handle the load, the patient lives; if not, bacteria spread through the bloodstream, affecting multiple organs. Malaise, fever, and delirium result, and the patient dies in about a week. If bacteria in the bloodstream are of a high enough quantity, death is swifter due to "poisoning" called septicemia. This deadly variation is septicemic plague, which kills so quickly that buboes have no time to form. Pneumonic plague results from *Y. pestis* bacteria being breathed into the respiratory system and acting quickly, and usually fatally, on the lungs. Though bubonic and septicemic plague forms require flea carriers for transmission, with pneumonic plague simple coughing or sneezing can transmit *Y. pestis* to one or many others. Of course, at no point during the Second Plague Pandemic did anyone anywhere develop an understanding of the roles of bacteria, fleas, or rats. Medical practitioners and researchers, whether Christian, Muslim, or Enlightened, had much experience with plague but acquired little insight and no effective medical responses beyond isolation of the sick. Despite the Renaissance, Scientific Revolution, and Enlightenment, plague remained a matter of poisoned air (miasmas), and many continued to blame God and planets as the ultimate causal agents.

The Origins of Public Health Procedures

By 1500 plague was becoming an urban disease, though infected refugees or travelers might spread it to rural areas as well. At the same time, both Europeans and Muslims had learned to live with plague. Sixteenth-century European governments began adopting approaches pioneered by rulers of Italian city-states such as Venice, Milan, and Florence. Exercising a newfound willingness and ability to coerce their people, they imposed quarantines on suspect people, goods, and ships, and health cordons (no-go zones) around areas struck by plague. Closing city gates, erecting cordons, and quarantining merchant ships interrupted trade and interfered with profit, encouraging city officials to delay plague declarations until the outbreak was well established. Wealthier folks fled a city when plague was declared—usually determined by a certain number of confirmed plague cases reported within a set time. Authorities then locked victims in their houses, built inadequate pest houses or lazarettos to house poorer victims, and had vagrants, beggars, prostitutes, and other undesirables expelled from their cities. London, Amsterdam, or Rome could become a ghost town in a week's time, leaving servants, apprentices, and the "lower sort" to fend for themselves. Shops closed, food became scarce, searchers patrolled streets for the dead, and corpses were tossed into rumbling carts and eventually mass graves. Bodies were also heaved into rivers that simply sluiced them downstream; they were also thrown into or dumped at sea, which in turn rejected them in horrible high tides of flesh and bone.[5]

In the Islamic World

People in Muslim countries, especially those around the Mediterranean Sea, experienced plague as often as Europeans did and for a longer

Figure 6.1 Doctor Schnabel of Rome sports the latest in plague-time protective clothing. The wide-brimmed hat protects the head and face from poisonous precipitation; the oilcloth gown is impervious to the poisonous plague mists; the distinctive beak is filled with air-purifying herbs and flower petals; his hands are gloved; and he carries a wand signaling his profession to warn others. The illustration is from a poster dated 1656, and the wand is tipped with a winged hourglass, suggesting that "time flies." (Bettmann/Corbis)

period. Cities such as Istanbul, Alexandria, Cairo, and Damascus were drawn together more tightly after Ottoman Turks took control of Egypt in 1517. Increased contact, as among European port cities, meant increased opportunities for infection. But Muslims, even more than pious Christians, saw the hand of God in plague and adopted an acceptance of the disease that seems to have blunted attempts to prevent it. For the righteous, death by plague was martyrdom; for the wicked, it was just punishment. Therefore, as plague repeatedly swept through port cities, Turkish authorities did little to interfere. During the early modern era they did rationalize the region's administration, paid more attention than previous rulers to sanitation and health care, and some sultans adopted elements of European medicine, but these advances did little to make life safer or more comfortable for the empire's peasants or workers. Islamic areas outside the Empire also continued to suffer: in the 1770s a reported 2 million Persians died of plague, including 250,000 in Basra alone.[6]

The Second Pandemic's End Game

Between about 1650 and 1772, one major European city after another underwent one last, major epidemic episode, followed by liberation from the pestilence. Civic responses were as sophisticated as they were going to get, as governments systematically engaged the tools they had acquired: civic bonfires to "fix" the corrupted air, quarantine, cordons, isolation, killing stray animals (even rats sometimes), burning the goods of victims, and executing those who bought or sold "infected" goods. Naples and Rome experienced their final plague epidemic in 1656 (together 173,000 died, though Rome suffered far less). Amsterdam in 1664 (35,000 dead) and London in 1665 and 1666 (70,000); Stockholm in 1711 (15,000) and Vienna in 1712–14 (8,644 reported dead); Marseille and surrounding Provence in 1720–22 (40,000 and 85,000 respectively); Messina, Sicily, in 1743 (50,000 of a population of 65,000); and Moscow in 1770–72 (over 60,000): each in turn suffered and was seemingly immunized by the experience. Historians have long disputed why the disease retreated from Europe, but the dominant opinion is that human attempts succeeded in blocking recurrences due to importation of rats and fleas, especially by ship. Authorities bolstered efforts at cordons and quarantine, especially in the Mediterranean, as they saw Ottoman and other Muslim ports suffer repeatedly into the 1840s until they, too, successfully adopted these efforts.[7]

MOSQUITOES, MALARIA, AND YELLOW FEVER

Medieval and early modern people lived with rodents and fleas as common elements of their environments. This familiarity may have helped blind people to their roles in spreading plague. Malaria and yellow fever were Old World diseases spread by other ubiquitous pests, respectively the *anopheline* and *Aedes* mosquitoes. Early modern medical science was as ignorant of this connection as it was of the plague's bacterium-flea-rat-human chain, hence the name malaria, or "bad air" in Italian.

Malaria

Malaria is caused by parasitic protozoa of the *Plasmodium* family that are carried most effectively by mosquitoes of the *anopheline* family. The family is large, and 70 species can carry the protozoon. The mosquitoes prefer warm temperatures and still, stagnant water in which they lay eggs and that supports early stages of the insect's life cycle. Outside of humans the protozoon reproduces sexually, but inside the human bloodstream it does so asexually inside red blood cells, which are destroyed in the process. This happens over a two- or three-day cycle that accounts for the recurring "tertian," or third-day, fevers characteristic of malaria. Fever and anemia result, and the sufferer is weakened terribly by the combination. The protozoa can also hibernate in the liver for three- to five-year periods, emerging and causing the recurring fevers also associated with malaria.

Plasmodium has four types that can affect humans, and two—*P. vivax* and *P. falciparum*—that were common to Southern Europe and Africa, respectively. *Vivax* is the less virulent and plagued marshy areas as far north as England's Kent and East Anglian marshes. *Falciparum* is less discriminating about which red blood cells it invades, so far more cells are killed off within a victim, and many more victims succumb. *Falciparum* was far more common in Africa, and, despite its lethality, Central and Western Africans developed some natural defenses. Children who were bitten and survived gained a measure of immunity, and many developed and passed along the "sickle cell" trait that can lead to anemia but protects from *vivax* and, less so, *falciparum*.[8]

Before the Age of Discovery, yellow fever was strictly an African disease, caused by an arbovirus (<u>ar</u>thropod-<u>bo</u>rne virus) spread from victim to victim by the female *Aedes* mosquito. The virus requires the mosquito for reproduction, which it carries out in the insect's mid-gut. From there it travels to the salivary glands from which it is deposited in the monkey or human bloodstream. Like other mosquitoes, *Aedes* reproduces in still water: pools, marshes, wheel ruts, or containers. For about a week after acquiring the virus, a victim suffers flu-like symptoms including chills, fever, and head and muscle aches. In a serious case the kidneys shut down and jaundice results from liver failure. The patient spews black vomit and hemorrhages. Within about a week, between 10 and 60 percent of patients die. Those who survive, however, do acquire immunity.[9]

Yellow Fever: The Tropical Scourge

Africans who lived with yellow fever and the more virulent *falciparum* form of malaria understood in their own terms the two diseases and had long developed ways of coping, both medicinal and cultural. When large numbers of these people were uprooted from their land and shipped as slaves to the Western Hemisphere, they and mosquitoes that lived and bred in ships' stagnant water supplies carried the pathogens with them. As the tragic cargoes spilled onto the wharves of colonial ports from Boston to Brazil, the diseases accompanied them. The mosquitoes fed indiscriminately on the immune and the uninfected alike, cross-infecting Europeans, natives, and blacks who had avoided infection or had been born in the colony.

The first major wave of yellow fever cases in the Caribbean began in the 1640s. As victims either died or were immunized, the epidemic cooled off for about 50 years. Spanish Havana, for example, suffered epidemics of yellow fever in 1649, 1651, 1652, and 1654, and again in 1709, 1715, 1730, 1731, 1733, 1738, and 1742. In 1762, during the Seven Years' War, an invading army of British troops was all but destroyed by the fever, while the largely immune Hispanic and slave population of Havana remained unscathed. After a 60-day siege and with the aid of North American militia, the British seized the city, which they had to return by treaty a year later. Though 696 British soldiers died of disease during the siege, during the two months following the surrender in mid-August, the hot season for yellow fever, over 4,000 British troops died of disease.[10]

Yellow fever, whether in the form of an urban epidemic or a military expedition-squashing outbreak among unseasoned troops, had a mortality rate that varied between 30 and 70 percent, depending on environment and season. *Vivax* malaria kills perhaps 1 percent of those infected, and the more lethal *falciparum* on the order of 10 percent. With *vivax*, the debilitation of the fever was the principal problem, one encountered in marshy European environments as well as colonial ports and plantations. Fever-weakened bodies were subject to a host of secondary diseases and conditions, and of course needed medical care. While European population growth was accompanied by the mosquito-friendly expansion of cultivated land, with its irrigation and furrows, trenches, and other water-collecting features, by the seventeenth century Europe was in a climatic cooling period that tended to curb the insects' activity. At the same time, the discovery of malaria-inhibiting "Jesuit bark," or cinchona bark from the New World, made effective treatment a possibility, if an expensive one.

Despite their curative bark, the main ingredient in quinine, native Americans died of malaria at rates second only to the slaughter of smallpox, some scholars believe. Relatively benign *vivax* may have been present in low-lying coastal areas before European contact, but *falciparum* was clearly imported from Africa. Historically, yellow fever (largely a problem in settled areas) and malarial fevers killed or debilitated huge portions of the native populations, allowing much easier domination of the New World by the conquerors from the Old.

FILTH AND PARASITES: TYPHUS AND DYSENTERY

Early modern cultures differed widely in their understanding of what was an acceptable level of personal hygiene or cleanliness. Whether or how often a person bathed or changed clothes did, however, dictate whether and how parasites on the skin or lodged in dirty clothing next to it were eliminated. People living in hot climates tended to wear little in the way of clothing of any sort, and what they did wear tended to be very light and well ventilated. Northerners, however, had developed cultures that required coverage from head to toe, often with heavy woolens and furs. Cool temperatures and a medical prejudice against opening the pores during bathing made Europeans among the filthiest people on earth. And along with filth came parasites.

Typhus

Typhus[11] results from human body lice that live in clothing of dirty people. The louse feeds up to six times daily on human blood. If it is infected by *Rickettsia prowazekii* bacteria, it will transmit the pathogens to the human bloodstream or deposit them on human skin in its feces. Human scratching opens skin and rubs in the bacteria. Like a virus, these bacteria enter human cells and reproduce. Incubation takes 5 to 15 days, after which sudden fever, chills, nausea, and debilitation strike down the victim. A serious case will result in prostration, neurological damage to hearing and mental sharpness, collapse of the circulatory system, and death. Untreated victims tend to recover from epidemic typhus from 75 to 95 percent of the time, gaining a limited immunity from the experience. Though lice die from the bacteria, they can live long enough to invade other sets of clothing and spread the disease; uninfected lice consume human blood infected with bacteria, find new human hosts, and the cycle becomes an epidemic.

Typhus tended to be found where weather was cold at least part of the time, people wore layers of clothing without cleaning it or their

Figure 6.2 Illustration from 1639 depicting a boy combing lice from his hair. The parasites, which thrive in unsanitary environments, transmit typhus. They also lay eggs on human scalp hairs, which have to be carefully removed—a task that gave us the phrase "nit-picking." (National Library of Medicine)

bodies, and they lived closely together, which facilitated exchange of lice. Village families huddled together around the winter fire comes to mind, as do crowded prisons and campaigning soldiers with their filthy uniforms or stolen clothing. The list of early modern military campaigns that were cut short or protracted by typhus and attendant diseases is long indeed. Troop mobilizations were the largest population movements of the period, and they grew larger over time. When outbreaks erupted, they affected the troops, their camp followers, the enemy, and the populations through whom they moved and with whom they were billeted or with whom the wounded were left behind. Europeans' first notice was among Spanish troops in Cyprus around 1490. Redirected to Italy, they quickly spread the novel disease to Italy and thence it migrated to France, Germany, and the rest of Europe. Its symptoms were reported in Latin America, though heavy clothing was rare and bathing common, at least in healthy communities.

Dysentery

Dysentery is a disease of the lower digestive tract passed through the oral-fecal route. A person ingests infected food or water and the pathogens exit the body through bloody diarrhea. Where control of human waste is lax, released pathogens taint food or water by direct contact (often by unhygienic infected food handlers) or by flies that light on waste and then food; and the cycle continues. Inside the human colon pathogens use and destroy the body's defensive cells, killing the organ's healthy cells and causing inflammation. A number of bacteria, including *Campylobacter*, *Escherichia coli* (*E. coli*), *Shigella*, and *Salmonella*, and the protozoon *Entamoeba histolytica* can cause the disease. *E. histolytica* become destructive only after they burrow into the colon's walls, causing bleeding, destruction of the walls, and possibly blood poisoning. Bacillary dysentery, caused by bacilli (bacteria), is clinically very similar to amebic dysentery, causing ulcers in the colon, bleeding, bloody diarrhea, and potentially acute dehydration.

Today, even though understood and treatable, dysentery kills tens of thousands each year. Usually dysentery becomes epidemic in large prison or refugee camps, third-world urban slums, or other environments where people are jammed together with little provision for cleanliness or waste disposal. In early modern times dysentery regularly visited armies, both encamped and on campaign, and burgeoning cities of the eighteenth century with little public sanitation. Cortés's conquistadors spread (if they did not introduce) the disease to Mexico by campaigning and creating refugees. Among the natives in Portuguese Brazil dysentery became epidemic in 1560, leading the colonists to begin importing Africans as slaves to do the work the sick natives could not. Dysentery may have helped Akbar the Great, Mughal ruler in India, expand his empire in 1601 by weakening and killing the defenders of the fortress at Asirgarh. Ironically, after reigning 50 years he died of dysentery in October 1605.[12] Dysentery often accompanied other diseases, especially when customary sanitation and hygiene broke down, as in armies and besieged towns during the Thirty Years' War (1618–48) in Europe, or London in 1623. Besiegers also suffered, as did the English during the siege of Jacobite Dundalk, Ireland, in the spring of 1689. A combination of deadly typhus, dysentery, and syphilis killed half of the English army and forcing its withdrawal, but not before striking the civil population as well. Until public sanitation and safe water, even Paris could suffer dysentery outbreaks, as in the winter of 1740, when it joined with influenza, tuberculosis, and typhus to slaughter thousands, especially among the poor. Epidemics accompanying filth often include several diseases since unhygienic and inadequate living conditions give rise to many related and unrelated conditions, from insect poisoning to digestive and respiratory illnesses.

WHEN THE AIR IS DEADLY: SMALLPOX, INFLUENZA, AND MEASLES

Many infectious diseases do not require insect vectors but are spread through the air by coughing or sneezing, as is pneumonic plague. Unlike plague bacteria, pathogens of smallpox, influenza, and measles are viruses that enter the human bloodstream rapidly through the respiratory system, invade human cells, and reproduce. Survivors of smallpox and measles gain immunity from the body's development of adequate defenses. Influenza, or flu, virus strains are extremely mutable, however, and the human immune system has to adjust to each new outbreak. Though smallpox has been eradicated from nature—thanks in part to its having only human hosts—and the flu and measles are either mild or easily controlled, each was a major epidemic killer during the early modern period.

Smallpox

Deadly smallpox was caused by a poxvirus, later named *Variola major*. It was passed in tiny aerosol droplets by coughing, sneezing, or even breathing, or by human contact with bedding or clothing on which the virus had been deposited. Around 12 days later, the victim suffered flu-like symptoms and malaise; but within another few days, pustules erupted on the skin. If they dried, scabbed over, and the scab fell off, the crisis was passed and he had immunity thereafter. In many cases, however, the pustules caused permanent pockmarks that permanently marred one's face, hands, and feet. The virus could also leave the survivor blind or, if male, infertile. But smallpox could also rapidly destroy the body, causing blood poisoning (septicemia), hemorrhaging, and death in 25 to 30 percent of its victims.[13]

By 1700, medical practitioners in Asia and Africa had long used various methods of introducing a powder of dried scabs into healthy people's skin to trigger a mild, immunity-conferring form of the disease. Known to the West as variolation or inoculation, the procedure came to Europe from Islamic Turkey in the early 1700s and even earlier to its colonies in the Americas with African slaves. The major problem was that the recipient underwent a form of the disease—from mild to deadly—and required rest and patient care. In 1798 English physician Edward Jenner did traditional medicine one better by replacing the smallpox material with biologically related cowpox material—vaccination—which immunized but did not debilitate recipients.

The Flu

Like all other diseases, influenza (from Italian for celestial "influence") was a mystery to early modern societies around the world. As we know from contemporary media reports, humans can catch the various forms of Orthomyxoviridae virus from animals as varied as birds and swine, and the strain of virus can mutate wildly. This makes modern vaccination programs problematical, since they tend to be effective against last year's version and not necessarily this year's. The famous "flu-like symptoms" of so many diseases make the disease difficult to pinpoint historically. Often called catarrh or grippe in early English sources, the disease was first clinically described in the mid-1650s by Thomas Willis. But influenza is an ancient disease, and its lethality was proven in the great pandemic of 1918 that swept the world and killed tens of millions.[14]

Transmitted in the same manner as smallpox, the victim undergoes about five days of incubation before showing symptoms. During this time he does not know that he is infected, but he is also infecting others unknowingly, since the virus can be passed along almost immediately after infection. This makes flu especially contagious and dangerous. The virus causes respiratory symptoms of coughing and sneezing—which help spread the virus—sore throat, fever, head and muscle aches, malaise, disorientation, vomiting, and diarrhea. Clearly, these symptoms weaken the victim, allowing other germs to invade and do further damage, often leading to death in the very young or elderly. The weakened respiratory system invites pneumonia, which can injure or even shut down the lungs. Unlike plague or smallpox, the flu opens the door to killer microbes that do the real damage.

Measles

Measles is caused by an airborne virus of the paramyxovirus family, which is related to several viruses that cause animal and other human diseases, including mumps. The fever and skin discoloration of measles created confusion with scarlet fever and rubella in doctors and even microbiologists until the 1880s. Though related to rinderpest, canine distemper, and other animal ailments, the virus that brings on measles is a strictly human pathogen, which has made measles a likely—though so far unsuccessful—candidate for eradication from nature through mass MMR (measles-mumps-rubella) vaccinations.

Early modern victims suffered a predictable and unvarying set of symptoms. After 10 days of incubation, respiratory inflammation, cough, and conjunctivitis develop, along with fever, a distinctive spotted rash on the inside of the cheeks, and the familiar raised, red itchy rash on the skin. The last tends to begin high on the body and move down, no doubt a frightening manifestation to cultures unaccustomed to measles. Complications included pneumonia, blindness, and encephalitis, and the disease was deadly to adults before modern medicine. Where it is endemic, as in early modern Europe, children tend to get the disease, which is generally mild and confers adult immunity. Among adult Native Americans mortality rates may have been as high as 35 percent. Measles and smallpox appeared similar enough to confuse even medical practitioners. Though medieval Arabs seem to have distinguished the two, in Europe this had to await the efforts of Thomas Sydenham, the "English Hippocrates," who studied English epidemics of the disease in the 1670s. That measles was infectious was not proven until the 1750s, though no one understood how it spread.

Epidemics and Pandemics

An ancient disease, influenza was common in Europe, and it probably arrived in the Americas with Columbus's men. The period 1556–60 saw a major European outbreak, which spread to North Africa and the New World. It appears often as an epidemic or even pandemic disease in the eighteenth century, beginning in Rome in 1708. Geographically isolated areas such as Spain, England, and Scandinavia were spared, but the disease struck across the rest of Europe. It returned with greater strength in 1712 and 1729, the latter outbreak affecting life from Central Asia to Iceland. This also spread by ship to the Americas. The years 1732–33 saw another major outbreak, which swept even more widely, as it did again in 1742 and 1762. By 1762 European nations were fighting a world-encircling war (Seven Years' War) that probably served to reintroduce the virus to the Americas and India. In 1780 flu was reported in China and it traveled widely in 1781 and 1782; and a Russian outbreak spread worldwide in 1788 and 1789.

Influenza may have been present in the Americas, but it would not have been the strain(s) brought over by Europeans during the sixteenth century. Historical sources often confuse flu, measles, and smallpox, or provide too little information for modern diagnosis of historical diseases. Nonetheless, it seems clear that the three tended to appear together with devastating results in the New World. They often arrived in a region long before the invaders, since carriers who were messengers, refugees, and travelers moved far in advance of European explorers. Unused to the frightening symptoms, natives responded to the fevers and rashes in ways, such as hot baths, that were dangerous rather than healing. Though infection conferred at least temporary immunity, which allowed the diseases to be endemic in Europe, they rapidly tore through the "virgin soil" of the Western Hemisphere, killing untold millions. As whole villages were stricken, there were few if any to tend the sick, providing them with vital food and water. Fever-ridden children quickly dehydrated and died. Frightened adults fled the horrors, spreading them further if they were carriers. Medicine proved fruitless, and rituals that ordered life and death disappeared as living conditions became intolerable and community leaders died off. Throughout the Americas infectious disease eliminated entire cultures.[15]

By contrast, in Japan the result was vastly different. Though isolated by sea, Japanese people had long been in contact with many different peoples from the Indian and Pacific Oceans and Asia's mainland. The islands boasted many dense cities, including Edo/Tokyo, which had over a million residents in the seventeenth century. Smallpox and influenza were endemic, though smallpox outbreaks reached epidemic levels in 1523, 1531, 1550, 1619, 1654, 1679, 1682, 1702, 1708–9, 1711–12, 1720, 1723, 1746, 1748, and 1773. About mid-eighteenth century the Japanese adopted smallpox inoculation from China, perhaps accounting for the fall-off in epidemics after 1748. Excellent Japanese records show that most deaths (in one study 95%) were of children 10 years of age or younger. Measles, popularly imagined as a large, bearded, black-robed man or speckled females, apparently never became endemic. Epidemics in 1506, 1513, 1523, 1535, 1578, 1587, 1607, 1616, 1649, 1690–91, 1708, 1730, 1753, and 1776 were sparked by importations of measles, at least some by Europeans, who were allowed access to Japan only from 1543 to 1639. Both younger adults and children suffered most of the deaths, probably due to the immunizing effect of the recurrent outbreaks. That none of these deadly diseases had deep effects on Japanese society may well have been because the Japanese understood the value of isolating the sick, or isolating the well from the sick.[16]

WATERBORNE DISEASES: CHOLERA AND TYPHOID FEVER

The human body requires water to live, but not any water will do. It will reject salt and sulfurous waters, but the really dangerous waters are those that appear to be clean to the sight, smell, and taste but are in fact home to various pathological microbes. When ingested, these could cause uncomfortable conditions such as "Montezuma's revenge," or even potentially deadly diseases, such as cholera and typhoid fever. Whereas ancient Rome drew its water from the surrounding hills through aqueducts and aerating fountains, burgeoning early modern cities around the world had water supply systems that presented the end user with a biological soup, however clear it might have appeared.[17]

Cholera

Cholera erupted onto the world stage in 1816, beginning a series of pandemics that circled the globe well into the twentieth century. Before advances in travel such as steamships and trains, it tended to be confined to cities and narrow ribbons along polluted water routes. It had, however, long been endemic to China and the Ganges River Basin in India. After the Portuguese landed in India in 1498, they began chronicling cholera (*moryxi*) outbreaks, including one in 1503 that struck 20,000 Indian soldiers, killing many. In 1563 the Portuguese physician García de Orta first clinically described cholera. Colonial records from India between 1503 and 1817 contain 64 references to cholera outbreaks, which is no doubt the tip of the iceberg.

The pathogen is a rod-shaped bacterium called *Vibrio cholerae*. Being motile, it can move through water and needs no further vector. Transmission is a chicken-and-egg problem: A sufferer has it in her digestive system and passes it though her feces. When these pollute a water source, for example a ground aquifer or surface stream, the bacterium is passed to one who drinks and digests the water. After a day or two in the body, *Vibrio* creates a toxin that induces cramps, as well as diarrhea and vomiting, which help spread infected waste even further. Up to 20 liters of fluid could flow out of a person in a single day, with 10,000,000 bacteria in a single milliliter. Other symptoms follow, but the acute expelling of bodily fluids dehydrates the sufferer, who may lose 10 percent of her body weight, including important electrolytes. Without rehydration, death is the likely outcome.

Typhoid Fever

Similar in many ways to typhus, typhoid is an enteric (intestinal) fever brought on by ingestion of a salmonella bacterium (*Salmonella typhi*) in infected food or water. Like *Vibrio*, it is transmitted within human groups through feces that may affect water supplies. Often, flies land on improperly treated infected waste and transmit it by their feet to human food. Unlike some other food-poisoning agents, typhoid pathogens enter the human bloodstream and various organs. Symptoms are slow to manifest, making identification of the source difficult to pinpoint. Fever, abdominal pains, headache, and diarrhea slowly reduce victims to a malaise that may last up to four weeks. Because typhoid affects the whole body, complications may occur in many organs from brain to spleen, and even bones may suffer from osteomyelitis. Death rates from such complications were about 15 percent before modern medicine.

Well-ordered communities that cared for the sick and maintained high levels of waste disposal had little to fear. Where people were crowded together and water supplies were subject to contamination, typhoid fever was always a threat. Armies in camp and on campaign were prime candidates, as were cities struck by war or disaster. As European cities grew, they often paid scant attention to water supplies and sewerage; in some cases the two were barely distinguishable. In such cases water, so necessary for human life, became a deadly poison.

WHEN SEX NEEDED DRUGS: SYPHILIS AND OTHER VENEREAL DISEASES

Transmission of a disease through sexual intercourse is labeled venereal in honor of Venus, the goddess of love. Low levels of hygiene can make sex a rather filthy act for a woman by allowing all sorts of bacteria to enter the vagina, whether from lingual, penile, or instrumental insertion. Males, too, may contract parasites or bacteria from contact with a woman's genitals, as early modern customers of prostitutes no doubt experienced. True venereal diseases are transmitted only through sexual contact, oral-genital, oral, or genital. Syphilis, or the pox, burst into the historical record in 1494 as a sidelight to the French attack on Naples, and gonorrhea was first described by a London physician a few decades later. In both cases the means of transmission was fairly clear, though no one understood the diseases' causes or how to treat them effectively and safely.[18]

Syphilis

Syphilis is transmitted by a carrier of the motile spirochete bacterium *Treponema pallidum*. During the three weeks after introduction through the mouth or genitalia, the pathogens enter the bloodstream and begin to affect the body's organs. A sore or chancre appears, probably at the site of infection. The lymphatic system sweeps many of the invaders and dead defenders to the groin's lymph nodes, which swell uncomfortably. After several weeks a range of symptoms develop, depending on which organs are most affected. A red rash may develop; other lymph nodes swell with the bacteria and pus; skin spots, open sores, and large skin swellings filled with the active bacteria may appear in the groin and between the buttocks. Major organs swell up, anemia develops, and involvement of the nervous system can result in hearing and vision problems. About 60 percent of victims who survive slide into a long latent period during which the symptoms subside (though marks may well remain). The remainder move into a third stage, or tertiary syphilis, which badly weakens major organs such as the heart, and the nervous system. A pregnant woman syphilis carrier may find that the disease crossed the placenta and infected her baby.

Gonorrhea

During the early modern period, gonorrhea was considered a symptom of syphilis rather than a separate disease. In fact, it is a bacterial infection by the gonococcus, which is related to meningitis-producing meningococcus and several bacteria typically found in the human mouth. It affects both men and women, causing a distinctive cloudy discharge from the penis, urethral swelling, joint pains, and eye problems in men. Women develop arthritic joints, inflammation of the pelvis, and scarring in the reproductive organs.

Early Modern Spread and Treatment of Venereal Diseases

The armies that departed Naples in 1494 spread syphilis far and wide. Within only a couple of years, it was reported across Europe. Most observers regarded it as sexually transmitted—a penalty for illicit sex—though some reused the standard theory of miasma, or poisoned air, and others the conjunction of the planets Saturn and Jupiter. Prostitutes and bathhouses were regulated or forbidden by civic authorities accustomed to stanching plague outbreaks. In 1497 the Scots isolated sufferers on the Isle of Inch until they recovered or died. The sixteenth-century Italian physician Girolamo Fracastoro gave the pox its Greek name, that of the main character in his poem *Syphilis*. The Portuguese took it to India in 1498, the same year it appeared in Azerbaijan; then China (1502) and Japan (1512) began seeing cases. Whether it began in the New World or was imported from Europe remains an open question (the first reported date of 1494 is very suspicious), but it was soon found among American natives and colonists alike.

Arabs had long used mercury as a treatment for skin diseases, and around 1500 some European practitioners began using the potentially lethal substance on victims of syphilis. Symptoms of mercury poisoning were ascribed to the disease, and its use continued through the eighteenth century. In 1517 Spaniards discovered the value of guaic bark, which was harvested in South America. Known to many as "Jesuit bark," it was expensive and only moderately effective when boiled in water and the liquid drunk. Pox wards in hospitals and entire facilities devoted to syphilitics appeared across Europe and in its colonies. Moral and hygienic imperatives, such as avoiding prostitutes, washing before sex, and inserting sponges into the vagina, may have had some effect in reducing the initial onslaught of syphilis (and gonorrhea as well), but it also appears that the disease lost some of its initial virulence. When disease pathogens are too deadly, they kill their hosts and cannot survive or reproduce in the long run.

Taken together, infectious diseases killed millions across the globe and damaged the lives of many millions more. Records of the premodern world allow for only a partial reconstruction of even the best-documented outbreak or epidemic, but those that survive paint a grim picture indeed.

NOTES

1. For a deeper discussion see, for example, Sherwood L. Gorbach, John G. Bartlett, and Neil R. Blacklow, eds., *Infectious Diseases* (Philadelphia: Lippincott, 2003).

2. On historical epidemics see Joseph P. Byrne, ed., *Encyclopedia of Pestilence, Pandemics, and Plagues* (Westport, CT: Greenwood Press, 2008); Kenneth F. Kiple, ed., *Cambridge Historical Dictionary of Disease* (New York: Cambridge University Press, 2003).

3. For premodern theories of contagion see Claire L. Carlin, *Imagining Contagion in Early Modern Europe* (New York: Palgrave, 2005).

4. On the Black Death and early modern plague generally, see for example John Aberth, ed., *The Black Death: The Great Mortality of 1348–1350: A Brief History with Documents* (Boston: Bedford/St. Martin's, 2005); Joseph Byrne, *Daily Life during the Black Death* (Westport, CT: Greenwood Press, 2006).

5. For responses to plague in Europe, see, for example, Byrne, *Daily Life*; and Carlo Cipolla, *Faith, Reason, and the Plague in Seventeenth-Century Tuscany* (New York: Norton, 1981).

6. On plague in the Islamic world see Stuart J. Borsch, *The Black Death in Egypt and England: A Comparative Study* (Austin: University of Texas Press, 2005); Michael Dols, *The Black Death in the Middle East* (Princeton, NJ: Princeton University Press, 1977).

7. Byrne, *Daily Life*, 281–97.

8. On malaria see Randall M. Packard, *The Making of a Tropical Disease: A Short History of Malaria* (Baltimore: Johns Hopkins University Press, 2007); James L. A. Webb Jr., *Humanity's Burden: A Global History of Malaria* (New York: Cambridge University Press, 2009).

9. On yellow fever see J. R. McNeill, *Mosquito Empires: Ecology and War in the Greater Caribbean, 1620–1914* (New York: Cambridge University Press, 2010), 32–52, 137–91; Kenneth F. Kiple and Stephen Beck, *Biological Consequences of the European Expansion, 1450–1800* (Brookfield, VT: Ashgate, 1997), and John R. Pierce and Jim Writer, *Yellow Jack* (Hoboken, NJ: Wiley, 2005).

10. McNeill, *Mosquito Empires*, 175–91.

11. The classic work is Hans Zinsser, *Fleas, Rats and History* (Boston: Little, Brown, 1963); see also Irwin W. Sherman, *The Power of Plague* (Washington, DC: American Society for Microbiology, 2006); and Sheldon Watts, *Disease and Medicine in World History* (New York: Routledge, 2003).

12. Valerie Berinstain, *India and the Mughal Dynasty*, trans. Paul G. Bahn (New York: Abrams, 2001), 71.

13. The standard work on smallpox remains Donald R. Hopkins, *The Greatest Killer: Smallpox in History* (Chicago: University of Chicago, 2002).

14. K. David Patterson, *Pandemic Influenza, 1700–1900* (Totowa, NJ: Rowman and Littlefield, 1986); Tom Quinn, *Flu: A Social History of Influenza* (London: New Holland, 2008).

15. On the broad range of diseases introduced into the New World from the Old, see Suzanne Austin Alchon, *A Pest in the Land: New World Epidemics in a Global Perspective* (Albuquerque: University of New Mexico Press, 2003), and Noble David Cook and W. George Lovell, eds., *Secret Judgments of God: Old World Disease in Colonial Spanish America* (Norman: University of Oklahoma Press, 1991).

16. Ann Bowman Jannetta, *Epidemics and Mortality in Early Modern Japan* (Princeton, NJ: Princeton University Press, 1987).

17. On both diseases and others related see Paul Hunter, *Waterborne Disease: Epidemiology and Ecology* (New York: Wiley, 1997).

18. There are many fine sources on venereal disease; for our period see Jon Arrizabalaga, John Henderson, and Roger French, eds., *The Great Pox: The French Disease in Renaissance Europe* (New Haven, CT: Yale University Press, 1997).

CHAPTER 7

Environmental and Occupational Hazards

Where and how one lives is sometimes a choice and sometimes dictated by genes, culture, technology, economics, or history. Some environments present regular, natural threats to human safety and life, and some suffer extraordinary and unexpected disasters. The following section scans some of the many endemic biological threats to human life in sub-Saharan Africa during the early modern period; and it focuses on two unforeseen ecological disasters in eighteenth-century Western Europe. The second half of the chapter outlines the hazards associated with certain early modern occupations.

ENVIRONMENTAL HAZARDS

The concept of environmental health is as ancient as Hippocrates and China's oldest medical texts. The climate, air, winds, water, seasonal changes, and other environmental factors played important roles in medical theory throughout history, as they still do. Endemic disease could be a major factor if it was potentially fatal and the society had no effective way of limiting it. Unusual conditions or events sometimes have complex or terrible effects on human populations. Hurricanes, tornadoes, volcanic eruptions, droughts, floods, deep freezes, and earthquakes are some of the environmental events that have marked the history of human health. Epidemic outbreaks of infectious diseases may also be considered environmental hazards, but these are specifically outlined in chapter 6.

The Sub-Saharan African Environment

Apart from a few major population centers, most early modern sub-Saharan Africans lived fairly close to nature in small settlements. Though some were influenced by Muslims from the east and north, and after 1500 by Europeans landing along the west coast, most lived tradition-circumscribed lives shaped by their physical environments. Africa is a huge continent possessing many types of landscape, and generalizations should be either avoided or highly qualified. One that is unavoidable is that the climate is hot and often very humid, though in certain regions prone to drought. Heat can cause many medical problems, even for those used to it, including dehydration and heat stroke. Another is that there is a very rich endemic disease environment in central and southern Africa. Both of these factors prevented the very mobile and aggressive Europeans from doing more than seizing much of the population of the central westcoast between 1500 and 1800.

Every region of Africa did not host every major disease, but an overview of some of the major examples is instructive. Oliver Ransford divided them into the epidemic, the crippling or deadly, and the debilitating.[1] Of course, no one in the world understood how any of these diseases functioned or how they might be effectively battled. The epidemic diseases included typhus, bubonic plague, yellow fever, smallpox, relapsing fever, and meningitis.[2] Today they all still plague the continent, but modern medicine reduces their carnage. Some deadly and crippling endemic diseases included the following:

Malaria[3] has four forms, the most dangerous of which, caused by the *Plasmodium falciparum*, was very common throughout southern Africa. Some historians believe it was so devastating to local populations that it prevented the type of historical urban and civilizational development found in other areas of the world. The female *Anopheles* mosquito loves heat and standing water and transmitted the protozoa among the people off of whose blood she fed. The previously unexposed victims, especially pregnant women and children, died very rapidly, while others suffered recurring fever and chills that effectively crippled the individual. Africa's pattern of rural settlement was conducive to the *Anopheles*, and its tropical climate made malaria a year-round problem.

Sleeping sickness[4] affected both humans and animals and was caused by a protozoon (*Trypanosoma*) that was spread by the tsetse or Glossina fly. The protozoa in the victim's body created mild symptoms, including

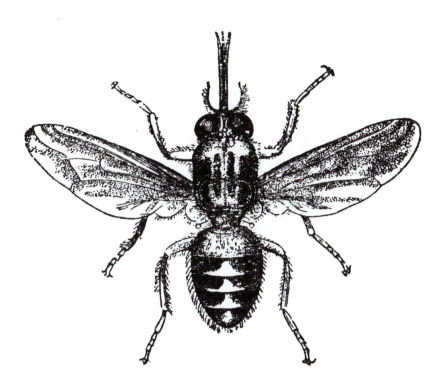

Figure 7.1 Engraving from 1880 of a tsetse fly, or Glossina morsitans (from *Meyers Lexikon*). Found living between the Sahara and Kalahari Deserts of Africa, the insect transmits the protozoon trypanosoma, which causes sleeping sickness in humans. (*Meyers Konversations-Lexikon*, Bibliographisches Institut: Leipzig, 1888/90.)

sluggishness and lack of balance, sores, inflammation and lung problems. When they attacked the central nervous system the brain swelled (encephalitis), often leading to coma or death. Animistic natives blamed witchcraft while Muslims pointed to God's punishment of apostates.

River blindness or onchocerciasis was caused by the residence of pairs of male and female worm-like flukes, *Onchocercus volvulus*. These were carried about on flies known today as *Simulium damnosum*, which preferred life in proximity to fast moving fresh water. Growing up to 50 cm in length, the female fluke burrowed into human skin and rolled up into a ball with her much shorter mate. They produced up to a million offspring annually, and these moved about inside the human host, creating irritation that could even be maddening. The real problem occurred when these entered into the eyes and eventually caused blindness, which was far from unusual. Though the sightless were often given light agricultural tasks, many communities abandoned prime riverine areas to avoid the disease.

Filariasis was caused by round worms or nematodes of the family *Filariodea*. These were also carried by biting flies and mosquitoes that fed on infected human and animal—cattle, horses, dogs—blood. The parasites lived under the skin or within the lymphatic system, causing symptoms that differed with the parts of the body affected. These, too, could cause river blindness, swelling of the joints (arthritis), skin rashes, and the deformation of the skin known as elephantiasis.

Hookworms were roundworms (helminthes) that lived in warm, moist soil and as larvae could burrow into human skin. They traveled through the victim's circulatory system to the heart and lungs, and from there to the pharynx from which they were swallowed and eventually settled in the small intestine. Eggs were passed out in human feces and into the soil. They fed on the human host's blood, resulting in protein loss and anemia. This weakened the victims' resistance to other diseases and made them very weak and sluggish.

Ransford's debilitating and less severe diseases include:

Dysentery was a disease of the gastrointestinal system caused by *Shigella* and similar bacteria. The bacilli were carried on the legs of flies that had landed on contaminated human waste to feed and then landed on humans' food and contaminated it. In the body the bacteria attacked the intestines, inflaming them, killing their cells, and shutting down their function. The victim suffered from bloody diarrhea and dehydration, but in modern cases many recover naturally as the body's defenses flush out the bacteria and repair the damage. While climate has nothing to do with the spread of *Shigella* and its equivalents, human waste management does. They often struck where normal ways of life were disrupted, as by natural disaster or war: to which early modern Africa was no stranger.

Leprosy was also a bacterial disease, one probably passed along by direct human contact—though modern research is questioning this. The bacteria prefer the cooler surface regions of the human body and thus caused skin and extremity deformities from scaly rashes to the falling off of toes or noses. The nerves were also susceptible to attack, resulting in symptoms from local numbness to blindness. Carriers were often asymptomatic and lived perfectly normal lives, but the symptoms could be disturbing and even revolting to those around one, resulting in a community's banishment of the sufferer, or worse.

Yaws was a condition of the skin caused by direct contact in the environment with the spirochete *Treponema pertenue*. Infection probably occurred when the germ entered the feet or legs through an open sore or wound, and in modern times it especially affects children, who are more likely than adults to go barefoot. The deep open sores were limited to the lower leg but recurred repeatedly even after a single exposure. Over time the disease could attack the bones and so weaken them as to cripple the person. Among the African slaves in the Caribbean, yaws was so common that some plantations had special "houses" for treatment of the disease.

Worms and flukes entered the human body through the skin or orifices and lived as parasites inside the person. The Guinea worm lived under the skin consuming the body's fluids and could reach a meter in length. Lacking ways to kill the invader, African healers waited until the victim's skin opened to release the worm's larvae and tried to hook the worm itself, pulling it out by winding it around a spool. Schistosomiasis[5] is also known as bilharzia, named for the European scientist who first discovered how the disease worked. As larvae the *Schistosoma* flukes penetrated the victim's skin within a few minutes of contact in fresh water. They traveled through the circulatory system and within a few days matured and mated. The female then anchored herself in such a way as to release her eggs into the host's urinary system or large intestine. From here the eggs reentered the freshwater environment and the cycle continued. These flukes could live half a dozen years, and they evolved to have a rather minimal effect on their hosts. Nonetheless, urinary and enteric complications certainly arose as cycle followed cycle.[6]

European Disasters: The Great Winter in Lyon, 1709

Lyon, France, was a center of French finance and the silk industry at the confluence of the Rhône and Saone Rivers. Its 90,000 souls relied on imported foodstuffs for survival, and these arrived via both rivers and the several roads that met at the city's bridges. In May of 1708 unusually heavy rains struck the region, destroying or retarding much of the region's young wheat crop that would feed the city in the fall. Nervous citizens hoarded grain, and merchants gouged locals with high prices, as grain was shipped away to feed Louis XIV's military. Discontent rose until government interaction ensured that there would not be a winter of shortages.

Nature turned on the French, however, as temperatures plummeted in early January 1709. Rain-saturated land froze hard, killing or retarding all manner of trees and vines. Frozen rain destroyed winter crops; the rivers froze at Lyon, and ice blocked or impeded much of that lifeline for several months. Deep snows and icy winds joined the bone-chilling temperatures in February, killing herds of animals and taking a further toll on agricultural resources. Some people froze to death, and many more suffered frostbite from exposure. People stoked great fires trying to keep warm, which sometimes turned into conflagrations, laying waste to homes and warehouses. It was a legendarily brutal season.

In March many peasants defied a royal edict and plowed under the ruined wheat crops, planting barley, oats, or buckwheat, which promised to grow more quickly. Faced with another greatly reduced crop, prices rose and people panicked, with serious rioting breaking out on March 25, usually around bakeries. As supplies dwindled and prospects soured further mobs, soldiers and royal officials seized grain shipments bound for Lyon even as increasingly desperate peasants began to swell the city's population. Economic disaster hit the city's elites as creditors called in accounts and debtors defaulted, ruining Lyonaise credit and cascading through the society. Imports dropped off, and even wine shipments fell by a third. State bread donations rose six times to 60,000 pounds in May, even after "foreign" poor had been herded out of the city in April. By May the price of wheat had risen by 300 percent in the small village of Grenette, and royal troops had to guard the roads and waterways so grain could pass to Lyon unmolested. Surrounding regions were as desperate as Lyon's, and foreign wheat seemed the only answer. In late July, 15 barges loaded with wheat began the trip from Toulon to Lyon, but nature again intervened as red coral banks blocked the Rhône's mouth. On September 28, however, the barges arrived and the grain flowed into the granaries.

For many this was too late. For numerous reasons August was the year's deadliest month, the average death toll for August rising half again as high as the July average. In 1709 August saw nearly twice the average number of deaths (366 as opposed to 190), as the weakened population succumbed. As usual, during this crisis period most deaths did not occur from starvation—few usually do starve—but malnutrition leads to anemia and gastrointestinal illnesses and weakens people's resistance to disease. The influx of rural folk introduced unusual pathogens; the lack of wine led to the drinking of tainted water (typhoid fever and dysentery); the cold winter led to unusually close living conditions and a lack of hygiene, which fostered lice-borne typhus and skin diseases. In the winter endemic influenza and tuberculosis thrived, and children were stricken with smallpox and diarrhea. Though conditions never became epidemic, urban dependence, natural forces, and delayed human action combined to undermine or destroy the health of thousands during the crisis of 1708 and 1709.[7]

European Disasters: The Lisbon Earthquake, 1755

My right arm hung down before me motionless, like a great dead weight, the shoulder being out, and the bone broken; ... my legs covered with wounds, the right ankle swelled to a prodigious size, with a fountain of blood spouting upwards from it: the knee was also much bruised, my left side felt as if beat in, so that I could hardly breathe: all the left side of my face was swelled, the skin beaten off, the blood streaming from it, with a great wound above and a small one below the eye, and several bruises on my back and head.[8]

The British merchant Thomas Chase was 26 years old when the great earthquake leveled the city of Lisbon, Portugal, at 9:30 a.m. on All Saints Day (November 1) 1755. He was living in the same house in which he was born, and which collapsed atop him (he survived, recovered, and lived another 33 years). This was the 8.7 to 9.0 Richter scale earthquake that shattered the philosopher Voltaire's optimism in man's capabilities and led him to write his masterpiece, *Candide*. Like most of the 30,000 to 60,000 who died in the quake, Chase was struck and buried by falling debris. The well-built residences of the wealthy fared better than the ramshackle tenements of the poor, but even the best were damaged. Many who survived and were trapped were incinerated by conflagrations started by disrupted kitchen fires, shop lights, and the thousands of candles in the well-lit churches on that religious feast day.

But the earthquake also spawned three tidal waves whose backwash swept into Europe's third-busiest harbor, engulfing debris, ships, docks, warehouses, and people and washing them out to sea. Barbados and Martinique in the far-distant Caribbean felt the tsunamis. When the major tremors and tidal events subsided, both the desperate and the criminal took what they wanted in the ensuing anarchy. With the city's food supplies gone or spoiled, and the infrastructure for resupplying it in tatters, the survivors made for the countryside or rioted until order was restored. Dysentery and other diseases of the disrupted human environment swept the survivors. To this was joined the fear of miasma and plague from the rotting corpses, many being washed up from the ocean. For all of their wealth and culture, before the fury of nature and nature's God the Portuguese stood humbled.[9]

OCCUPATIONAL HAZARDS

Many early physicians recognized that people in certain occupations tended to suffer from the same ailments. Hippocrates discussed the problems of tailors, horse wranglers, fishermen, dyers, metalworkers, and farm laborers. Galen noted patterns of sickness in wet nurses, students, farmers, and wrestlers. Sixteenth- and seventeenth-century physicians wrote about soldiers, miners, metalworkers, melancholic scholars, mothers, and other specific groups and the risks they faced. The real founder of what we can call occupational health, however, was the Italian physician Bernardino Ramazzini.

Bernardino Ramazzini, Father of Industrial Medicine

Ramazzini spent most of his productive life in and around the city of Modena, at whose university he held a chair of medicine. Rather than being a medical theorist, he spent much of his time as a healer and observer of the sick and well. He visited and interviewed workers in many occupations but also read widely among the ancient and modern medical authors. His writings are liberally sprinkled with references to Hippocrates, "the Divine Teacher." He discussed his interest in the medical problems common to people in various trades with other physicians. He was a keen observer and a man of the early Enlightenment who wanted to see the improvement of working conditions and medical care for the men and women of his day.

To this end he penned *The Diseases of Workers*,[10] which was published in 1700. This first edition contained descriptions of the health risks for workers in 43 occupations. A second appeared in 1713, which included an additional 12 trades. In this case he published it in a size that was easy for the practicing physician to carry with him, firmly believing that one of the first questions a patient is asked should be "What is your occupation?" Two common themes that came out of his research were that a person should be physically and temperamentally suited to his or her occupation and that most "diseases" stemmed from environmental causes, such as noxious vapors from materials, or from the "violent and irregular motions of the body" required by the job. Though he was perhaps the first medical writer to rely solely on statistics for a study, in *Diseases* he used little in the way of quantification.

Women Workers in Ramazzini

Of the 55 chapters in the 1713 edition of *The Diseases of Workers*, only 3 dealt specifically with women. Midwives were susceptible to any diseases the child might have, but he was less clear about the mother's passing along any illnesses. The nature of contagion was still an open question, and as close as he came is to note that if the mother had syphilis, the infected lochia could cause the midwife's hands to become inflamed. Even uninfected but "corrosive, acrid" lochia could damage the skin, as could the "poisonous" menstrual fluid that was released as part of the afterbirth. He did cite several authorities who dismissed the ancient fiction of poisonous menses but concluded that the fluid did have "a certain latent malignant quality." Even breathing the vapors could sicken one. He recommended often washing the hands with water and wine or vinegar during labor. Oddly, it was to protect the midwife and not the mother. Ramazzini also noted that Italian midwives used the birthing chair unlike women elsewhere. This required the midwife to lean out over the mother's legs with her arms outstretched to receive the baby. In the short run fatigue set in, but over time this posture could cause real skeletal damage, he noted.[11]

In his lengthy chapter on wet nurses and nursing women in general, Ramazzini summarized that they were subject to "gradual wasting, hysteria, pustules and scabies, headache, vertigo, respiratory trouble, and weak eyesight." The very act of holding or carrying the nursing infant could cause "itching irruptions," and a mother could suffer from curdling milk, cracked nipples, and abscesses. Since lactating suppressed the menses, Ramazzini could blame many of the side effects on the accumulation of the "poisonous" stuff. He recommended the typically Galenic remedy of letting blood. A wet nurse who lived in a rich man's house, away from her husband, had two other problems. One was that she consumed rich foods to which her body was not accustomed. The other was the absence of sexual intercourse. These combined with the menstrual suppression to cause hysteria in many women, Ramazzini believed. The fathers would do well, he wrote, to allow the nurse to have sex with her husband from time to time to prevent this condition. Finally, the nurse could suffer "wasting" from feeding the infant too often. On the other hand, women who nursed often tended to have even fewer breast tumors than nuns who never did, Ramazzini wrote.[12]

Laundresses worked in a constantly damp environment, which damaged the lungs and skin. Having their feet and lower legs immersed supposedly suppressed their menses, as did the clogging of their skin pores with moisture. He cited lung problems resulting from breathing the boiling lye soap and inhaling of the remains of "a thousand kinds of filth" that saturated bedding, underclothes, and other laundry. Like the midwives', laundresses' hands suffered, becoming inflamed by the lye, which could also cause fever, he averred. He noted the value of their service to the community and wrote that he always urged them to avoid all fumes as much as possible, to use butter to soften their hands, and to change their wet clothing after work. Women workers also appear in the chapter on textile workers and on Jews (seamstresses). In the latter he mentioned the eyestrain caused by the close work their craft entailed.[13]

Anthrax: The Woolsorters' Disease

In his chapter on textiles Ramazzini discussed flax, hemp, and silk but not the far more common wool. This was because Frenchman Nicholas Fournier had yet to articulate the connection of wool and anthrax (1750s), a disease typically associated with wool workers, especially female woolsorters. It is a disease of animals (zoonosis) that humans catch from contact with infected animals or their products. The bacterium traveled inside spores and could live in the soil or animal hides, meat, hair, or wool. In 1758 there was a report from Finland of a bear that died from having eaten an infected animal. The man who skinned the bear caught the disease and died, as did four other men who prepared the skin. It produced toxins similar to cholera or tetanus and was quite deadly depending on where on the body the initial infection occurred. The French blamed "cursed fields" whose vegetation fed and contaminated the animals that butchers then slaughtered and marketed. By this means what was an occupational hazard became an epidemic disease. Major outbreaks occurred in Southern Europe in 1613, when some 60,000 died, and in Guadeloupe and Saint Domingue in the Caribbean in the 1770s, when 15,000 people and thousands of animals perished. With no understanding of bacteria, Fournier and his followers located the cause of the disease in tainted animals. How the animals became diseased was another question: miasma, nonspecific contagion "germes," and spontaneous generation were all suggested. Modern science indicates that periodic floods disturbed the spores in the fields, grazing animals inhaled them, and an outbreak was set off.[14]

Bookkeepers and Scholars

While Ramazzini does not specifically address the plight of scholars, he does have a chapter on "scribes and notaries." Such workers, he says, suffer from three qualities of their profession: constant sitting, continual movement of the hand and in the same direction, and the mental strain of striving to copy the material correctly. Our culture is well aware of the problems of a "sedentary lifestyle" and carpal tunnel syndrome, and Ramazzini seems like something of a prophet. He cites medical problems such as "obstructions of the viscera ... indigestion ... numbness of the legs, a considerable hindrance of the circulation of the blood, and an unhealthy habit. In a word, they lack the benefit of moderate exercise." His take on repetitive-motion problems is equally modern, and he mentions a notary whose right hand had become paralyzed by his profession. Worst, he thought, was the mental strain from concentration that resulted in "headaches, heavy colds, sore throats, and fluxes."[15]

Eighty years before Ramazzini the English physician Robert Burton penned his lengthy *Anatomy of Melancholy* (1621). Melancholy was a recognized medical condition and not just an emotional state. It was caused by an excess of black bile (melan = black; choler = bile), associated astrologically with the planet Saturn, and a curse of the depressive and introspective scholar and artist. Early in the 1500s German artist Albrecht Dürer created a remarkable woodcut entitled *Melancolia I* in which an angelic figure representing genius sits frustrated and impotent though surrounded by intellectual tools and symbols. This creative blockage was the result of the buildup of black bile due to a sedentary lifestyle. The Galenic explanation was that excessive contemplation or study had a drying effect on the mind and ultimately the whole body. The student's natural poverty meant that the stomach and liver were not properly fed, and the body became "desiccated." Burton wrote that this led to a bevy of symptoms: "gouts, catarrhs, rheums, wasting, indigestion, bad eyes, stone and colic, crudities, oppilations, vertigo, winds, consumptions and all such diseases as come by oversitting." Emotionally, of course, the melancholic person, whether a scholar or not, is still associated with depression and deep, unshakeable sadness. Burton's is a complex work with layers of moral teaching and not merely a medical manual, but the condition he described was taken very seriously.

Even before Burton, William Shakespeare gave his audiences Hamlet, the "melancholy Dane." The young man is a student at Wittenberg University. Home for break, he has to confront the death of his father and sketchy remarriage of his mother. Like the textbook melancholic he is very smart but confused, unsure of himself, and frustrated from acting to avenge his father. He even contemplates suicide. Those around him are uncertain of and fearful for his sanity. In his brilliant monologues Hamlet explores the anatomy of his own melancholy, a study that ultimately takes him down a path of death and destruction.[16]

European and Colonial Metal Mineworkers

In the early modern world, deep-shaft mining was common in many regions. In his treatment of miner's diseases, Ramazzini mentions mines for gold, silver, and copper, but also mercury, vitriol, nitre, and arsenic. The dangers of work in the deep-shaft metal ore mines were legendary. In the classical world only slaves, criminals, or prisoners of war were cast into the earth to reap its shiny bounty. In early modern Europe miners were respected laborers—Martin Luther's Saxon father was one—and their problems and issues were noticed. Sixteenth-century German medical reformer Paracelsus wrote a three-volume work on the diseases of miners, and in 1551 German scholar and physician Georgius Agricola discussed a range of illnesses related to mining in his *De re metallica*. At Joachimsthal small contributions from miners supported the "brother houses" in which disabled miners lived.

Figure 7.2 Tin mining methods as depicted in Georgius Agricola's *De Re Metallica* from 1556. The author noted that the method of heating sealed tunnels unleashed a "foetid vapour," exposure to which was one of the many hazards of early mining techniques. (Eon Images)

Spain had long had its own mines and in gaining the New World imposed the industry on hapless natives. Critics at court decried exploitation of Indians as early as 1511. The royal Burgos Statutes of 1512 and regulations articulated the following year sought to limit the exposure of women and children under 14 to the rigors and hazards of the mines. At the Guadalcanal mines near Seville in Spain itself, the monarchs provided a physician with a nice house and high salary to treat the victims of fumes, "smoke and noxious vapors." Eventually the Spaniards imported German miners, whom they thought naturally better suited to the work.

At Almadén, Spain, the miners extracted mercury, a deadly toxin that was used in treating syphilis and in purifying silver from ore. This was shipped to South America until mercury was discovered and mined by natives and slaves at Huancavélica in Peru. For Spaniards, Indians, and African slaves alike, the exposure to and use of mercury were crippling. Nerve damage, palsy, and extreme debilitation; tooth loss and mouth sores; and outright madness were not atypical results. Later in our period the use of mercury in making headgear gave rise to the phrase "as mad as a hatter."

High in the Andes Indian workers chewed coca leaves, the high from which dulled some of the pain they had to endure. Colonial authorities did try to humanize working conditions by insisting on changes of clothing after shifts, reasonable working hours, and no forced labor. At the Potosí mines, officials imposed standards for shoring up the mineshafts and employment of a single daylight shift each day. Eventually a hospital with a physician, surgeon, and apothecary was mandated and established for the workers, which was funded from a 1 percent tax on the mine operators.

In Germany, Agricola emphasized the lung diseases, headaches, vertigo, and podagra from which miners suffered, and his contemporary the physician Paracelsus also concentrated on the vapors and fumes that led to pneumonia and what he believed to be a mix of tuberculosis, lung cancer, and silicosis. Andean mummies show clear signs of this last disease, with their lungs coated with the dust of silver, iron, copper, and silica. This condition was at least as deadly as black lung disease in coal mining. One of the main problems, of course, was poor ventilation in the shafts and the lack of respiration-protecting masks.

Ramazzini chose to open his work with miners' diseases, and his text reminds us that there were many early modern authors who either discussed the occupation and its dangers or mentioned miners when discussing diseases of lungs and brain. Early on, Ramazzini lists miners' problems as "dyspnoea, phthisis [tuberculosis], apoplexy, paralysis, cachexy, swollen feet [from the damp], loss of teeth, ulcerated gums, pains in the joints, and palsy." In the course of his discussion he added asthma, ophthalmia, suffocation, and the threat of "certain small creatures that look like spiders," and "little demons and phantoms" that were "no fable as I used to think." True to his reformer's program he wrote, "We ought study carefully the diseases of those workers with a view to their safety and suggest precautions and remedies." For the demons he recommended exorcisms; for the others his program was scanty: ventilation pumps, gloves and leggings, masks, milk and butter in the diet, and various medicines for specific complaints. What he does not address is what a general audience might regard as the most dangerous hazards: flooding and cave-ins that either trapped or buried miners. Nor does he treat the strains on the human body of mining, including hernias and repetitive-stress injuries, injuries from mishandled tools or falling objects, heat exhaustion, and eye strain, just to name a few.[17]

It was a dangerous world out there.

NOTES

1. Oliver Ransford, *Bid the Sickness Cease: Disease in the History of Black Africa* (London: John Murray, 1983), 36.

2. For most see chapter 6.

3. Ransford, *Bid the Sickness*, 92–108.

4. Ibid., 109–32.

5. Ibid., 149–59.

6. This subsection is based on discussions in Ransford as well as Joseph P. Byrne, ed., *Encyclopedia of Pestilence, Pandemics, and Plagues* (Westport, CT: Greenwood Press, 2008); and Richard S. Osterfeld, Felicia Keesing, and Valerie T. Eviner, eds., *Infectious Disease Ecology* (Princeton, NJ: Princeton University Press, 2008).

7. See W. Gregory Monahan, *Year of Sorrows: The Great Famine of 1709 in Lyon* (Columbus: Ohio State University Press, 1993).

8. Nicholas Shrady, *The Last Day: Wrath, Ruin, and Reason in the Great Lisbon Earthquake of 1755* (New York: Viking, 2008), 17.

9. Ibid., 3–49; and see Edward Paice, *Wrath of God: The Great Lisbon Earthquake of 1755* (Waltham, MA: Quercus, 2010).

10. Bernardino Ramazzini, *The Diseases of Workers* (Chicago: University of Chicago Press, 1940); see also G. Franco, F. Franco, and L. Paita, "Focusing Bernardino Ramazzini's Preventive View in Health Protection," in *Contributions to the History of Occupational and Environmental Prevention*, ed. Antonio Grieco, Sergio Iavicoli, and Giovanni Berlinguer (New York: Elsevier, 1999), 31–41.

11. Ramazzini, *Diseases of Workers*, 157–67 on midwives.

12. Ibid., 167–201 on wet nurses.

13. Ibid., 253–55 on laundresses, 257–61 on silk workers, 287 on Jewish seamstresses.

14. Susan D. Jones, *Death in a Small Package: A Short History of Anthrax* (Baltimore: Johns Hopkins University Press, 2010).

15. Ramazzini, *Diseases of Workers*, 421–25.

16. Robert Burton, *Some Anatomies of Melancholy* (1621) (New York: Penguin Books, 2008); see also Jennifer Radden, ed., *The Nature of Melancholy: From Aristotle to Kristeva* (New York: Oxford University Press, 2000; includes excerpt from Burton).

17. Ramazzini, *Diseases of Workers*, 15–33; A. Pretel and M. Ruiz Bremón, "Social and Medical Protection for the Working Population in the Age of Philip II," in Grieco, Iavicoli, and Berlinguer, *Contributions*, 159–70; C. Piekarski, "Some Aspects of Early Developments in Occupational Health Care in the German Mining Industry," in Grieco, Iavicoli, and Berlinguer, *Contributions*, 187–93.

CHAPTER 8

Surgeons and Surgery

The learned traditions of China and the West clearly defined medical practitioners. Physicians were experts on intricate theories of human physiology and the food, drink, and medicines necessary to maintain health and cure illness. This was the high road to health and healing in both cultures. They distinguished other medical practitioners who, essentially, worked with their hands as inferior. For theirs was an art or craft, not a profession: it lacked the theoretical or "philosophical" underpinnings that marked the physician and his training. Yet the human body often needed the physical manipulation that physicians shunned. Wounds needed bandaging; broken bones needed to be set; babies needed to be delivered; cataracts and urinary stones needed to be cut away; teeth needed to be pulled, blood drawn, hernias removed, boils lanced, dislocations repositioned, and the list goes on. In some cultures, such as the Aztec, the African, and the Afro-Caribbean, these tasks simply fell to the healer's skills, with some known for what we might call specialization. In China, such needs literally fell to lower-class healers, often itinerant, who had no relationship to the learned profession. In the West the situation was complex. Some specialized healers—lithotomists, wound doctors, bonesetters, oculists—operated under the radar of the physicians and most civic authorities. Others, with broader skill sets gained through formal apprenticeships, were given the name surgeon and organized into self-regulating guilds—like

Figure 8.1 Painting from the 17th century in the style of Flemish painter David Teniers the Younger (to whom it is sometimes attributed), depicting a man having his foot bandaged by the village surgeon. (National Library of Medicine)

physicians, but of inferior education and status. During the early modern period, the roles and status of European surgeons underwent some major changes that reflected larger trends in society and culture.

THE AZTECS

Truly effective healing requires a fairly sophisticated understanding of human anatomy and physiology, but there is little evidence of this among the Aztecs. They were empirics in the true sense of relying upon their own experience, often guided by others. The Nahuatl *texoxtl* was the equivalent of "surgeon" and indicated a wide range of skills. More specialized was the "bloodletter," or *tecoani*. Medicinally, letting blood flow was simply a means of reducing certain types of swelling. The *tecoani* used flaked obsidian knives or maguey tree thorns to open veins. He had another important societal use, too. He carried out the human sacrifices required by the Aztec religion. He knew how to use certain narcotic plants—jimson weed, marijuana—to drug the victims, ensuring their cooperation.

The *texoxtl* learned his skills from others and worked in cooperation with herbalists, spirit healers, and other practitioners. Unlike Europeans, Aztec surgeons valued cleanliness, though having no conception of germs. This was especially useful in treating wounds, which could so easily become infected. According to one instruction, the wound was to be washed clean with water; further cleansed with fresh, warm urine (which is aseptic); slathered in agave sap, salt, and lampblack; then wrapped airtight. In his Nahuatl herbal of 1552, the native physician Martín de la Cruz recommended the following: "An inflicted wound will heal if the juice from the bark of the *ylin* tree, the root of the *tlal-ahuehuetl* bush [a low-lying cypress], wax salve and yolk of egg be injected."[1] They had numerous poultices and knew how to suture a wound or incision, using a long human hair cleansed with honey and salt. If not bled, a swollen wound would be cleansed with papaya juice.

Maintaining dental health was important, and tooth powders (dentifrices) included combinations of salt and charcoal, or white ashes in white honey. Caries or cavities resulted, they believed, from the rapid succession of hot and cold fluids in the mouth. If decay and toothache should occur, the tooth was to be punctured with an incisor and the damage cleared away. De la Cruz offered a compress to dull the pain.[2] They also knew how to drill away and fill caries. For some reason the eyes were often treated with powdered human excrement, yet Aztec surgeons could successfully treat cataracts. They also carried out trepanation, the drilling of holes in the skull, though whether it was to release fluid pressure on the brain from traumas or let spirits escape is unclear. Fractures received splints to immobilize the bone until it knitted itself back together. Bleeding or plasters were used to reduce swelling. If the bone failed to heal, they used a tool not seen again in the West until the twentieth century: the intramedullar nail. A "resinous stick" was inserted into the halves of the bone to hold them together.[3]

The first European surgeon arrived in Mexico City in 1525, and more soon followed. Other colonists valued these men and their ways, leaving the healing of natives, especially outside the major towns, to the old ways. In cities, though, the Spanish reproduced the pattern of surgical practice and its oversight that they knew in Old Spain.[4]

THE CHINESE

China's ancient Confucian heritage revered the human body and shunned deliberate violations of it. This included not only invasive forms of medical treatment but even the study of anatomy and dissection of corpses. True medicine was learned medicine, and this involved balancing the yin and yang, strengthening the qi, and keeping channels of their flow open through daily regimen and largely herbal medicinal drugs.[5] Kidney or bladder stones were treated with tea; no one cut for cataracts but instead there were medicinal herbs; and amputations were out of the question as far as formal medicine was concerned. Not surprisingly, the earliest Chinese work on surgery or external medicine, *Remedies Left over by Ghosts*, was rather late (c. 500 CE) and largely military in its concerns (wounds).[6]

Yet popular medicine had long run its parallel track, developing what we might call surgical specialties. By the early modern period, many physicians (*ruyi*) accepted the need for skilled mechanics of the human body and accepted them the way architects accept plumbers. The early modern period did see the appearance of numerous works on wounds, boils, burns, fractures, and other typical surgical concerns. But the period was one of neo-Confucianism, and critics such as late-seventeenth-century physician Wang Weidei resented their interference and undermined the role of invasive medicine and surgeons in society. He represented one of three recognized early modern schools of external medicine (survival school). Chen Shigong and his school (the "orthodox") stressed a balance of internal medication and external approaches, and even the sterilization of instruments (*True Lineages of External Medicine*, 1617). The surgeon and *ruyi* Gao Binjun leaned toward internal approaches, noting that even skin diseases and carbuncles originate within the body. His followers were sometimes called the study school, and he expressed his ideas in his *Collection of Heart-Felt Experiences in Sore Specialty* (1805).[7]

They learned their trades from predecessors, much as Western empirics did. Many were itinerant, quickly identifying where in a community the healers gathered to meet or treat their patients (often a religious shrine or garden). Wounds were tended, abscesses drained, and eyes treated with something other than drugs; some specialized in teeth, others cupping and phlebotomy; some practiced massage, setting fractured bones, and tending dislocated ones.[8]

Acupuncture and moxibustion are two therapies associated with classical Chinese medicine and popular practitioners. Acupuncture dated back to at least the second century BCE, and the standard Nine Needles to the Han Dynasty. Each type of needle has a particular form and function: for example, a two-edged one is for releasing pus and a round, sharp one is used in the treatment of acute maladies.[9] Usually the needles were heated and carefully rotated or hammered into a very specific spot or spots on the body. The theory was that the needle was placed to open a closed conduit for blood or qi, whose blockage was causing the illness. The acupuncturist had to know the network of conduits that ran through the body, the best spots on the skin through which to contact the appropriate position on the conduit, and the most effective way to place the needle in the body. Many were Daoist priests.[10] Moxibustion, used by both Indians and Chinese, consisted of the burning of a small cone of dried mugwort on a very specific spot on the body with hopes of the same essential effect.[11] Throughout our period both practices, which could be quite painful for the patient, were losing popularity as people preferred to take medicines (and the *ruyi* preferred to prescribe them). In 1757 Hsü Ta-ch'un wrote, "[Recently the use of] prescriptions and drugs flourished widely while no one spoke of the method of needling anymore. . . . Today's physicians insert their needles at liberty and do not care about any schema."[12]

THE ISLAMIC WORLD

The Tradition by 1500

The Arabs, and by extension Islam, inherited the medicine of ancient Greece and Rome. Galenic humoralism emphasized the role of the humors and of regimens of lifestyle and, when necessary, pharmaceuticals. But Galen himself had tended gladiators, and most of their problems were not treated with "moist" or "dry" foods or herbs. The line between surgeon (*jarrah*) and physician (*tabib*) appears not to have been too broadly drawn, at least from the tenth century. Later medieval and early modern Persian and Arabic physicians seem to have performed certain surgical procedures themselves, leaving others to trained assistants, though no clear pattern of practice emerges. As in China, numerous manuals of surgical procedures circulated, and these display a truly sophisticated understanding of instruments and their use. This was true of even very meticulous tasks, such as work on the eye.

As for a working knowledge of human anatomy and physiology, however, despite some evidence to the contrary it seems that Muslim doctors had little beyond Galen's problematic legacy. Anatomical illustrations remain crude and there is no evidence of dissection for the sake of education. In the thirteenth century the physician and critic of traditional medicine Ibn al-Nafis wrote:

> The veto of the religious law and the sentiment of charity innate in ourselves alike prevent us from the practice of dissection. That is why we are willing to be limited to basing our knowledge of the internal organs on the sayings of those who had gone before us.

Little had changed by the eighteenth century. In working with living patients, Islamic laws of personal modesty limited the amount of the body that one could expose to a doctor without scandal: off limits were navel to knees for a man and neck to ankles for a woman. Ignorance was so deep that physicians argued over the number of bones in the human body (which in fact changes with age as bones fuse). In Persia it was said that a Jew had boiled a woman's body and found 248. This was confirmed by the ancient saying that one's number of bones was the same as the numerological value of the name of one's "original home." The value of the word *rahm*, or womb, was 248.[13]

When operating Muslim practitioners insisted on cleanliness, in part because blood was a ritual pollutant, but they had no notion of germs or the need for asepsis. In addition, anesthesia was limited to a few opiates, which would have made many procedures excruciating. Amputation of the hands, however, was a well-understood procedure since it was a judicial punishment. Certain routine concerns, such as bloodletting, dentistry, bone setting, and suturing wounds, apparently fell to specialist craftspeople on whom the physicians relied. Some of these were women, especially in areas related to reproduction, but their wider participation was a matter of local culture.[14]

Ottoman Turks and Safavid Persians

The Muslim Turks who conquered Constantinople in 1453 and seized the Levant and Egypt in the 1510s inherited the Arabo-Persian medical system. Galen and Avicenna retained their pride of place, as did the surgical writings of the eleventh-century Spanish Muslim al-Zahrawi. Nothing of medical knowledge seems to have been lost due to the conquest, but the Turks had little to add (with the possible exception of inoculation for smallpox). The surgeon (*cerrah*) and other specialists in external medicine worked in the urban hospitals alongside the physicians. They also served in the Turkish fleets and army, both to maintain the men's health and to do what they could in the wake of battle.[15]

The Safavid Empire that centered on Iran suffered from the same antiquity of theory and practice, and yet their practitioners could be quite effective. They had barbers who cut, shaved, and dyed men's hair, bled, performed dentistry, cleaned ears, massaged, cauterized, cupped, and circumcised males (near puberty in Muslim Persia). They had bonesetters who had expertise in all of the bones and tools such as retractors, pulleys, ropes, and wheels. They knew how to set splints, what ointments to help bones heal, and which anesthetics were most effective. These included opium, marijuana, and drugs that were said

Figure 8.2 Illustration of bonesetters setting a fracture, from an Ottoman medical manuscript. (The Art Archive/University Library Istanbul/ Gianni Dagli Orti)

to "induce unconsciousness" and "put the patient to sleep." They knew how to recognize cancers and cut many out successfully. They operated with a range of knives and other instruments whose edges were kept razor sharp by preservation in olive oil. Their suturing needles were made of steel or copper and were probably the same as those used by tailors and shoemakers. To stitch wounds they used silk or cotton thread, horse or human hairs, harp strings, and even the heads of biting ants as tiny clamps, snapping the bodies off after setting them.[16]

One last, disagreeable area of Safavid surgical performance was in using surgical removals to punish wrongdoers. Eyes were cut up and removed, gouged out, or skewered with a red-hot needle that penetrated the lens and optic nerve. Red-hot pokers and corrosive materials that ate away the eye were also used. When a new shah took the throne it was customary to blind anyone who might threaten the throne, so even the oldest prince generally lost his sight as a matter of course: a man who could not see could not rule. Spoken insults or blasphemy easily resulted in one's tongue being cut off; a few teeth might be pulled out; ears, hands, and feet were amputated. Hands were not sawn off but hammered off with a mallet at the wrist, and the stump shoved into flaming tar to cauterize the wound. It may not be fair to end this discussion of Islamic surgery with this list of horrors, but it remains a reminder that under an autocratic regime even healers could be used as instruments of torture and death.

THE EUROPEANS

Later medieval Europeans derived a great deal from Muslim sources. Some included medical manuals from antiquity and subsequent Muslim commentators and practitioners (in translation), knowledge of and access to pharmaceuticals, and certain surgical skills and practices gained from direct contact with Islamic medicine in the Near East, Sicily, or southern Spain. Of course, Christian healers had long used a wide array of their own traditional techniques for handling wounds, fractures, rotten teeth, and dislocated shoulders. Skilled and unskilled technicians could be found at noble courts, monasteries, and pilgrim hospices, and with armies in the field. Since its inception at Salerno in the twelfth century, formal European medical education was based on Galen, balancing humors, and the use of dietary regimens and pharmaceuticals. Medical schools, at least outside Italy, had little to teach about treating the body for nonhumoral problems. Physicians, then, recommended, diagnosed, and prescribed. Virtually everything physical—from bloodletting to setting a broken leg—was left to the trained, but not "educated," surgeon or other specialist.

Organization

By 1500, however, a recognized craft of surgeon had emerged across Europe to the point that in towns and cities they had organized into guilds. Guilds regulated the education of young apprentices as well as the practices of their masters, and limited access to those they deemed fit. They kept themselves busy by restricting the number of surgeons who could practice, and often regulated scales of charges for typical procedures. One of the most typical was bloodletting, understood as important for regulating that humor in the body. This was often linked to the cutting and shaving of hair, which of course also required the use of extremely sharp cutting tools. Barbers and surgeons were often joined in the same guild, and were often the same people, as in Paris from the fourteenth century. Scotland's James IV required combining when he created the Incorporation of Barber-Surgeons in Edinburgh in 1505. In 1540 England's Henry VIII raised the status of barbers by

Figure 8.3 Oxford-educated John Banister—surgeon, medical author and teacher—lectures at the Barber-Surgeon's Hall, London, 1581. Like Vesalius he himself conducts the lesson, using a corpse, text and display skeleton. Note that the onlookers are well-dressed men who are probably practicing surgeons. (National Library of Medicine)

linking their Guild of Surgeons with the Company of Barber-Surgeons (the largest of London's 39 guilds with 185 members in 1537). The result was the United Company of Barbers and Surgeons. Oddly, perhaps, only barbers could cut hair or pull teeth, and the regulations required seven years of apprenticeship. This arrangement lasted until 1745, during a period when surgeons across Europe were trying desperately to raise their status. In 1800 London's achieved this with foundation of the Royal College of Surgeons (a society, not a school). Spain's Philip II imposed the Barber-Surgeon's Guild in Amsterdam in 1556. By the later seventeenth century, Dutch tastes were craving French-style hair salons and stylists—no surprise that so many hair-preparation terms are French: coiffure, barrette, stylist, pomade, even salon—and by the eighteenth high-status barbers sought separation from the bleeders and wound stitchers.[17]

Anatomical Dissections and Medical Education

No one today has to argue that any medical training should require a strong background in anatomy and physiology. Yet Galenic medicine, that of the physician, required a bare minimum. The oldest anatomical handbook, Mondino de' Liuzzi's *Anathomie*, dated to the early fourteenth century and its many misunderstandings and fallacies remained unchallenged for almost two centuries. Dissections were not unknown—even the pope called for autopsying some of the local plague victims in 1348—but they were conducted rarely before the seventeenth century. Students sat at a distance while a surgeon opened the body up and the physician/ professor droned on from an error-filled Latin text. This began to change in the sixteenth century with the new teaching and illustrating techniques of Andreas Vesalius. The Netherlander studied in Italy and here established his new model: the professor needed to perform the actual dissection, as Vesalius did, and anatomical texts needed to be rewritten to reflect reality. He also insisted that text illustrations had to rise to the same level of realism as contemporary painting and sculpture. Though the last of nine new anatomy works published between 1490 and 1543, his *Construction of the Human Body*, illustrated by a partner of the artist Titian, rose to a new level of verbal and visual accuracy. Vesalius alone corrected over 200 of Galen's verbal anatomical errors.[18]

The value of anatomical education was such that dissection/lectures were usually open to surgeons as well as well as medical students. They were offered more regularly and increasingly were required for medical licensing or degrees. Over the following 250 years three trends unfolded: first, Galenism underwent a slow decline; second, the line between physician and surgeon began to blur; and third, the surgeon's status rose in recognition that his expertise in the mechanical—as opposed to the humoral—body was directly related to the major advances in medicine of the seventeenth and eighteenth centuries.

Empiricism and Medical Advances

Rooted in experience rather than theory and models, practicing surgeons in the sixteenth century began publishing manuals and studies that reflected their findings in real cases. Pierre Franco published his *Treatise on Hernias* in 1561 and other works on urinary tract stones and cataracts based on his own experiences and experiments. In 1597 Gaspare Tagliacozzi of Bologna first described a successful skin graft: arm skin to make a new nose. The Scotsman Peter Lowe helped organize the Guild of Surgeons in Glasgow (1599), but only after writing Britain's first full surgical manual, *Chirurgerie*, in 1597. Most famously, the French barber-surgeon and army surgeon Ambroise Paré published many works in which he shared his widely ranging new and successful surgical techniques. Like other surgeons he wrote in his vernacular to make his works accessible. He very consciously sought to reform surgical practice, perhaps in a way like contemporary Protestants were reforming Christianity. Some of his advances came from the battlefield, such as employing ligatures to stop blood flow to a limb before amputation (instead of merely cauterizing afterward), or the prosthetic mechanical hand he invented for those who had undergone a successful amputation. Others ranged from improved methods of treating cataracts to an infant feeding bottle.[19] He and others experimented with and made advances in the treatment of urinary stones, gunshot wounds, tumors, and fractures, among many other ailments. Theirs was the spirit of the Scientific Revolution, which questioned authorities (Galen, Aristotle), trusted their own empirical evidence, shared their successes and failures, and sought to improve people's lives though their efforts.

Formal Education for Surgeons

Seventeenth-century discoveries about human anatomy and physiology joined with the practical and successful application of new surgical techniques to raise the social status of the surgeon close to that of the physician by the mid-eighteenth century. Their tools were being made with greater skill and to standardized designs and quality by gold- and pewter-smiths rather than armorers and blacksmiths. Surgeons sought to raise their status, and they were enabled by separating themselves from barbers and their guilds. They did this by supporting the repression of empiric practitioners and even moving in on the practice of female midwives. Monarchs prized the surgeons that saved the lives of their precious soldiers and sailors, and increased their presence among the field ranks and shipboard. Few eighteenth-century British surgeons had not served in the military or navy. In 1752 Parliament's unpopular Murder Act guaranteed that the corpses of executed criminals would go to the Company of Barber-Surgeons for dissection. The British Royal Navy valued the advice of Scots naval surgeon James Lind to use citrus fruits to prevent scurvy aboard ship, testing it in the 1750s but refusing to adopt their use until century's end.[20] The Italian medical schools had long combined surgical education with Galenic humoralism, but Padua, Bologna, and other once renowned centers fell into a slump. In 1742 the overlord of Bologna, Pope Benedict XIV, set up a local "short-course" school of surgery: over 20 days students would study cadavers from two hospitals.

France was in the forefront of establishing surgical education, with the foundation in Paris of the royal School of Surgery in 1724. Barbers and surgeons in Paris were divorced in 1743, and the Royal Academy of Surgery was established in 1748. In Paris widows were barred from continuing their husbands' practice in 1755, and after 1768 formal surgical education was required in place of outdated apprenticeships. In 1775 the school became the Collège de Chirurgie with a curriculum including anatomy, chemistry, and physiology.[21] Several German states followed Paris's lead by instituting state surgical schools, often as a way of ensuring a supply of trained surgeons and undermining powerful local guilds.

Perhaps following the Italian model, Spanish medical schools sponsored chairs of surgery at Salamanca (1561) and Alacalá de Henares (1590). In 1617 a royal decree mandated all universities have chairs of anatomy and surgery. Filling these positions remained difficult, and many professors were second-rate practitioners and teachers. Because the law required either two years' apprenticeship plus two of school, or four as an apprentice (after 1603 a total of five years), most Spanish surgeons had apprenticed and received little or no anatomical education. Since university-educated surgeons knew Latin and most apprenticed did not, society made the distinction between "Latin surgeons" and "romance surgeons" who knew only Spanish or Catalan. From 1583 Madrid's *Confradía* or Brotherhood of Saints Cosmas and Damian, two early Christian physicians, included all the city's surgeons. Consisting mostly of romance surgeons, the group existed almost exclusively to protect its members and reduce competition from outside. It did virtually nothing to advance surgical practice and by its conservatism probably retarded innovation and change. In 1701 the Hospital General in Madrid received its first chair of anatomy, and four years later its anatomy theater for dissections.

Like many eighteenth-century Scots, enlightened Spaniards tended toward useful knowledge and practical projects for improving life in their country. The Benedictine monk and royal adviser Benito Feijóo helped found Madrid's Academy of Medicine and Surgery in 1734, and in 1748 a group of naval surgeons successfully lobbied to found the Royal School of Surgery, Spain's first, in the busy port city of Cadiz, and a second in Barcelona in 1760. The same year, Madrid's General Hospital began teaching a regular three-year anatomy course, but it was limited to physicians. The capital finally received its first surgical school, the Royal College of San Carlos, in 1787. San Carlos was built adjacent to Madrid's General Hospital and by 1790 had a 40-bed clinical ward for its students' use. The curriculum was based on those of the naval surgery's schools and was both practical and up-to-date.[22]

The training of surgeons took a different tack in Enlightenment London. The island's premier medical school was in Edinburgh, and it followed many of the reforms pioneered at Leiden in the Netherlands. One of these was having the professor and medical students "doing rounds," or making regular visits to patients in hospital beds. Young Scotsman John Hunter (d. 1793) avoided what he considered the nonsense of medical school and went to London to learn the surgeon's craft from his brother. He also apprenticed with William Cheselden, noted for his success in removing urinary stones with a mortality rate of 10 percent or less (despite advances the norm was closer to 40%). Hunter practiced surgery at St. George's and St. Bartholomew's hospitals and became the premier teacher of apprentice surgeons from England, Scotland, and even North America. He is believed to have trained 449 apprentices in 40 years of practice. He was an empiricist in the spirit of John Locke and the English and Scots Enlightenment: "Do the experiment," he taught his students. Hunter tried new methods, observed carefully, and recorded his findings. He studied the lymphatic system, the reproductive systems of pigs and dogs, and bone regrowth after fracturing, and worked with running tubes down the trachea (intubation). The age of the professional surgeon had arrived.[23]

A Range of Practitioners

As in China and the Islamic world, the European medical landscape was populated with more or less skilled craftspeople practicing surgical specialties. The poor and rural folk usually had to make do in silence with what they knew. Some household medical books from the seventeenth and eighteenth centuries contain recipes for rough casts to immobilize a fractured bone and oral solutions to unroot rotted teeth. The local blacksmith could usually pull teeth and reposition dislocated joints. In Germany, bathhouses made a comeback by the eighteenth century, and bathmasters were allowed to shave, cut hair, and let blood, as long as it was done in the bathhouse. Germany also had "wound doctors" who dealt with open sores, wounds, and bad bruising.[24] Other specialists either set up shop and were tolerated, or moved itinerantly plying their craft(s). Lithotomists extracted urinary stones; oculists treated cataracts and a variety of eye diseases; hernia cutters removed these and other growths, often caused by the strain of hard work; and phlebotomists let blood. In general medical guilds and colleges fought against these unlicensed empirics, though in times of need, especially during wartime or plague, authorities were happy to bend the rules. Another trend was to license skilled practitioners. In 1699

Paris licensed *bandigistes*, a category that included hernia cutters, lithotomists, bonesetters, occulists, and dentists, and Bourbon Spain followed some years later with the same list of special licenses.[25]

But was the public in 1800 better served by all the licensing, educating, and organizing? Paré's insistence on applying a tourniquet above the wound before amputating no doubt saved some lives, but the horrible pain from the four minutes of bone sawing, the shock, and the nearly inevitable infection that followed no doubt killed as many as before. Anesthesia remained a major problem, and surgeons had their own concoctions, including alcohol and/or opiates, and made few real advances. Stone cutting, even by an expert and lasting only 30 seconds, often meant not only pain but hemorrhaging, shock, and infection. Complicated fractures or poorly set bones could knit together badly and result in loss of the limb or gangrene and death. Most surgeons, even formally educated ones, had limited knowledge of anatomy, even less of physiology, and no respect for cleanliness. Even the finest surgeons avoided invasive surgery beyond cutting for stones, hernias, or some tumors, knowing that deep, especially thoracic penetration simply invited hemorrhage, shock, and infection. Despite medical academies and manuals that spread news of discoveries, these often had little impact on the practicing surgeon, and less on the unlicensed practitioner. Perhaps the widest range of practical surgical advances came from men who had served as army or naval surgeons, which, following a major conflict such as the Seven Years' War, might include a large percentage of practicing surgeons.

Dentistry

Maintenance of good teeth and removal of troublesome teeth was a major concern of early modern Europeans. Many factors had always threatened dental health, such as poor diet, trauma, or cavities, but new ones appeared between 1500 and 1800. Scurvy from months at sea damaged the mouth, gums, and teeth; the increased use of cheap sugar helped rot teeth away; and the increased use of mercury as an ingredient in cosmetics and as treatment for syphilis introduced a poison that undermined the teeth and gums. Poor dental and oral health more generally led to halitosis, ugliness, and disruption of speech, all of which were especially unwelcome in polite European society. Home recipe books almost always included tooth painkillers and tooth powders—including such abrasives as ground amber or coral—to cleanse the teeth, and many had herbal mouthwashes, heavy on the alcohol and mint. Across the period a few professional works appeared, including sections

Figure 8.4 *The Dentist* by Lucas van Leyden, 1523. This satiric Dutch engraving shows a traveling, dishonest—and probably phony— toothpuller, who is decked out in fancy clothing decorated with human teeth. His assistant is disappointed by the empty purse she is trying to steal from the patient. A certificate to practice on the table could be either a fake or van Leyden's comment hanging above legitimately licensed dentists. (National Library of Medicine)

of Paré's books in France and the German *Teeth Doctoring* (*Zene Artzney*), which was published around 1530 and saw 15 editions by 1576. England's first was Charles Allen's *Curious Observations in That Difficult Part of Chiurgery, Relating to the Teeth* of 1685–87.[26]

Barbers, surgeons, and tooth pullers handled most of society's needs. All could clean and pull, but only the talented, or skilled jewelers, could make artificial dental work. Artificial teeth date from the sixteenth century, when carved animal bone, agates, or tusks did the job. Human teeth, too, often pulled from dead soldiers on the battlefield, were fitted into new owners and secured by gold wires. Teeth specialists could drain abscesses, use a hand drill to remove decay, reroot teeth that had fallen out, and whiten teeth with acids or bleaching compounds. By the mid-seventeenth century tooth pullers had morphed into "operators for the teeth." One such, London's "High German Operator," John Schultim, advertised his abilities: "He also draweth broken teeth, and sets in artificial ones in their room, as firm as if they were natural, so that you may eat and bite with them: he helps loose teeth, restoreth decayed gums, and cureth the scurvy in the mouth."[27]

The dentist, properly labeled and considered a professional, had emerged by about 1760. With license in hand, at least in Paris and Spain, the dentist emphasized his "painless" methods, and by the end of the century artificial teeth of porcelain and metal began to appear. In that often gullible Age of Enlightenment, many charlatans and outright frauds peddled dentifrices, painkillers, cures for halitosis, and other oral remedies, but tooth pulling remained the standard procedure for professional and itinerant alike.[28]

NOTES

1. William Gates, *An Aztec Herbal: The Classic Codex of 1552* (Mineola, NY: Dover, 1939/2000), 84.

2. Bernard R. Ortiz de Montellano, *Aztec Medicine, Health, and Nutrition* (New Brunswick, NJ: Rutgers University Press, 1990), 155; Gates, *Aztec Herbal*, 27–28.

3. On surgery among the Aztecs in addition to Ortiz see Gordon Schendel, *Medicine in Mexico: From Aztec Herbs to Betatrons* (Austin: University of Texas Press, 1968).

4. For surgeons in colonial Mexico see Sherry Fields, *Pestilence and Headcolds: Encountering Illness in Colonial Mexico* (New York: Columbia University Press, 2008).

5. Ilza Veith, *The Yellow Emperor's Classic of Internal Medicine* (Berkeley: University of California Press, 2000), 3.

6. Zhenguo Wang, *History and Development of Traditional Chinese Medicine* (Beijing: Science Press, 1999), 141–42.

7. Ibid., 233–37.

8. Linda L. Barnes, *Needles, Herbs, Gods, and Ghosts: China, Healing, and the West to 1848* (Cambridge, MA: Harvard University Press, 2005), 118.

9. Wang, *History*, 24.

10. On advances in acupuncture during the early modern period see Peter Eckman, *In the Footsteps of the Yellow Emperor: Tracing the History of Traditional Acupuncture* (San Francisco: Long River Press, 2007), 81–86.

11. Barnes, *Needles*, 110–15, 181–85.

12. Paul U. Unschuld, *Forgotten Treasures of Ancient Chinese Medicine: The I-hsüeh Yüan Liu Lun of 1757, by Hsü Ta-ch'un* (Brookline, MA: Paradigm, 1998), 244, 247.

13. Cyril Elgood, *Safavid Medical Practice: The Practice of Medicine, Surgery, and Gynecology in Persia between 1500 and 1750* (London: Luzac, 1970), 131–39.

14. Peter E. Pormann and Emilie Savage-Smith, *Medieval Islamic Medicine* (Washington, DC: Georgetown University Press, 2007), esp. 121–35.

15. Miri Shefer-Mossensohn, *Ottoman Medicine: Healing and Medical Institutions, 1500–1700* (Albany: State University of New York Press, 2009), 45–56.

16. Elgood, *Safavid Medical Practice*, 141–70.

17. Harold Ellis, *The Cambridge Illustrated History of Surgery* (New York: Cambridge University Press, 2009), 37–39, 61; see also Margaret Pelling, "Occupational Diversity: Barber-surgeons and Other Trades, 1550–1640," in her *The Common Lot: Sickness, Medical Occupations and the Urban Poor in Early Modern England* (New York: Longman, 1998), 203–29.

18. Andreas Vesalius, *On the Fabric of the Human Body (1543)*, 5 vols., trans. William Frank Richardson (Novato, CA: Norman, 2003–9).

19. See Ambroise Paré, *The Apologie and Treatise of Ambroise Paré Containing the Voyages Made into Divers Places with Many of his Writings upon Surgery*, ed. G. Keynes (Mineola, NY: Dover Books, 1968).

20. On Lind see David I. Harvie, *Limeys: The Conquest of Scurvy* (Stroud, UK: Sutton, 2002).

21. See Toby Gelfand, *Professionalizing Modern Medicine: Paris Surgeons and Medical Science and Institutions in the Eighteenth Century* (Westport, CT: Greenwood Press, 1980).

22. Michael E. Burke, *The Royal College of San Carlos: Surgery and Spanish Medical Reform in the Late Eighteenth Century* (Durham, NC: Duke University Press, 1977).

23. Zachary B. Friedenberg, *Surgery over the Centuries* (London: Janus, 2009), 193.

24. Mary Lindemann, *Health and Healing in Eighteenth-Century Germany* (Baltimore: Johns Hopkins University Press, 1996), esp. chap. 3.

25. Burke, *Royal College*, 29–35.

26. A. S. Hargreaves, *White as Whales Bone: Dental Services in Early Modern England* (Leeds, UK: Northern Universities Press, 1998); see also Roger King, *The Making of the "Dentiste," c. 1650–1760* (Aldershot, UK: Ashgate, 1998).

27. Hargreaves, *White as Whales Bone*, 78.

28. Colin Jones, "Pulling Teeth in Eighteenth-Century Paris," *Past and Present* 166 (2000): 100–145.

CHAPTER 9

Mental and Emotional Health and Disorders

When a person fractures a bone, suffers from a high fever, or hemorrhages after giving birth, there is little doubt that some treatment is needed. Practitioners may argue over the cause of the fever or what damage is causing the hemorrhage, but not over the need for setting the bone or stanching the flow of blood. When a person is uncharacteristically sluggish or excited, suddenly passes out, or begins talking to himself, both the need for intervention and what remedy is needed are far less obvious. Today's psychology and psychiatry may have answers about the underlying conditions that cause this series of symptoms. These may be serious and require medical treatment, or they may be simply situational: low blood sugar resulting from poor diet or preoccupation due to anger. We look to doctors to sort these out.

In premodern societies the interactions among the brain, nerves, and outward behavior were understood only very tentatively if at all. People, including physicians, accepted and thought they understood divine or demonic actions, magic and curses, vapors released by bad humors into the brain, poisons, and negative astrological influences as causes for aberrant behaviors. Depression, panic attacks, epileptic fits, multiple personalities, rage, idiocy, senility, paranoia, and madness were often considered spiritual rather than medical conditions, or spiritually caused medical conditions. Different cultures approached those afflicted with mental problems in different ways, depending in part on the level of disruption their behaviors caused. Across the early modern period, most mentally or emotionally ill people whose symptoms were tolerable were probably treated by the appropriate priest, shaman, cunning woman, or "mad doctor" and then hidden away by the family. A much greater problem was posed by those unfortunates whose behaviors were extreme and threatened themselves and others around them.

THE AZTECS

Much of what is known of Aztec medicine was transferred through the Spanish, though some writers were themselves of Aztec origin. Aztecs believed the heart and not the brain was the seat of mental activity. Thus the root of behaviors such as epilepsy, idiocy, and mania was to be found in the heart. They did not have as wide a set of labels for mental illness as the Europeans did, and most behaviors were categorized as either passive or active insanity. It seems that passive indicated those symptoms that made the person quiet and easily manageable, such as depression, lack of affect, dementia, or catatonia. Active insanity would have made the person unpredictable and difficult to manage, such as epilepsy or frenzy. Aztecs blamed both behavior patterns on what the Europeans called phlegm collecting in the area of the heart.[1]

This could occur naturally but could also be the result of self-poisoning with certain drugs used for their psychotropic or other effects. In this case, detoxification by purging and withdrawal of the person from the offending substance was supposed to return him or her to normal. In the 1552 Aztec herbal, written in Nahuatl by native Martín de la Cruz, appear several entries dealing with what we would call mental problems. The first is for epilepsy "recently aroused." First the patient drinks the juice of a purgative root, then a wicked mixture of hot water with stones found in specific bird stomachs, the root of a highly odiferous plant (*quetzal-atzonyatl*), deer's horn, white incense, human corpse hair, and the ashes of an incinerated mole. This should cause him to vomit profusely. Right before a fit begins he is to undergo a second treatment including the consumption of boiled wolf and weasel brains, and incensing with the "odor of a mouse's nest." The very macho Aztecs treated "fear or timidity" with a potion made of several plants and a poultice made of "the blood of a wolf and a fox, a worm, the blood and excrement of the *acuecueyalotl*, laurel, [and] swallow's excrement." Temporary "stupidity of mind" was treated first with a vomit-inducing purge; days later a drink including the "heart plant" should drive out "the evil humor in the chest." Then a cocktail of

Figure 9.1 Sixteenth-century religious brother Bernardino Álvarez, founder of the earliest mental hospitals in the Americas. He came to New Spain as a soldier and became a wealthy businessman who used his wealth to build health facilities. He founded a religious order named for his asylum of San Hipólito in Mexico City, which is still operating and is now named in his honor. (National Library of Medicine)

powdered bird stomach stones and precious stones was to be drunk and poured over his head. After this, if he takes to carrying around yet another bird stomach stone, "his sanity of mind [will] be restored." Just in case, his head should be anointed with ravens' brains and he should wear an amulet of a swallow's stomach stone around his neck.[2]

As with other maladies, however, a cause other than nature or self was also possible: evil spirits. Some of the elements of each of the remedies above probably contain elements that were meant to propitiate or drive away malevolent entities. But priest-practitioners, at least in pre-Christian Mexico, had their exorcisms and other rites for restoring the mentally troubled to their communities. The Catholic Church did what it could to eliminate the Aztec priesthood, replacing native with Catholic exorcisms, but the low state of sixteenth-century mental health practice meant that the Spaniards had little to teach the Indians. The first mental hospital in the Western Hemisphere was San Hipólito in Mexico City, used exclusively for the insane from 1589.[3]

CARIBBEAN SLAVES

Over the 300 years covered by this book, several million Africans were forcibly taken from their homes, held as captives in dank, prison-like conditions, then shipped under utterly inhumane conditions to a strange land where they were to serve in baking, disease-ridden land-scapes as field slaves for the rest of their lives. Perhaps the surprising thing is that any preserved even a shred of their mental health. Because slaves were gathered, sold, bought, and used as property, records on their mental health and illness are hard to come by. Slaveholders and their agents simply did not tolerate the kinds of manic, depressive, demented, or otherwise disruptive behavior that are often associated with mental illness. While a physician might have been called to treat a fever, a surgeon to mend a broken limb, or a mid-wife to help with a woman's labor, only the whip and other instru-ments of discipline waited on the bodies of the mentally or emotionally troubled.

While certain congenital conditions may have been sifted out of many African populations by the harsh and demanding realities of daily life in the tropics, the trauma of the descent into slavery would have left many in a miserable emotional state. From later slave narra-tives we know the terror imposed simply by the white-skinned slavers, by the unfamiliarity of the pounding surf and endless ocean, the rock-ing of the fetid ship. The new slave's sense of self was stripped not only by the shackles and chains but by the babble of strange voices, the loss of identity and freedom of action, and the utter uncertainty of the future. Anthropologists have pointed out that typically Africans built their senses of self through identification with their natural and social environments in Africa. We modern—or even postmodern—people define ourselves at least in part by our independence to define our-selves by our economic liberty and our choices. Africans defined them-selves as individuals who were a part of a larger whole, a kin group and tribe that provided for all of the individual's needs and whose circle was the source of personal fulfillment and happiness. Outside the circle was social death. The African was a person only in relation to his family, ancestors, and divinities. The living landscape, of which he was an integral part, not only provided food and shelter but was the matrix that gave meaning to life.

Capture, captivity, and enslavement ripped all of that away. Life became a matter of confusion, weariness, pain, disease, fear, and death. Many chose suicide, either at their own hands or at those of their armed captors. All had suffered a social death and had few resources with which to build a new self. Those whose bodies survived the Middle Passage intact found new homes as the property of Spanish, French, Dutch, or English masters. Their new communities were formed of people whose languages differed and whose customs and manners sometimes clashed. Foods, gods, and medicines were a mixture of the familiar and the strange. The hostile climate, numbing labor, and endless hours invited illness of mind and body, and weakness made the body susceptible to greater ravishment still. Slaves were brutalized by overseers and rented out to neighbors who had little incentive to treat them humanely. While slave owners would have recognized certain behaviors as medical illness among their own social group, the weariness of depression, epileptic fits, or unpredictable outbreaks of mania were simply intolerable breaches of discipline, no matter how involuntary. Those whose mental capacities dropped considerably were given tasks suited to their new conditions, while those whose behaviors became chronically disruptive often simply disappeared and were written off, as there was neither madhouse nor market for an insane slave.

THE CHINESE

Early modern Chinese medicine revered its ancient roots and the literature in which it was expressed. Like Aztec and African traditions, Chinese medical traditions held that the human body, mind, and spirit were all organically interconnected and that proper treatment accounted for all three aspects of the unwell person. Mental or emotional illness could be the result of physical or spiritual causes, and the two could appear very similar. For example, madness could be caused by an excess of "mucus" around the heart, requiring the administration of drugs that would break up and remove the troublesome substance. But spiritual forces including demons, angry ancestors, or the spirits of victims of injustice could also induce madness. Comprehensive treatment thus required a spiritual specialist's methods, such as exorcisms and sacrifices, as well as organic or physical remedies. The same held for emotional problems: for example, anger

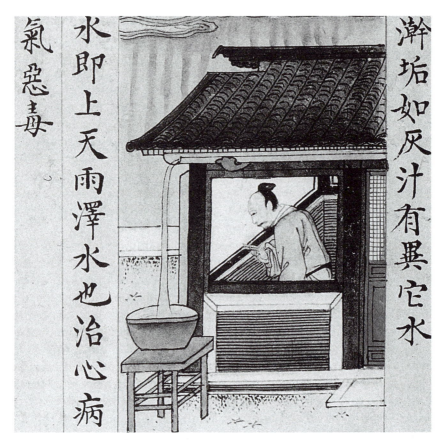

Figure 9.2 Illustration of a man collecting "mid-air river water," from the anonymous Ming-era dietetic herbal, *Shiwu bencao*. The accompanying text refers to rainwater as being pure and clean, and as such a useful tool to fight heart disease, madness from demonic infestation, malign *qi* and noxious poisons. (Wellcome Library, London)

was directly related to the liver, and if a person's proper liver functioning were disrupted, then uncontrolled verbal or physical manifestations of anger could result. Of course, spirits might also cause such displays.[4]

As early as the *Yellow Emperor's Canon*, Chinese physicians recognized the two types of causation. One was physical: imbalances in or among the body's yin and yang, Five Phases, emotional centers in the organs, or the seasons. The second included a wide range of spiritual conditions both particular to the individual, such as a "loss of soul," or external assaults such as spirit possession or disfavor by the gods. Alternative medical practitioners, the highly spiritual Chinese Daoist masters emphasized the role of religious ritual, such as sacrifices, and spiritually powerful objects such as amulets. When Catholic priests arrived the masters recognized and welcomed the power of the foreigners' healing rituals (the Mass, prayers, hymns, exorcisms) and variety of sacramentals (religious objects including rosaries, holy water and oil, communion wafers, icons, relics, crucifixes, and candles).[5]

The *Canon* also distinguished two main types of illness. *Dian* was an overabundance of yin that led to behaviors as different as depression or catatonia, and unwarranted euphoria or giddiness. Too much yang resulted in *kuan*, which manifested in many ways, including aversion to heat, loss of appetite and inability to eat, irrational anger, and uncontrollable urges to sing, undress, curse, climb things, or lord it over others. In the seventh century Sun Miao added "wind" as a cause: it entered the conduits of the body's yin or yang resulting in the disruptive imbalance. Twelfth-century Liu Wansu emphasized the importance of the "climatic influences" heat and fire in bringing on *kuan* behaviors. This immediately recommended physical therapies that reduced the body's heat and fire and sleep that naturally cooled it.

As part of their campaign to increase their status in Chinese society, physicians increasingly emphasized the "medical" causes of and remedies for mental illness and emotional distress. If a sufferer or her family consulted a physician, he would seek the organic cause and recommend herbs, potions, acupuncture, and/or moxibustion as means of addressing it. From the thirteenth century there was also a move toward what we would call psychological treatments. The physician might seek to provoke laughter from a person with no outward emotion or induce a person who refuses to eat with his favorite foods' sights and smells. Reverse psychology suggested countering exaggerated emotional states with their opposites: trying to anger or depress the giddy, for example. With the decline in physicians' emphasis on spiritual causes for mental or emotional illness, which often had moral guilt associated with its onset (what had the patient done to anger the gods or ancestors?), personal stigma tended to fall away. At least it happened among those urban Chinese who accepted the official medical community's conclusions.

Even in cities, however, there were thriving communities of alternative healers with whom even the most sophisticated might consult. In rural areas the range of choices was smaller, but the local healer was far more likely to be an empiric herbalist or religious master than a literate physician. As might be expected, older folk traditions held sway, and mental or emotional problems did imply moral failings, at least once home remedies failed. For Buddhists sins took many forms, from killing animals for food to homosexuality. Given their concept of karma, Buddhists insisted that such actions had consequences—including mental illness in this or future lives—and offered sufferers small certificates after proper prayers for release from retribution. Buddhist and other alternative healers seem to have especially credited sexual sins with the onset of mental or emotional troubles.

Early modern China had no governmental asylums until the 1730s. Those with debilitating illness found shelter in their homes or Buddhist care facilities. Others simply wandered the streets and roads —at least until officials across China cracked down on the mentally and emotionally ill. In 1731 an asylum for the insane was proposed for Sichuan Province; this was provided and the order extended to the country in 1740. The same law required all mentally ill to be housed, and in 1757 the government attempted to get the rural clans to register their mentally ill. Across China clans refused to comply: a matter of clan solidarity and the stigma of mental illness. A decade later the Board of Punishments declared the insane to be incapable of forming the necessary intention to commit criminal acts apart from murder or treason. From 1762 a mad murderer warranted imprisonment for life rather than execution. Also in 1766, the government insisted that the ill kept in homes or religious refuges had to be secure against escape or they would be forcibly confined. Governmental facilities were for men only; women had to be maintained securely at home, a bow to the culture's traditional gender distinction. Officially, at least, the Late Imperial Chinese had come to regard the mentally ill not as victims— whether of demons or organic failures—but rather as deviants who needed to be confined and controlled.[6]

THE TURKS AND PERSIANS

Early modern Islamic authorities considered madness to be an imbalance of both a spiritual and physical nature. As such, there were recognized degrees of madness, from those that caused mild behavioral problems to those that presented a real threat to the person or those around him or her. The first were generally accepted as colorful characters in society, often providing what we would consider unacceptable amusement by their babbling, dancing, or harmless emotional outbursts. Both medical and civic authorities allowed the harmlessly insane to wander as they would, living on what they could find, steal, or receive as charity. Public lunacy was often associated with substance abuse, and the line between intoxication and true mental illness could be easily ignored.

When symptoms became acute, however, the bimaristans took in the disruptively mentally ill person. In the Turkish world they were controlled in special wards, being chained when needed. For those who were believed to benefit from therapy, there were soothing fountains and even a form of music therapy. Baths played a role in the attempt to rebalance the superfluity of overly "dry" humors. Lest this create an image of paradise, however, visitors also described vile living conditions of filth and disorder among the incarcerated insane. In Persia physician recommendations apparently included severe beatings "about the head." In at least one case, staff were told that a patient "be shut up and so terrified that he dare not open his mouth."[7] "Therapy" for the acutely insane included shaving of the head, branding of the temples, pulling of all the teeth, and beating with a leather strap or on the soles of the feet with a cane. However barbaric, such treatment was disciplinary and not punitive in meaning. Maintaining social order was of prime importance to the Ottomans and perhaps even more so to the Safavids and their officials. When lunatics seemed to threaten this order, even by their mere presence, the state was more than willing to act.[8]

THE EUROPEANS

In several famous books, the recent French intellectual and historian Michel Foucault laid out an influential model of European (especially French) reaction to mental illness. As he saw it, up to the seventeenth century societies not only tolerated the presence of the mad in society but even celebrated their freedom from convention and alternatives to social norms. Renaissance works such as Erasmus of Rotterdam's *Praise of Folly*, Sebastian Brandt's *Ship of Fools*, Rabelais's *Gargantua and Pantagruel*, Cervantes's *Don Quixote*, and any number of Shakespeare plays featured disordered minds that often formed deeper truths than the day's philosophy.[9] Foucault described this acceptance withering beneath the burgeoning seventeenth-century state, which understood any deviance as a threat to its authority and power. The growth of the insane asylum paralleled those of the prison for the criminal and pest house for the plague sickened. Religious bigotry accompanied the targeting of "witches," and intolerance trumped diversity. Foucault's vision of our period has been refined and undermined, but it remains an important model for considering how a society defines and constructs a disease.[10]

Early Theories of Madness

Early modern Western philosophy no less than medicine was uncomfortable with the problem of the connection and relationship among the mind, soul, and body. That the corporeal body and the nonmaterial mind and—eternal—soul interacted was accepted as obvious, but neither religion nor philosophy nor medicine could clarify how this worked. It became an issue when a person's behavior—fits, inappropriate babbling, catatonia—seemed to indicate a problem that was not merely physical.

Christian Europe accepted the power and interference of the spiritual world no less than did the Aztecs or Chinese. Biblical accounts of demonic possession and popular tales of curses by devil-worshipping witches or wizards seemed to confirm the role of the unholy in causing at least some cases of insanity or emotional imbalance. On the other hand were the saints, whose irrational acts and meditative states indicated God's favor and possession by the Holy Spirit. The French girl Joan of Arc heard voices she identified as those of saints: was she deluded by Satan, mentally ill, or truly blessed? In her day her supporters considered her a prophet and her enemies considered her a witch, capturing and burning her as punishment. Today she would probably be given medication and be shunned even by her own church. In 1562 the prescient Dutch physician Johann Weyer published an entire book on how demons indeed deceive people, especially women, into serving Satan, but he insisted that self-confessed "witches" were really poor wretches who merely suffered from melancholy, an overabundance of the humor black bile, or bad dreams, drug abuse, or hallucinations.[11]

From the ancient Greeks, and to a lesser extent the medieval Arabs, Europeans inherited a natural model of mental and emotional illness. Most problems were a matter not of spiritual interference, whether possession or curse, but of a physical imbalance in the body itself. That this affected the body's behavior—hallucinating, passing out, uncontrollably cursing—was not an issue, but how this was caused by the mind, or itself affected the mind, was not at all clear. The Greek medical paradigm of Galen posited the body's four humors—blood, phlegm, black bile, and yellow bile—as the determiners of most forms of illness, including mental or behavioral illness. Each humor and its associated organ needed to function properly and in balance with the others for good health.

For at least the early part of our period, many physicians also accepted that each person was influenced by the planet under which he or she was born, each of which was associated with a specific humor. This astrological effect was dominant in the sixteenth century, being heavily supported by the writings of Marsilio Ficino, a physician and head of the Medici Academy in Florence. The planet imprinted itself as a kind of genetic predisposition to a dominant mood. It did this by stimulating the production of its particular humor. For example, those born under Saturn's influence were subject to overabundance of black bile, and this buildup would stimulate a number of responses including creativity and emotional depression, or melancholia (literally "black bile").

In his *Three Books of Life* (1482), Ficino further explained that human behavior could be an important causal factor as well. The kind of intense mental work and concentration that was required of the artist or scholar had the physiological effect of drying up the brain. This eliminated the important moisture that retained important heat, making the brain cold and dry, which were the characteristics of the melancholic. Still further, the sedentary artist or scholar did not move about (exercise) in such a way as to "exhale" the "thick, dense, clinging, dusky vapors" that "overcome the soul with sadness and terrifies it."[12] How physical vapors could terrify the immaterial soul remains unexplained. For other practitioners melancholy was brought on by "vapors" that rose from one or more of the body's organs and dried out the brain. Warm and moist substances such as cinnamon, saffron, sandal, and "milky" foods could help prevent melancholia, while it could be treated with moist foods and baths or a warming ointment of lavender. Wearing a talisman with the properties of Jupiter could also ward off the effects of Saturn. Handling melancholy successfully was important because many believed that if unattended it developed into the more serious mania. But in 1549, the Montpellier physician Denys Fontanon wrote that mania resulted rather from yellow bile or too much blood around the brain.[13] Four decades later, in England's first treatise on *melancholia*, Timothy Bright distinguished melancholy caused by black bile, which could be treated successfully with typical dietary remedies and purging, from melancholy rooted in spiritual anguish or guilt, which called for repentance and religious healing.

In a broader sense, exercise, one of the six classic "non-naturals," along with rest, diet, evacuation (helped by purging), and healthy climate were believed to help maintain humoral balance, while ignoring a healthy regimen courted imbalance and illness. Galen taught that epilepsy, usually associated with divine disfavor, resulted from the rising to the brain of vapors of phlegm or black bile. Of course physical trauma to the head could result in diminished mental capacity or disrupted emotions, and emotional traumas such as losing a loved one or witnessing a shocking horror could also bring on a disordered mental or emotional state. Some believed trauma could unbalance the humors in the head, while others understood that "corrupted air" found its way into the head. Popular English sixteenth-century remedies for illnesses of the head included herbal plasters for headaches, a plaster of vinegar and mustard for a migraine, lily of the valley or rosemary for memory loss, primrose, sage, and powdered human skull for inability to speak, and for insomnia alcohol, poppy syrup (an opiate), or a mixture of valerian, hops, and passiflora.[14]

The Early Asylum

As our chapter on early modern medical institutions makes clear, many types of confinement or isolation facilities for special patients sprang up across Europe between 1500 and 1800. Yet family members, villagers, and townspeople either tolerated eccentricities or locked the more dangerous folk in sturdy rooms, attics, or cellars. This was in part to protect the dangerously ill from hurting themselves or others, but it was also to shield from the public the family shame. Throughout the period— across the globe—most insane people were cared for and isolated by their own families. Some hospitals and other semimonastic facilities had special wards or rooms for the seriously mentally ill—including those suffering from the madness brought on by late-stage syphilis— but many more excluded the disruptive and dangerous.

Housing the mad seems to have begun in the fifteenth century, with the Casa de los Inocentes (House of the Innocents, 1436) in the Spanish port city of Seville an early example. Perhaps based on Muslim models in Granada, others soon appeared in Valencia, Zaragoza, Valladolid, Toledo, and Barcelona. The beliefs that lunatics were insensitive to most sources of discomfort and that maniacs were possessed of extraordinary strength meant that madhouses needed few luxuries but strong doors, window bars, and at least some shackles and chains. The infamous Bedlam Hospital in London began life in 1247 as the Priory (religious residence) of St. Mary of Bethlehem (Bethlem). In 1403 it housed at least six insane men. During the Reformation the City took it from the exiled Catholic Church, stripped its incomes and chapels, and appointed the board of governors of Bridewell Prison to run it as an asylum from 1547 (to1948). Inmates could be discharged to known friends, but they were not allowed to beg. A 1598 report listed 20 inmates: 11 women and 9 men, 6 sent from Bridewell and 14 committed by courts or families (both poor and wealthy). Overseers treated physical wounds or sicknesses, but governors provided nothing in the way of mental therapy. Located between two open sewers, the place naturally stank, all the more so since it was never cleaned out. In 1618 King James I ordered conditions raised to the level of those at the City's hospitals. In 1643 the Puritan government

Figure 9.3 Engraving by William Hogarth depicting the interior of Bedlam Hospital in 1763. Based on Hogarth's earlier paintings for the series *A Rake's Progress*, the engraving shows the character of Tom Rakewell in the madhouse of Royal Bethlem Hospital in London. As in the real asylum of the time, in Hogarth's Bedlam fashionable ladies have come to observe the lunatics as a form of entertainment. (National Library of Medicine)

enlarged Bedlam and doubled the population but banned curious sightseers and insisted on more sanitary conditions.[15]

New Bethlem (1674) was the first purpose-built hospital in London since 1519. Located in Moorfields on the City's old moat and funded by loans and private donations, it was designed by Robert Hooke (of microscope fame) as a long neoclassical block 720 feet by 80 feet deep. Its 120 rooms were surrounded by walls 14 feet high, and for half a century it was London's biggest postfire (1666) building project after only the Exchange Building and St. Paul's Cathedral. Additional space for noninsane paupers was added in 1725 and 1733, allowing for a total population of some 220.[16]

From at least 1610 Bedlam became a place to visit to watch the residents' antics, like a zoo. Some moralists considered this a good thing, insofar as they viewed the inmates as morally fallen humans who were suffering for their sins. By the eighteenth century this practice was seen as degrading and disruptive to residents, but it provided some £400 annually of very necessary income, and visitations reached a peak in the 1760s. Nevertheless, gawking visitors were first limited in number and then banned altogether in 1770.

In France in 1657 Louis XIV established in Paris the *hôpitaux généraux* named Bicêtre (for men) and Salpêtrière (for women). They included the insane, increasingly specialized in holding them, and gained reputations for their horrible conditions and inhumane treatment of the sick. At their height early on, they housed some 6,000 residents. In 1788, 245 of the males in Bicêtre were mentally ill (the rest were beggars and decrepit old men).[17]

Central Europe lacked the metropolises of London and Paris and relied on churches and local governments to provide secure quarters for the mad when a family could not. From the later Middle Ages, many Catholic-run German hospitals housed "raving lunatics" in specially furnished rooms, but by the sixteenth century they resided together with the blind, elderly, and crippled in urban hospitals. In Protestant areas some old monasteries were converted for confining the insane, where strict discipline—even beatings and the use of cages —might be used to maintain order. Unlike hospitals in Catholic Europe, where friars, monks, or nuns often provided spiritual as well as physical care, Protestant hospitals in Central Europe were run as strictly secular institutions.[18] Given the Russian love for their mad holy men, it should not surprise that when a Russian family could or would not care for a mentally sick member he or she would be sent to a monastery.

Asylums were transplanted rather late to the New World, with the first in Mexico City in 1589: the Hospital of San Hipólito, which was hived off of the facility La Caridad y San Hipólito. In colonial Boston the Almshouse, which cared for the destitute, set aside a special ward for the insane in 1729, and the first public insane asylum appeared in Williamsburg, Virginia, in 1773. Ireland's first madhouse was St. Patrick's Asylum in Dublin, funded in part by reformer, cleric, and author Jonathan Swift.

Emerging Theories and Therapies

In early modern Europe more than any other part of the world, traditional medical models of mental illness were challenged by the discoveries and theories of scientists and physicians. In turn these suggested new treatments. For example the nerves, envisioned as tiny tubes that connected the brain to the rest of the body, were believed by some to circulate "vital spirits" that somehow provided sense data to the brain and directed the brain's commands to the body. Blockages in the nerve-tubes or other types of damage to them explained many types of illness and gave rise to the notion of "nervous disorders" and "neurosis" (coined by Dr. William Cullen in 1785). This mechanical model replaced "rising vapors," humoral imbalances, and the wandering uterus. It also opened the door to hydrotherapies that utilized baths of mineral waters, such as those found naturally at Bath, England; Spa, Belgium; Wiesbaden, Germany; and Plombieres, France. These and other "watering holes" drew Europe's elite and became seasonally fashionable to aristocrats and hangers-on. This fad grew with the notion that being a bit "nervous" was a sign of a "sensible" person of high breeding. By century's end, though, the elites had discovered the sea as a natural source of dissolved minerals and salts, and they abandoned the spas for the seaside resorts that canny entrepreneurs established along the Atlantic and Mediterranean shorelines.

The fad for bathing joined with the fascination for magnetism and early electrical experiments and resulted in Franz Mesmer's famous demagnetizing tubs. A number of doctors had identified vital spirits, or the force circulating through the nerves, with electricity. Mesmer began offering his therapy of bathing in tubs that supposedly contained "animal magnetism" in Vienna. Forced out of town, in the 1770s he settled into the capital of the Enlightenment, Paris, and seduced the aristocracy. Though wildly popular, an official committee that included the chemist Antoine Lavousier, Ben Franklin, and Dr. Ignace-Joseph Guillotin (he of the later guillotine) investigated and concluded that Mesmerism was bogus and Mesmer a fraud.

Confinement in the Eighteenth Century

Enlightened thinking among physicians and social reformers informed a great expansion of asylums—perhaps Foucault's real Great Confinement—and the broadening sense that madness or insanity was a sickness that warranted a therapy. Institutions should not merely house but seek to heal the mentally ill. Reflecting the societal abandonment of spiritual causes for insanity, Lady Mary Wortley Montagu, early proponent of inoculation for smallpox, wrote in 1755 that "madness is as much a corporeal distemper as the gout or asthma . . . Passion may bring on a fit, but the disease is lodged in the blood."[19]

The French provided a model of combining a workhouse for the indigent with a madhouse, in which the insane would be housed and chained to their work stations. This had the reasonable result of both securing the mad and making them productive, and was adopted by many German states. As major urban hospitals appeared in the later eighteenth century, many included wards or separate facilities for the insane. This both spurred and was spurred by the increasing medicalization of madness, which defined it as a disease and not just a social disability.[20]

During the 1700s asylums appeared in the English cities of Manchester, Liverpool, Norwich, York, and Newcastle. The traditional Galenic regimen of carefully controlled diets, exercise, light, good air, clean surroundings, and purgings recommended itself to humane and enlightened managers. In mid-century Bedlam was under the direction of Dr. John Monro, who had replaced his father, James. In 1751 one of Bedlam's governors, Dr. John Battie, opened St. Luke's in Moorfields near Bedlam as a competing charity hospital. Its simple unadorned lines contrasted with the fancy neoclassical decoration of Bedlam; and they differed in other ways as well.

In 1758 Battie wrote *A Treatise on Madness*, and his competitor, John Monro, immediately rejoined with his scathing *Remarks on Dr. Battie's Treatise*. Both supported their arguments with classical and contemporary authors, but more importantly, they relied on their own experiences. Battie believed that mental illness could be understood and even cured in many cases, since there were many different underlying causes. Some illness was "original," often hereditary, and could not be cured. The rest was "consequential": brought on by drug abuse, physical trauma, or emotional distress, and thus curable if understood. Battie advocated multiple types of therapy and isolating patients from "gawkers." Further, he adhered to the enlightened belief in progress in medical knowledge. Since medical schools still provided no training in treating mental illness, he urged that asylums allow medical students to learn from insane patients as residents in hospitals learned from diseased or wounded patients. He also welcomed constructive public scrutiny of his new institution. Each point was a criticism of Monro and Bedlam, and Monro rejected many of Battie's attitudes and methods. The insane should be managed with humane care, but they are confined because they cannot be cured. Mental illness was a single disease with many manifestations and thus a single Galenic regimen sufficed to control it. Gawkers were welcome, even physically interacting with the inmates, but medical students had no place, nor did the scrutinizing eyes of the public, at least as long as gentlemen ran the place. In many ways this was a dispute of Monro's old school against the progressive model championed by Battie.[21]

From the later 1600s London also hosted numerous private madhouses. Some were run as sidelines by physicians, surgeons, or apothecaries, while others were purely business ventures. Though often run-down old manor houses, they were expensive but discreet, and thus useful to the upper classes. And they proved to be very lucrative. "Mad doctors" like Monro and Battie had their own professional private practices, often recommending specific "houses" that they also served as medical consultants. Monro was a business partner in Brooke House, Hackney, a rebuilt seventeenth-century ruin. The site was waterlogged, but each individual room had its own fireplace. Though most private madhouses hosted fewer than 10, Brooke House managed 50 inmates. It remained to be demolished by the German Luftwaffe in 1940. In 1774 the Royal College of Physicians succeeded in getting passed the first parliamentary act for regulating madhouses, requiring registration and inspection. About 50 passed muster by 1800.

Both Battie and Monro, and many mad doctors in England and elsewhere, kept casebooks with notes on patients, though few of these survive. One of Monro's did and has been published. It is a rare glimpse into the physician's private practice and the life of mentally ill patients in the eighteenth century.

Late in the century, medical pioneers, of whom Battie was one, set the scene for nineteenth-century advances in treatment of the insane. In 1788 Florentine physician Vincenzio Chiarugi opened the renovated Bonifazio Hospital for mental patients from the Hospital of Santa Dorotea. Bonifazio was designed as a place of therapy and healing with clear rules for handling the patients in the most humane way possible. In 1793/94 Chiarugi published his three-volume *On Insanity*, which spread his ideas. In revolutionary Paris Philippe Pinel adopted Chiarugi's ideas at Bicêtre and Salpêtrière in 1793, striking off their chains (though he later introduced straightjackets).[22] In 1796 the Quaker Tuke family of York established a residence for the mentally ill. York Retreat rejected the confinement of residents, based on the Quaker belief that the divine Inner Light each person possessed would be stimulated to heal them.[23] Perhaps ironically, many English considered religious "enthusiasts" such as the Quakers and Methodists to be mentally ill simply by virtue of their religious choice.

NOTES

1. Gordon Schendel, *Medicine in Mexico: From Aztec Herbs to Betatrons* (Austin: University of Texas Press, 1968), 49–50.

2. William Gates, *An Aztec Herbal: The Classic Codex of 1552* (Mineola, NY: Dover, 1939/2000), 94, 97, 98.

3. See Clara Sue Kidwell, "Aztec and European Medicine in the New World, 1521–1600," in *The Anthropology of Medicine: From Culture to Method*, ed. Lola Romanacci-Ross, Daniel E. Moerman, and Laurence R. Tancredi (Westport, CT: Greenwood Press, 1997), 19–30; on San Hipólito see John S. Leiby, "San Hipólito's Treatment of the Mentally Ill in Mexico City, 1589–1650," *The Historian* 54 (1992): 491–98.

4. Paul U. Unschuld, *Medicine in China: A History of Ideas*, 2nd ed. (Berkeley: University of California Press, 2010), 216.

5. Vivian W. Ng, *Madness in Late Imperial China: From Illness to Deviance* (Norman: University of Oklahoma Press, 1990), remains the best Anglophone treatment of mental illness in early modern China, and this section relies heavily on its findings.

6. Ibid., 63–83.

7. Cyril Elgood, *Safavid Medical Practice: The Practice of Medicine, Surgery, and Gynecology in Persia between 1500 and 1750* (London: Luzac, 1970), 27–28.

8. Michael W. Dols, *Majnun: The Madman in Medieval Islamic Society* (Oxford: Clarendon Press, 1992); Miri Shefer-Mossensohn, *Ottoman Medicine: Healing and Medical Institution, 1500–1700* (Albany: State University of New York Press, 2009), 135, 139–40.

9. See Paromita Chakravarti, "Natural Fools and the Historiography of Renaissance Folly," *Renaissance Studies* 25 (2011): 208–27.

10. Michel Foucault, *Madness and Civilization: A History of Insanity during the Age of Reason*, trans. Richard Howard (New York: Pantheon, 1965); or Foucault's *Discipline and Punish: The Birth of the Prison*, trans. Alan Sheridan (New York: Pantheon, 1977); for critiques of Foucault see the essays in Norbert Finzsch and Robert Jütte, eds., *Institutions of Confinement: Hospitals, Asylums, and Prisons in Western Europe ad North America: 1500–1950* (New York: Cambridge University Press, 1996).

11. For Weyer see Jennifer Radden, ed., *The Nature of Melancholy: From Aristotle to Kristeva* (New York: Oxford University Press, 2000), 97–105.

12. Ibid., 90; for the full text see Marsilio Ficino, *Three Books on Life*, trans. Carol Kaske and John Clark (Tempe, AZ: Medieval and Renaissance Texts and Studies, 1998).

13. Roy Porter, ed., *Cambridge History of Medicine* (New York: Cambridge University Press, 2006), 243.

14. Katherine Knight, *How Shakespeare Cleaned His Teeth and Cromwell Treated His Warts: Secrets of the Seventeenth-Century Medicine Cabinet* (Stroud, UK: Tempus, 2006), 128–43.

15. Catharine Arnold, *Bedlam: London and Its Mad* (New York: Pocket Books, 2008); Leonard Smith, *Lunatic Hospitals in Georgian England, 1750–1830* (London: Routledge, 2007); Jonathan Andrews and Andrew Scull, *Undertaker of the Mind: John Monro and Mad-Doctoring in Eighteenth-Century England* (Berkeley: University of California Press, 2001).

16. Jonathan Andrews and Andrew Scull, *Customers and Patrons of the Mad-Trade: The Management of Lunacy in Eighteenth-Century London, with the*

Complete Text of John Monro's 1766 Case Book (Berkeley: University of California Press, 2002), 8.

17. Edward Shorter, *A History of Psychiatry: From the Era of the Asylum* (New York: Wiley, 1998), 6.

18. Christina Vanja, "Madhouses, Children's Ward, and Clinics: The Development of Insane Asylums in Germany," in Finzsch and Jütte, *Institutions of Confinement*, 117–32.

19. Andrews and Scull, *Undertakers*, 30.

20. Vanja, "Madhouses," 117–132

21. Andrews and Scull, *Undertakers*, 52–53.

22. Shorter, *History of Psychiatry*, 10–14.

23. Robert Kilpatrick, " 'Living in the Light': Dispensaries, Philanthropy, and Medical Reform in Late Eighteenth-Century London," in *The Medical Enlightenment of the Eighteenth Century*, ed. Andrew Cunningham and Roger French (New York: Cambridge University Press, 1990), 254–80.

CHAPTER 10

Apothecaries and Their Pharmacopeias

Between 1500 and 1800, the world became knitted together in ways it had never been before. Europeans were exposed to medical and pharmacological traditions of which they had never dreamed. China, Africa, and Central America exchanged foods, spices, and other health-related substances that remained limited to isolated cultures before 1500. Writing about the new materia medica that was beginning to circulate around the globe was largely a matter for Europeans, though most literate cultures produced new herbals, recipe books, and pharmacopeias that reflected the wide-ranging exchanges. For Europeans at home and abroad as colonists, merchants, or conquerors, the recent innovation of printing provided a revolutionary tool for recording and learning about world cultures and their medical traditions. Through trade and plunder Europeans acquired the newspices, barks, roots, fruits, and other riches, shipping them home and abroad as the markets demanded.[1] But they also shipped living specimens home to be planted in medicinal and botanical gardens to slake the Renaissance's thirst for new knowledge. Meanwhile, those who retailed herbal simples, compounds, and drugs integrated the new materia medica in with the traditional menu, bringing the world's healing secrets into the most humble lodgings.

TYPES OF *MATERIA MEDICA*

Materia medica is simply the Latin for "medical materials" and refers to the various substances that medical practitioners used in preparing drinks, pills, powders, fumigations, emetics, washes, poultices, clysters and other remedies. At their simplest a single ingredient was used, and this was a termed a "simple." A compound consisted of a mixture of two or more simples, perhaps in a pleasing medium such as sugar water, rose water, or wine. In the premodern period many choices by cultures reflected generations of experience, passed on orally or in writing. Others reflected what we might consider less rational criteria: a root looked like a human limb and could therefore fix that limb; or the red juice of a plant could help with menstrual problems.[2]

Simples

Simples could be animal, vegetable, or mineral, and each culture believed that each simple contained the power to stimulate some positive effect on the human body. Some simples had multiple effects—that intended and those we might call side effects—and the prescriber of these needed to know how much healed and how much could kill. Depending on the culture, animal simples could include blood, claws, feathers, brains or other organs, digestive stones (bezoars), pearls, coral, eyes, horn, tongues, tails, hair, teeth, ground bones, dried cartilage, and even urine and feces. Of course, humans are animals, and human material included the skull of a hanged man, a young boy's urine, "mummy," a virgin's blood, menstrual fluid, sweat, dried placenta, pus, as well as various other parts and waste.

Vegetable simples were often herbs (local) or spices (imported)—many still marketed for a range of assumed medicinal properties—but almost anything edible might be considered medicinal. These constituted the largest category of medical substances in any pharmacopeia, or list of recognized materia medica. Experts in a culture knew when in its life cycle each plant was most effective and what part to use: roots, stems, seeds, leaves, bark, flowers, berries, or other fruits. They knew how and when to harvest them and how to preserve them properly (drying, pickling, sugaring, powdering). They also knew how to prepare them appropriately: bruising, mashing, extracting juice; infusing like tea; boiling to decoct essences; boiling with sugar to make a syrup; mixing with alcohol to make a tincture; distilling in an alembic by boiling and condensing the steam in a separate container; or boiling down to purify or concentrate an essence. Spices and herbs both improved the flavor of foods and most had supposed medicinal properties. Organic theories of health and disease, like the Chinese and the Galenic humoralism of the Muslim and Christian worlds, relied heavily on organic—animal or vegetable—materia medica. One issue during our period of global exploration and discovery was how to categorize newly encountered plants from Asia or the Americas: was a given root or leaf hot or cold, moist or dry? Most worked backward from what effects the materia seemed to have, deducing its qualities.[3]

But there was still room for mineral or other inorganic medical ingredients. Certain earths such as clays were thought to be effective as drying agents; semiprecious and precious stones were thought to absorb celestial rays and focus them on the sick person, who either wore them or drank the crushed material. Some metals, especially gold (sun) and silver (moon), were thought to have medicinal value, since their shining surfaces supposedly reflected healing powers best. Sixteenth-century Western alchemists sought two things: the "philosopher's stone" and how to change (transmute) lead into gold. Interestingly, both the "stone" and transmuted gold were considered panaceas, or universal healing mediums, and worth a fortune in the age of plague.

Compounds

The blending of two or more ingredients into a single mixture might achieve any of several desired results. The effect of the main ingredient might be strengthened, or a side effect lessened, or secondary symptoms addressed; or multiple ingredients might make the compound effective against several conditions. Honey or sugar made bitter-tasting herbs palatable, and alcohol helped dissolve certain substances. Materia medica was humorally speaking wet, dry, hot, or cold, and in varying degrees (three in Islamic medicine), and some material was subject to astrological forces. The Western or Chinese herbalist's or apothecary's special skill was the blending of the materials in the correct proportions, and his recipe books were vital for that task. The lore of the African or American herbalists and shamans (medicine men and women) was passed along orally. Some of this was combined as African slaves brought their medical traditions to the Caribbean with its distinctive flora and native medical customs.

EARLY MODERN DISPENSERS OF MEDICINAL MATERIALS AND THEIR SOURCES

The Aztecs

The Native Americans had no equivalent of the West's apothecaries or China's herbalists, but Aztec healers and possibly even mothers commanded an ancient tradition of natural materia medica. The Spaniard Francisco Hernández traveled to Mexico at the order of King Philip II to discover what he could of native medicine and medicinal plants. He catalogued some 3,000 plants, of which 1,200 were considered to have medical value. The Aztecs themselves had a sophisticated categorizing system, some of which found its way into the first Aztec herbal, that compiled in Nahuatl in 1552 at Tlatelolco by Aztec physician Martín de la Cruz, *Little Book of the Medicinal Herbs of the Indies* (Latinized by Juan Badiano). They organized plants by taste, smell, feel, use, and natural environment. The ruler Moctezuma I is known to have had extensive botanical gardens of some 2,000 specimens cultivated for medicinal and research (often to discover poisons) as well as aesthetic and culinary purposes from 1467. Of course, medicine and supernatural ritual intertwined, so that healing included pacifying the spirits and religious ritual included drugs. For example, narcotics such as peyote, jimson weed, marijuana, and psilocybin mushrooms served as medical anesthesia and to dull the senses of human sacrifices. Of course, De la Cruz, Hernández, and other Christian writers filtered out the Aztec spiritual elements, presenting a very one-dimensional view of Aztec healing. Some point out that Spanish preconceptions and beliefs may have influenced even the native-produced medical works.

Healers were not limited to herbal simples or compounds, for they employed a wide range of animal products and minerals. For fevers they used pearls and cool green stones such as turquoise, jade and emeralds; red jasper was good for the kidneys and blood and to stanch hemorrhages. De la Cruz includes wild and domestic animal blood, flesh, urine, and organs in many of his recipes, and others recommend young alligators for scabies and ants for arthritis. When Spanish practitioners interacted with their Aztec counterparts, it was the native materia medica that the invaders best understood and respected. They brought their own apothecaries, and these remained open to discovering the next panacea.[4]

Africans and Caribbean Slaves

West African healing utilized a large and varied materia medica whose traditions were millennia in the making. As with the Aztecs, African communities prized their herbalists and healers who had mastered the lore of medicinal plants and their preparation. Likewise, they tended to rely on local plants rather than imported, though since tribal groups were far from stationary over time they brought important species with them to transplant. The penetration of Islam into Africa's interior and some western regions may have also introduced new plants and practices in some areas. West Africa in many ways had a patchwork of medical traditions. Their differences were evident after their forcible transplantation to the New World.[5] Sorting them out on Caribbean plantations was essential, since Africans strongly believed that what could heal could also kill.

Ripped from their homelands, the Caribbean slaves were forced to work and live with people from various regions of Africa or native-born Afro-Caribbeans. Unless physicians, whites generally respected the medical traditions of their slaves, and usually left them to their own healers. But for many these people were not *their* healers: these they had left behind in Africa. Medicines, they believed, worked in part because of the rituals that attended their preparation and administering, and who knew the rituals? Where were the familiar African plants? Did similar-looking specimens have the same powers? Were other local varieties better? Black healers had to adapt and empirically create their own pharmacopeias. The English physician Hans Sloane recorded some of this practice on the island of Jamaica in the late 1680s and noted some 800 plant species. He dismissed local healers in the same way his colleagues in London dismissed empirics and midwives: they lacked "philosophy" and Western medical knowledge. Yet for the slaves, establishing a working understanding of the local flora was essential to their very survival.[6]

The Chinese

Chinese materia medica as a medical science is as old as China itself. Shennong's *The Divine Husbandman*, from the first centuries CE, was one of the classics of Chinese medicine, listing 365 medical recipes. China's position and trade meant its herbalists and drug preparers had a great materia medica with which to work. From the eighth century CE, the state established pharmacies with reduced prices of simples and compounds for the poor, and by the ninth century Chinese materia medica included "precious stones, minerals, trees, fowl, quadrupeds, reptiles/worms, and fish," though herbs topped the list.[7] In 992 CE the *Taiping Prescriptions of Sacred Benevolence* contained over 10,000 recipes. Such works contained much but included much redundancy and lacked the organization that would make them useful.

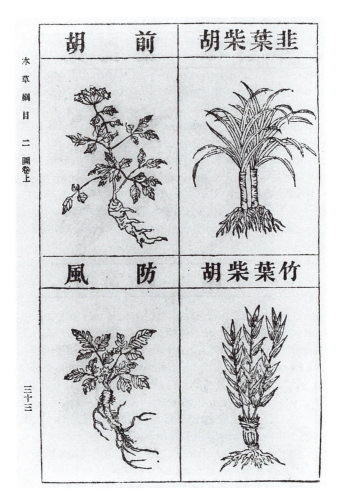

Figure 10.1 One of 1,160 woodcut illustrations of Chinese medicinal herbs from the enormous *Compendium of Materia Medica* (*Bencao gangmu*), written by Li Shizhen in the 16th century. His name and image are so famous that they are still used in relation to traditional Chinese medical institutions, companies, and products. (Library of Congress)

The early modern period opens with the imperial project to rationalize the state of Chinese pharmacy. In 1505 Liu Wen-t'ai presented the *Materia Medica Written on Imperial Order, Containing Essential and Important Material Arranged in Systematic Order* to the emperor. It was a compilation containing nothing new, but it reduced the list to 1,786 substances. The emperor died, and the *Materia Medica* was forgotten until about 1700. Several others of varying size and quality followed.

During the second half of the sixteenth century, Li Shih-chen, who worked in the Imperial Medical Office, produced the magisterial 25-volume *Materia Medica Arranged According to Drug Descriptions and Technical Aspects*, which appeared in 1596. It cut out some of Liu Wen-t'ai's and added 420 new simples for a total of 1,898 substances and 11,096 recipes. For each simple he included a description, its supposed medicinal qualities, how to prepare it, its uses and how to use it, and his own experiences with it. Huge and expensive, it had little circulation outside of the capital. Five smaller and more practical works between 1624 and 1778 as well as numerous specialized manuals followed it.[8]

Between 1500 and the later eighteenth century, little of note moved the field of pharmacy forward in China. Theory and practice remained stable, and writings rehashed what had become tradition. Even the title of a work such as Hsü Ta-ch'un's brilliant *Forgotten Traditions of Ancient Chinese Medicine* (1757) makes this dependence clear.[9] A few new substances, such as American tobacco and Canadian ginseng, entered the pharmacopeia but little changed.[10] Chinese medicinal products, however, spread worldwide in the bottoms of first Portuguese (1557–1685) and later exclusively British ships (from 1715). Camphor, rhubarb, ginger, cassia, china root (*smilax pseudo-China*), and later tea, were major simples exported from China to the West. Physicians, merchants, and missionaries wrote works on their discoveries in India and China, such as the physician and converted Jew Garcia D'Orta's *Colloquies on Simples and Drugs and Medical Things of India* (Goa, India, 1563) and Cristóvão Acosta's *Treatise on the Drugs and Medicines of the Oriental Indies* (Burgos, Spain, 1582). In 1656 the Jesuit missionary Michael Boym compiled the authoritative *Chinese Flora, or a Treatise on the Flowers, Plants, and Animals Particular to China*, with appropriate medical commentary; and in 1735 Jean-Baptiste du Halde published his encyclopedia of China in four volumes, three of which were taken up with medical matters.[11]

The Islamic World

The Arabs invented the apothecary (from the Greek for "warehouse") and inherited materia medica of both the East and West. Arabia was the linchpin connecting the Mediterranean Sea and Indian Ocean, and their dhows and caravans had carried fragrant cargoes since time immemorial. The markets of Cairo, Baghdad, and Damascus sold culinary and medical herbs and spices from throughout the Islamic world and beyond. Muslim scholars and physicians studied the first-century

CE Greek *On Medicinal Substances* by Dioscorides, whose thousand or so animal, mineral, and especially vegetable simples were known to and written about by Galen a century later.[12] Scholars translated Dioscorides into Arabic in the tenth century. One of the translators, Ibn Juljul of Cordoba in Spain, wrote a work on materials used by Muslim doctors but not in Dioscorides, beginning a tradition of original Islamic works on medicinal materials. The most influential was the thirteenth-century *Comprehensive Book on Simple Drugs and Foodstuffs* by the Spanish Muslim Ibn al-Baytar, with some 1,400 simples.[13] Books known as formularies contained the many compounds and specific recipes known to Islamic medicine. Given the many cultures and linguistic groups included in the Islamic world, multilingual synonym books were attempts to provide the many names for simples and compounds. The task proved too daunting, however, and the results were disappointing.

An important healing tool often sold with other materia medica was the talisman. Carried on the person or worn around the neck, the supposed effect of the stone or other object was to focus astral forces or rays down and into the body in such a way as to activate it to respond to the poison or other danger. This was a kind of astrological magic that literally used the skills of a magus, but instructions for creating these were commonly available.[14]

With the rise of the Savafids in Persia and the Ottoman Turks around the Mediterranean, popular and classic Arabic works were translated but, as in China, little development in theory or practice occurred. Medicine remained Galenic and carefully monitored pharmacists sold their goods—most commonly simples—from market stalls and dispensaries attached to hospitals distributed cheap or free remedies to the needy. Yet studies of Ottoman gardens, even attached to hospitals, show no interest in growing medicinal herbs or fruits. Among the Ottomans, at least, compounds seem to have been available at court and to elites. There were, however, some inroads of European influence in Istanbul at the Turkish court in the seventeenth and eighteenth centuries. Some materia medica from the Western Hemisphere found its way into otherwise traditional formularies, and the new chemical medicine of European Paracelsians (see below) found interested scholars, physicians, and bureaucrats. Yet outside of the Topkapi Palace Galenic traditions dominated, "with the new only lightly sprinkled here and there."[15]

The Europeans

During the twelfth and thirteenth centuries, contacts with the Islamic world made numerous Islamic medical works and Islamic versions of

Figure 10.2 Two doctors give instructions for the preparation of prescriptions inside a pharmacy; from an Ottoman manuscript at University Library Istanbul. (The Art Archive/University Library Istanbul/Gianni Dagli Orti)

classical medical works available to European scholars and physicians. Medieval Europeans likewise borrowed the apothecary and stocked his shelves with spices and other materia medica purchased in Islamic markets.[16] By 1500 European apothecaries were on a par with their Muslim contemporaries. Yet the era of the Renaissance, Discovery, and Scientific Revolution saw major advances in European pharmacopeias. Renaissance trends such as the editing, translating, and printing of classical medical works—including Galen and Dioscorides—forced the reconsideration of their Arabic inheritance. Printing helped extend literacy and created markets for medical self-help books and patent medicines advertised in pamphlets. New materia medica of all sorts poured into European markets from the Americas, Asia, and the islands of the Indian and Pacific Oceans, expanding pharmacopeias, both professional and popular. The pseudoscience of alchemy began its long metamorphosis into the science of chemistry with the help of the bombastic sixteenth-century German empiric Paracelsus. Paracelsus rejected "pagan" Galenic humoralism and laid out a model of human physiology that emphasized the roles of minerals, salts, and metals instead of organic materials.[17] By the eighteenth century biology had been reorganized around the system of Carl Linnaeus, which created a system of relating and labeling all living things, including organic materia medica old and new.

The provision of medical simples and compounds had essentially crystallized by 1500. Officially, local apothecary guilds oversaw the education and operations of their members. One entered the guild after an apprenticeship during which the necessary skills and knowledge were mastered. Only during the sixteenth century did medical schools begin formally teaching about materia medica (Padua, 1533; Bologna, 1534; Pisa, 1544), but this was for physicians only. Socially, apothecaries were closer to surgeons, who were also trained as apprentices. Apothecaries worked from well-stocked shops, selling to doctors and the public alike. When in need of recipes for specific prescriptions they referred to formularies, sometimes required by guilds, and created their own blends.[18]

Their direct competition was from empirics who lacked formal training and guild membership but provided local herbs and other substances directly to the suffering. Midwives specialized in women's reproductive problems, while herb- or drug-peddling itinerant charlatans sometimes offered their wares through gaudy and eye-catching "infomercials" performed in town squares from colorful carts or stages (mountebank = to climb on a bench).[19] In England the so-called patent medicines, advertised in print, played the same role in self-medication from the 1650s (see below). The gardens of monasteries[20] and old "wisewomen" also produced the herbal simples for remedies demanded by the poor and villagers. Medicinal spices were supposed to be a monopoly of the apothecaries, though spicers and grocers sold many of the same items for cooking. Apothecaries distinguished themselves by displaying a stuffed crocodile representing their exotic wares, or the mortar and pestle in which spices were ground to powder, or signs with images of them.

New treatments appeared for old diseases—tobacco smoke for plague prevention and cinchona bark for malaria—and new treatments for new diseases, such as mercury and guaiacum for syphilis. Books on

Figure 10.3 Eighteenth-century depiction of the interior of a European pharmacy with a young lady having her throat examined by the robed and bespectacled apothecary. The walls are lined with jars of herbs and medicines, and an aloe vera plant, still used as a skin-healing plant, sits prominently in the foreground. (National Library of Medicine)

newly discovered medicines flourished during the seventeenth and eighteenth centuries, with exotic titles such as Herman Grimm's *The Medical Treasury of the Island of Ceylon* (1677) and Hendrick van Reede's three-volume *Garden of Malabar* (1678–82).[21] Women also published recipe books, including the English Countess of Arundel, whose collection of 397 entries was arranged by illness (1606), and French midwife Louise Bourgeois (*Collection of Secrets*, 1626), whose 280 recipes called for almost 300 herbs, 45 animal products, and 27 minerals.[22] But European medicine was undergoing a movement toward professionalization by around 1650, and society was becoming convinced that only well-educated males should be making medical decisions.[23]

Through their guilds, licensing, royal favors, and increased educational opportunities, surgeons and apothecaries were gaining power and authority over their rivals. Wise women and even midwives were being slaughtered as witches possessed of demonic powers and intents. In England, self-medication took the form of advertised and retailed patent medicines (see below), and across Europe male medical voices eclipsed those of even the most experienced women practitioners.

THE WORLDWIDE PHARMACOPEIA

Cultures naturally developed their pharmacopeias around the plants, minerals, and animals most readily available. These increased through local discoveries and trade but more dramatically through commerce and other contact with distant cultures.

Tobacco

Tobacco was a New World plant whose active ingredient, nicotine, was rather stronger than in today's varieties. Native Americans used it (*petum*) as a hallucinogen for spirit journeys, as a painkiller for toothache and snakebite, and to treat asthma and curb hunger. Italian Amerigo Vespucci was first to write of it, in 1505, and the Dutchman Rembert Dodoens first included it (*henbane*) in an herbal in 1553. The same year the Portuguese gave the French ambassador, Jean Nicot, some specimens that flourished in his garden, and Europeans have never stopped smoking. The word "tobacco" came from the hollow reed through which Caribbean natives smoked the dried leaf, but it was also chewed and inhaled as snuff and used externally in plasters. Considered healthful, Europeans used tobacco smoke from clay pipes to counteract the "poisoned" air that most thought caused plague. Seventeenth-century English physician Nicholas Culpeper recommended as a cure-all a salve of boiled-down tobacco juice, hog grease, and red wine.

The Portuguese shipped it to Africa and Macao from Brazil, and from Macao to Guangdong in China and Japan from about 1605. Spaniards brought it from Mexico to the Philippines, and from Manila plantations to Fujian, China. Chinese physician Yao Lu believed it helped block malaria, cleared the lungs, and aided digestion, and herbalist Zhang Jiebin included it in his pharmacopeia. India accepted tobacco as a luxury stimulant and not a medicine, and appears to have introduced the water pipe (hookah). These spread to Persia and eventually Turkey, and Chinese women used hookahs to mellow the harsh yang of the smoke through the cooling yin of water.[24]

Opium and Opiates

Opium is derived from the opium poppy that grows naturally and has long been cultivated in south central Asia (Afghanistan, Iran). An intense relaxant and painkiller, its cultivation spread to the Ganges Valley in India, Iraq, Turkey, and Egypt along Muslim-controlled trade routes. Mongols traded it to China from the fourteenth century. Indian Ayurvedic medicine considered it hot and dry, but Greeks believed it to be "cold and dry" when used to adjust the humors. Galen claimed it was useful for "venomous bites, headaches, vertigo, deafness, epilepsy, apoplexy, eyesight, bronchitis, asthma, bloody sputum, colic, jaundice, spleen hardening, kidney stones, urinary problems, fever, dropsy, leprosy, menstrual issues, melancholy, pestilences."[25] Muslims noted it intensified sexual pleasure, and the Qur'an did not forbid it, though custom banned its use during the month of Ramadan. It was typically used to calm and control the insane.

Crusaders and Venetian merchants imported small quantities to Europe before 1500, and navigators such as Columbus and Magellan sought its sources. Traditionally taken in the form of a pill, opium was exported from India by the Dutch and spread throughout its trading empire. It seems to have been smoked first in Taiwan, where it was mixed with tobacco to form the very potent madak. It was also mixed with Indian hemp (marijuana; *gange* to Arabs), which Robert Hooke both used and recommended for "lunaticks."[26]

The drug laudanum (from Latin *laudare*, "to praise") was apparently developed by the sixteenth-century German alchemist and medical practitioner Paracelsus. He found that he could suspend certain opium alkaloids in brandy and deliver the supposed benefits of both. His recipe contained 25 percent opium, along with tobacco juice, crushed pearls, amber, coral, musk, "unicorn" (narwhal) horn, and bezoar stone. In the late 1600s Dr. Thomas Sydenham, called the English Hippocrates, standardized a formula that consisted of one pint of sherry, two ounces of opium, and one ounce each of saffron, powdered clove, and powdered cinnamon.[27] Like many other secret mixtures containing opium, and often alcohol, laudanum was easily marketed as a patent medicine to kill pain and level moods. It had a long life on European and American shelves, well beyond 1800. Opium's addictive quality was well known and regretted, a point made in the first European book about the substance, *Mysteries of Opium Revealed* by Dr. John Jones, himself an addict. This unfortunate quality led to opium's ban from time to time in Safavid Iran and in China in the 1720s and 1790s. The ban on madak led to the practice of smoking straight opium purely for the intoxicating effect, and to the infamous opium dens of nineteenth-century China.[28]

Alcohol (Spirits)

Unlike tobacco or opium, drinkable alcohol does not occur naturally but needs to be produced through the controlled fermentation of certain carbohydrate-rich fruits, grains, and even roots, such as grapes, rice, and potatoes. Most early modern cultures drank alcoholic beverages such as mead, sake, wine, or beer in place of or along with water, on a daily basis. Of course alcohol was intoxicating and could be addictive, leading to broken lives of lethargy and poverty, or wild mood swings. Islam theoretically banned the use of alcoholic beverages, though both early modern Safavid Iran and the Ottoman Empire struggled to keep its use under control.[29] Distillation as a chemical process was invented by the Muslim Jabir ibn Hayyan in the eighth century, but German monks were among the first to apply it to wine, creating "burnt wine," or brandy, just before 1500.[30] Other starchy or sugary foods quickly followed, including grains (whiskey, from *uisge*, Gaelic for "water of life," expanded from monasteries in sixteenth century; gin from Holland, c. 1650; schnapps, developed in sixteenth-century Germany), sugar (rum; Barbados, first mentioned in 1651 but much older), and potatoes (vodka; noted in Poland from fifteenth century). This "spiritous" liquid had concentrated properties of normal beverages, could dissolve many substances, burned very readily, and as aqua vitae (water of life) became a medium for many compounds and drugs, including laudanum.[31] Eventually in the West spirituous liquors became less a calmative or stimulant and more a means of getting drunk quickly, as in the eighteenth-century stereotypes of gin-swilling London denizens, whiskey-guzzling Irish, or vodka-soaked Russians. In India alcoholism was treated with an opiate tonic called *filuniya*, much as methadone is used today.

Coffee

The coffee plant's original home was the eastern Indian Ocean. Its bean was harvested and dried or roasted, which dehydrated it out and reduced its weight tremendously. It was ground to a powder and infused—not dissolved—in boiling water to produce the thick, bitter hot drink the West knows as Turkish or Greek coffee, or espresso. After 1500 it spread north through Turkish trade routes to Cairo, Egypt, by 1520, and Damascus, Syria, where the first known coffeehouse appeared in 1530. Constantinople's first opened in 1554, Baghdad's in 1601, and coffee reached India in 1609. Muslims valued the boiled bean as a stimulant where alcoholic drinks were banned, and Sufi poets adopted it as a mild narcotic. Iranian physicians recommended coffee as a remedy for fatigue, "boiling blood," measles, hemorrhoids, nightmares, colic, and "vapors." Like tea, coffee required boiled water, which made the water safe to drink, but the dried beans required grinding, which relegated coffee to the special houses. The buzz stimulated conversation and in cities coffeehouses became common gathering places during the day (a trend revived in the 1970s).[32]

Coffee arrived at the French court via Marseille merchant De la Roque in 1644; Venice boasted Europe's oldest coffeehouse, opened in 1645; and in Oxford a Lebanese named Jacob first served coffee at the Angel in 1652. But coffee was always part beverage and part medicine. European coffeehouses became important meeting places for medical practitioners—especially quacks—and their patients and many establishments sold pills, potions, and other patent medicines. Important in the history of early newspapers, coffeehouses also distributed handbills and other advertisements for medical remedies and services. For the Galenic, coffee was "cold and dry." In his *Sylva sylvarum* of 1627, the English scientist and statesman Francis Bacon insisted "the drink comforteth the brain, the heart, and helpeth digestion"; while a printed handbill from London's Pasqua Rosée coffeehouse in 1652—its first year of business—claimed it prevented miscarriages and cured dropsy, gout, and scurvy. Another advertisement praised coffee's value to sexual males: "It collects and settles the spirits, makes the erection more vigorous, the ejaculation more full, adds a spiritual escency [*sic*] to the sperm, and renders it more firm and suitable to the gusto of the womb." Despite such powers, tea replaced coffee in England and elsewhere, while cheap liquor (gin, schnapps, brandy) and cheaper beer kept the masses content.[33]

Tea

The delicate leaves of many types of camellia tree have been harvested and dried for later infusion in boiling water to make what the Japanese and Chinese called *chiaa*. Like coffee it contains caffeine and is a fairly mild stimulant. Green tea is noted for its antioxidants today, and the generally healthful effect may have helped popularize it in East Asia. Though the Japanese developed the famous tea ceremony, they also drank it freely throughout the day. Portuguese and Dutch merchants shipped tea around the Indian Ocean and it arrived in Portugal about 1650. England's queen from 1660 was Catherine of Braganza, a Portuguese princess, who brought the drink to the island, beginning England's long love affair. The Dutchman Cornelis Bontekoe popularized tea with his 1678 *Treatise on the Excellence of the Herb Called Tea*, which earned him the nickname "The Tea Doctor." He suggested many (up to 50!) daily small cups of weak tea, since when strong it "spoiled" the "stomach, the blood and the brains."[34] Otherwise, it was considered a panacea, especially good for treating urinary stones and gravel, fevers, and "almost all defects of the blood." Easy to prepare at home, it eclipsed coffee as a stimulating hot drink of choice in many places. Once European merchants wrestled the plants from Canton, they established tea plantations in Ceylon, India, and Java, which reduced the price to the colonial powers and increased its popularity with the lower classes.[35]

Cocoa or Cacao

The Olmec and Mayan peoples first cultivated the *Theobroma cacao* to use for a variety of medical conditions. Its flowers in a bath battled fatigue; the seeds, dried and powdered, helped with digestion, diarrhea, and fever, menstrual issues and conception, as well as the liver. Among the Aztecs it was the beverage of choice, after water, and the conquistadors were welcomed with the stimulating stuff (it does contain caffeine). Europeans, especially the Dutch, originally drank it in its bitter, natural form, but once they discovered what could be accomplished by adding sugar and then milk or cream, hot chocolate took off among women and children.[36]

Sugar

Sugar cane was produced among the Polynesian peoples and highly valued in the Pacific and Indian Ocean regions for its sweetening properties. Muslim traders circulated sugar north into the Mediterranean, where Muslims and Christians valued it as an ingredient in medicinal syrups, juleps, and electuaries: its sweetness masked the often bitter or otherwise unpleasant tastes of simples and compounds, and it dissolved readily in water and alcohol. In the fifteenth century Spanish sugar plantations appeared in the Canary Islands, and Columbus, who stopped there on his second voyage, carried specimens to Santo Domingo in the Caribbean, where planters established the earliest refinery in 1515. Antwerp became the center of European refining, with

19 factories in 1556. Before the sixteenth century sugar's rarity and close association with medical formulas meant that in Europe it was handled only by apothecaries. But as its availability spread and its price dropped, it replaced honey in many cuisines and came to be considered a food at least as much as a medicine.[37]

Spices

When is cinnamon a spice and when a prophylactic against diabetes? Of course the answer lies in why and how it is used, for it has long been both. The world bordering on the Indian Ocean had had a thriving network of exchange among spice-producing regions and islands long before Muslim ships began supplying the souks and bazaars of Islamic southwest Asia and North Africa. European Christians encountered spices used for flavoring food and as medicines in Spain and Sicily, and while on Crusade. Peppercorns, cinnamon bark, ginger, turmeric, cloves, allspice, saffron, and a literal boatload of other aromatic seeds, barks, stems, roots, and other plant portions sat on apothecary shelves in tightly sealed jars to treat poisonous bites, colic, and poor vision; to prevent epilepsy, digestive problems, and colds; and to promote sweating, urinating, and a sound appetite. The spices that Columbus and others went in search of during the Renaissance were not to make rancid meat taste better but to serve the medicinal needs of those who could afford them, cutting out the Muslim middleman. To shorten supply lines Europeans often tried to establish plants in distant parts of the world, for example growing ginger in Mexico.[38]

Ginseng

The root of the *panax ginseng* was considered by the Chinese to be so powerful a panacea that only the emperor was supposed to have access to it. During the early modern period, ginseng was one of only two plants to have its own book written (the other was mugwort, used in the important Chinese practice of moxibustion). By the sixteenth century it circulated in East Asia, with finer qualities being grown in Manchuria and Korea. A Canadian version of ginseng was discovered in 1715 and exported to Europe and even China at a huge profit. Alvaro de Semedo in 1655 was the first European to mention the plant, calling it "the panacea, and the remedy that dispenses immortality."[39] The Chinese prized it especially as an inducer of "heat," a purifier of blood, a fortifier of the stomach, and an exciter of the pulse. English doctors found it humorally cooling, restoring the appetite and acting against fevers.[40]

Guaicum

Many early modern Europeans believed that God always provided a remedy in the region where a particular illness was found. When syphilis was first observed in southwestern Europe in the 1490s, it was thought to have been imported from the New World. While many American medicinal imports were tried, including the sudorifics sarsaparilla and sassafras, the resin of the guaiac tree proved to have value. It may have appeared as early as 1508 in Spain and 1517 in Italy. After mocking other attempts, the German author and knight Ulrich von Hutten, himself a sufferer, first mentioned the remedy in 1519, and the Fugger banking family of Augsburg quickly wrestled a monopoly from the cash-strapped Charles, emperor and king of Spain. The guaiacum was decocted and drunk to excite copious sweating, which was believed to cleanse the body of the syphilitic poison. Known as Holy Wood among Catholics and lignum vitae (wood of life) elsewhere, its only real competition was the rather hideous chemical treatment with mercury. From the 1520s demand for the wood was huge, with a single Roman hospital in a single purchase acquiring 7,287 pounds of the stuff. As household recipe books and herbals show, it remained popular throughout our period for both the pox and other maladies requiring profuse perspiration.[41]

Cinchona or Quinine

Cinchona trees (*kina-kina* to the Peruvians) grew in the Andean highlands and their bark had long been used by locals as a drug against fevers. Jesuit missionaries are thought to have linked its healing properties to malaria, and the Peruvian bark, Jesuit bark, or Jesuit powder arrived in Europe in 1630s. It worked by killing parasites in the blood and reducing fever (except with *vivax*). Its popularity—despite its terribly bitter flavor—led to attempts to transplant it but to no avail. In Europe, apothecaries tended to cut the bark powder with sugar and other substances, reducing its effectiveness. China's introduction seems to have been via Jesuit missionaries who treated the Emperor K'ang Hsi for malaria in 1693. It remained essentially a Spanish monopoly throughout the period, with Colombia alone shipping out 500 tons in 1794.[42]

Theriac/Treacle

Galen wrote of theriac, and his Muslim and Christian successors venerated the complex drug. Both taken orally and used as an ointment, theriac was originally believed to counteract poison. With time, its powers expanded to those of a panacea. By the sixteenth century Venice produced the best theriac in Europe. Consisting of 70 or 80 ingredients, including viper's flesh, snake venom, and opium, apothecaries prepared it once a year in an open, festival setting, before storing it away in tightly sealed jars to develop its magic. Such a drug was, of course, quite expensive, and in the Ottoman Empire was restricted to elites. It was a standard remedy and prophylactic in European plague manuals and in household medical books down to the eighteenth century. In England it was known as treacle, but after 1700 treacle became synonymous with molasses.[43]

Patent Medicines

Medical entrepreneurs who peddled their pills, potions, salves, and creams were found throughout Europe. One of the earliest German producers of a popular proprietary drug was Dr. Caspar Kegler in early sixteenth-century Leipzig. An alchemist, physician, entrepreneur, and author of popular vernacular works on the plague, he advertised with printed pamphlets and peddled his electuary widely north of the Alps. A generation later, the Italian Leonardo Fioravanti was likewise selling his own medicines directly to consumers.[44] The English, with a wide self-help streak and relatively few doctors, had developed a ready market by 1650. Apothecaries, bookstores, printers' shops, taverns, and coffee shops offered variously labeled remedies, such as Dr. Lockyer's Pills and Daffy's Elixir Salutis. Lockyer's advertising pamphlets from the 1660s listed 174 different distributors in and around London. English law recognized property rights in inventions (patents), and apothecaries, quacks, and empirics began using the laws to protect their medicinal compounds and their names. The earliest was Anderson's Scots Pills, granted royal letters patent in 1687. The earliest patented compound was Timothy Byfield's 1711 "sal oleosum volatile." Unlike most apothecaries' compounds, these carried distinctive names, brand names, really, that competitors were not allowed to copy: Epsom Salts (1695), Dr. Stoughton's Elixir Magnum Stomachicum (1712), or Turlington's Balsam of Life (1744). Many contained opium, relaxing the user, and most were purgatives that induced sweating, vomiting, or defecating, clear signs to the user that the drugs were working. Daffy's Elixir was the first to be shipped to New England, where it was advertised in newspapers and found a ready market among the colonists. Ships' surgeons, physicians, merchants, hypochondriacs, and a multitude of other Englishmen and women carried these products throughout the world, a world that was rapidly shrinking.[45]

NOTES

1. For recent studies see Londa Schiebinger and Claudia Swan, eds., *Colonial Botany: Science, Commerce, and Politics in the Early Modern World* (Philadelphia: University of Pennsylvania Press, 2005).

2. On materia medica in history see Stuart Anderson, *Making Medicines: A Brief History of Pharmacy and Pharmaceuticals* (London: Pharmaceutical Press, 2005).

3. For example see Cyril Elgood, *Safavid Medical Practice: The Practice of Medicine, Surgery, and Gynecology in Persia between 1500 and 1750* (London: Luzac, 1970), 16, 17.

4. For an edition of De la Cruz's herbal see William Gates, *An Aztec Herbal: The Classic Codex of 1552* (Mineola, NY: Dover, 1939/2000).

5. Oliver Ransford, *Bid the Sickness Cease: Disease in the History of Black Africa* (London: John Murray, 1983); and Robert Voeks, "African Medicine and Magic," *Geographical Reviews* 83 (1993): 66–79.

6. Mark Harrison, *Medicine in an Age of Commerce and Empire: Britain and Its Tropical Colonies, 1660–1830* (New York: Oxford University Press, 2010); Richard Sheridan, *Doctors and Slaves: A Medical and Demographic History of Slavery in the British West Indies, 1680–1834* (New York: Cambridge University Press, 1985); Karol K. Weaver, *Medical Revolutionaries: The Enslaved Healers of Eighteenth-Century Saint Domingue* (Chicago: University of Illinois Press, 2006); and James H. Sweet, *Domingos Álvares, African Healing, and the Intellectual History of the Atlantic World* (Chapel Hill: University of North Carolina Press, 2011).

7. Paul U. Unschuld, *Medicine in China: A History of Pharmaceutics* (Berkeley: University of California Press, 1986), 13.

8. Ibid., 140–47; for an English edition of the *Materia Medica* see Li Shih-chen, *Chinese Medical Herbs: A Modern Edition of a Classic Sixteenth-Century Manual* (Mineola, NY: Dover, 1973).

9. For the English translation see Paul U. Unschuld, *Forgotten Traditions of Ancient Chinese Medicine: The I-hsüeh Yüan Liu Lun of 1757by Hsü Ta-ch'un* (Brookline, MA: Paradigm, 1998).

10. Much of *Forgotten Traditions* is taken up with prescriptions; see Unschuld, *Forgotten Traditions*, 19–23, 146–224.

11. On the European pharmacopeias see Linda L. Barnes, *Needles, Herbs, Gods, and Ghosts: China, Healing, and the West to 1848* (Cambridge, MA: Harvard University Press, 2005). Early modern Chinese pharmaceuticals are also discussed in Volker Scheid, *Currents of Tradition in Chinese Medicine, 1626–2006* (Seattle, WA: Eastland Press, 2007).

12. See John Riddle, *Dioscorides on Pharmacy and Medicine* (Austin: University of Texas Press, 1985).

13. Peter E. Pormann and Emilie Savage-Smith, *Medieval Islamic Medicine* (Washington, DC: Georgetown University Press, 2007), 53.

14. Liana Saif, "The Arabic Theory of Astral Influence in Early Modern Medicine," *Renaissance Studies* 25 (2011): 609–26.

15. Pormann and Savage-Smith, *Medieval Islamic Medicine*, 162, 171. On the Ottomans and Safavids see Miri Shefer-Mossensohn, *Ottoman Medicine: Healing and Medical Institutions, 1500–1700* (Binghamton: State University of New York Press, 2009), 34–45; and Elgood, *Safavid Medicine*. For pre-Ottoman (to 1517) Egypt see Leigh Chipman, *The World of Pharmacy and Pharmacists in Mamluk Cairo* (Boston: Brill, 2010).

16. On the later medieval medical spice trade see Paul Freedman, *Out of the East: Spices and the Medieval Imagination* (New Haven, CT: Yale University Press, 2008), 50–75.

17. On alchemy and medicine see Bruce T. Moran, *Distilling Knowledge: Alchemy, Chemistry, and the Scientific Revolution* (Cambridge, MA: Harvard University Press, 2005); on Paracelsus see Charles Webster, *Paracelsus: Medicine, Magic, and Mission at the End of Time* (New Haven, CT: Yale University Press, 2008).

18. Among many see Anderson, *Making Medicines*; Richard Palmer, "Pharmacy in the Republic of Venice in the Sixteenth Century," in *The Medical Renaissance of the Sixteenth Century*, ed. Andrew Wear, R. K. French, and I. M. Lonie (New York: Cambridge University Press, 1985), 100–117.

19. On charlatans and mountebanks see for example David Gentilcore, *Medical Charlatanism in Early Modern Italy* (Oxford: Oxford University Press, 2006).

20. Sharon Strocchia, "The Nun Apothecaries of Renaissance Florence: Marketing Medicines in the Convent," *Renaissance Studies* 25 (2011): 627–47.

21. On the Dutch search for exotic materia medica in the seventeenth century see Harold J. Cook, *Matters of Exchange: Commerce, Medicine, and Science in the Dutch Golden Age* (New Haven, CT: Yale University Press, 2007).

22. On Bourgeois see Wendy Perkins, *Midwifery and Medicine in Early Modern France: Louise Bourgeois* (Exeter, UK: University of Exeter Press, 1996); for a later "kitchen book" authored by a woman see Vincent DiMarco, *It Has Helped to Admiration: Eighteenth-Century Medical Cures from the Kitchen Book of Bridget Lane, 1737* (Bloomington, IN: iUniverse, 2010).

23. See Rebecca Laroche, *Medical Authority and Englishwomen's Herbal Texts, 1550–1650* (Burlington, VT: Ashgate, 2009).

24. On medicinal uses of tobacco see Sander Gilman and Zhou Xun, *Smoke: A Global History of Smoking* (London: Reaktion Books, 2004); Anne Charlton, "Medical Uses of Tobacco in History," *Journal of the Royal Society of Medicine* 97 (2004): 292–96.

25. Colin R. Shearing, *Opium: A Journey through Time* (London: Mercury Books, 2004), 15.

26. Timothy Brook, *Vermeer's Hat: The Seventeenth Century and the Dawn of the Global World* (London: Bloomsbury Press, 2008); and Frank Dikötter, Lars

Laamann, and Zhou Xun, *Narcotic Culture: A History of Drugs in China* (Chicago: University of Chicago Press, 2004); Shefer-Mossensohn, *Ottoman Medicine*, 39–45; Rudi Matthee, *The Pursuit of Pleasure: Drugs and Stimulants in Iranian History, 1500–1900* (Princeton, NJ: Princeton University Press, 2005), 97–116; Elgood, *Safavid Medicine*, 44–46.

27. Thomas Dormandy, *The Worst of Evils: The Fight against Pain* (New Haven, CT: Yale University Press, 2006), 130–32.

28. See Zheng Yangwen, *The Social Life of Opium in China* (New York: Cambridge University Press, 2005).

29. For example, Shefer-Mossensohn, *Ottoman Medicine*, 90–92; Elgood, *Safavid Medicine*, 39–41.

30. Iain Gately, *Drink: A Cultural History of Alcohol* (New York: Gotham Books, 2009), 91–94.

31. See Moran, *Distilling Knowledge*.

32. Matthee, *Pursuit*, 144–74; Shefer-Mossensohn, *Ottoman Medicine*, 87; Elgood, *Safavid Medicine*, 41–44.

33. See Markman Ellis, *The Coffee House: A Cultural History* (London: Orion, 2005); quote from David Brandon, *Life in a 17th Century Coffee Shop* (Stroud, UK: Sutton, 2007), 20.

34. H. J. Cook, *Matters*, 293–97.

35. Matthee, *Pursuit of Pleasure*, 237–45; Li Shih-chen, *Chinese Medical Herbs*, 81–87.

36. Bernard R. Ortiz de Montellano, *Aztec Medicine, Health, and Nutrition* (New Brunswick, NJ: Rutgers University Press, 1990), 141; Gordon Schendel, *Medicine in Mexico From Aztec Herbs to Betatrons* (Austin: University of Texas Press, 1968), 116–19; see also Sophie Coe and Michael Coe, *The True History of Chocolate* (New York: Thames and Hudson, 1996).

37. On the market in sugar see Freedman, *Out of the East*; and H. J. Cook, *Matters*.

38. Freedman, *Out of the East*, 50–76; Shefer-Mossensohn, *Ottoman Medicine*, 32–39; H. J. Cook, *Matters*; Barnes, *Needles*; and see Li Shih-chen, *Chinese Medical Herbs*.

39. Barnes, *Needles*, 104

40. Li Shih-chen, *Chinese Medical Herbs*, 301–4; Unschuld, *Forgotten Traditions*, 179–81; Barnes, *Needles*, 100–106, 173–179, 275–279.

41. Jon Arrizabalaga, John Henderson, and Roger French, *The Great Pox: The French Disease in Renaissance Europe* (New Haven, CT: Yale University Press, 1997); Valeria Finucci, " 'There's the Rub': Searching for Sexual Remedies in the New World," *Journal of Medieval and Early Modern Studies* 38 (2008): 523–57.

42. Fiammetta Rocco, *Quinine, Malaria and the Quest for a Cure That Changed the World* (New York: HarperCollins, 2003); Li Shih-chen, *Chinese Medical Herbs*, 107. See also Saria Shah, *The Fever: How Malaria Has Ruled Mankind for 500,000 Years* (New York: Farrar, Straus, Giroux, 2010); James L. A. Webb Jr., *Humanity's Burden: A Global History of Malaria* (New York: Cambridge University Press, 2009).

43. For examples see Christiane Nockels Fabbri, "Treating Medieval Plague: The Wonderful Virtues of Theriac," *Early Science and Medicine* 12 (2007): 247–83; J. P. Griffin, "Venetian Treacle and the Foundation of Medicine's Regulation," *British Journal of Clinical Pharmacology* 58 (2004): 317–25; Elgood, *Safavid Medicine*, 46–48.

44. Erik Anton Heinrichs, "The Plague Cures of Caspar Kegler: Print, Alchemy, and Medical Marketing in Sixteenth-Century Germany," *Sixteenth Century Journal* 43 (2012): 417–40.

45. There is a large body of work on patent medicines and their market; see for example Patrick Wallis, "Consumption, Retailing, and Medicine in Early Modern London," *Economic History Review* 61 (2008): 26–53; Roy Porter, *Quacks: Fakers and Charlatans in Medicine* (Stroud, UK: Tempus, 2001; especially chaps. 2 and 4); David Boyd Haydock and Patrick Wallis, *Quackery and Commerce in Seventeenth-Century London: The Proprietary Medicine Business of Anthony Daffy* (London: Wellcome Trust, 2005); Peter Issac, "Pills and Print," in *Medicine, Morality and the Book Trade*, ed. Robin Myers and Michael Harris (New Castle, DE: Oak Knoll Press, 1998), 25–48 ; and moving beyond England, Andreas-Holger Maehle, *Drugs on Trial: Experimental Pharmacology and Therapeutic Innovation in the Eighteenth Century* (Atlanta, GA: Rodopi, 1999).

CHAPTER 11

War, Health, and Medicine

The early modern world was marked by nearly constant warfare. European kingdoms fought to consolidate their political boundaries, impose dynasties, or expand territories; religious groups battled each other for the sake of Truth; colonial powers waged war with natives and each other over islands, territories, and wealth. Even while Europeans perched nearby like vultures, different factions of Aztecs, Incas, Indians, and African warlords fought among each other. For example, in the 1720s and 1730s Agaja of Dahomey, Africa, carried out a brutal expansion of his kingdom with a ferocity compared to that of Genghis Khan. Smallpox swept his armies, refugees spread diseases, and the conquered were enslaved locally or sold into European slavery.[1] Revolts, revolutions, and rebellions tore states apart, some leading to the birth of new ones, from the Netherlands to the United States and Haiti.

During the same period and led by Europeans, warfare underwent its own revolution. Firearms and artillery consolidated their roles on the battlefield, ultimately replacing the pike and sword. This required a new form of discipline as ranks of men had to line up shoulder to shoulder to load, fire, and mow each other down on command, and then to withstand the same fire from the other side. This took training, drilling, and professional commitments not seen since the Roman Empire. Armies grew in size as royal budgets did, making the killing

Figure 11.1 A German military surgeon removes an arrow in a woodcut from the 1528 edition of Hans von Gersdorff's *Feldtbüch der Wundtartzney* (*Fieldbook of the Treatment of Wounds*). (National Library of Medicine)

fields ever larger and more crowded. The Muslim states of Mughal India, and the Safavid and Ottoman Empires became known as the "gunpowder states" because of their adoption of the new weapons. Huge Ottoman cannon had made the conquest of Constantinople possible in 1453. The Turks then rapidly swept through the Near East and Egypt, defeating the less innovative Mamluks who refused to use guns. The technology spread as Asians adopted European tools and methods of warfare; European slavers armed African warlords at the rate of four to six guns per slave; and English colonists in North America traded guns and ammunition with the Indians.

The simple act of building larger and larger national or imperial armies with men from different regions allowed the era's infectious diseases unique opportunities to spread among those with lowered resistance or no immunity. During European wars civilians in theaters of war were dragged in as companies of soldiers milled about awaiting their next call to action. But camp life was no picnic, and even between battles soldiers faced many medical dangers from plague to depression. On the march, soldiers lived with the hapless civilians, and their wounded were left with the nearest community, friend or foe. Lacking the discipline of the battlefield, they often took what they pleased and otherwise brutalized the defenseless populace, inevitably exchanging diseases along the way. Growing cities with improved defenses were besieged for months; swollen with residents, defending soldiers, and refugees and cursed by famine, they became hotbeds for physical suffering of every kind.

At sea, ships became ever-larger platforms for artillery, ready to bombard coasts and port cities as well as one another with devastating fury. Global colonial and trade empires required sailors to serve for months at sea with horrible food and tainted water, as well as limited facilities for recovery when one fell ill, injured, or wounded. Colonial conflicts often pitted men-of-war against canoes and professional soldiers against stone-age warriors in asymmetrical confrontations, usually resulting in massacres.

By the eighteenth century, political and military leaders came to appreciate the investment they had in each trained soldier. Advanced states such as France and Britain provided unprecedented resources for preserving the soldiers' and sailors' health before and after battle. Surgeons and health officers, field hospitals, and veterans' hospitals appeared in greater numbers to hasten the sick and wounded back onto active-duty lists. They also came to realize the toll that tropical warfare in the Caribbean took, as whole armies melted away from epidemics of imported yellow fever and malaria. Indeed, in every early modern army disease always took a far greater toll than all the bullets and cannonballs combined. In the long run, military concerns led to important advances in disease control, though before 1800 this was limited to some surgical advances, widespread inoculation for smallpox, and the defeat of scurvy.[2]

THE AZTEC WAY OF WAR

Aztec society was built on a warrior ethic like those of Homer's heroes, the Japanese Samurai, or Europe's medieval knights. They had

Figure 11.2 Late 16th-century illustration of the Battle of Azcapotzalo, from the second section of the Tovar (or Ramírez) Codex, attributed to the Mexican Jesuit Juan de Tovar. Soldiers fight with war clubs and shields; at left is a jaguar warrior, one of the elite soldiers of the Aztec, with the glyph of a flowering cactus above him. At right an infant is being sacrificed by a priest at a temple while two victims lie dead on the ground. (Library of Congress)

established their hegemony by battle and maintained it the same way. Every free male was trained to fight from childhood, with the best forming the elite Jaguar and Eagle units. Negotiations preceded formal conflicts, so a pitched battle was something of a last resort. On both sides men were protected by flimsy hats and padded body armor, and round wooden shields. A battle opened with ritual noise making and the hurling of javelins, arrows, and other missiles. The two sides closed and men fought with flaked obsidian-edged wooden swords, jabbing spears, and obsidian knives. Since obsidian can be flaked to a greater than razor sharpness, the knives and slashing swords could cause deep cuts where blows were landed. Arrows were often tipped with obsidian, increasing their ability to penetrate the light armor and skin. The skillfully handled spear could also pierce deeply into the victim's body, severing blood vessels, disrupting organs, and causing sepsis if not immediate death.

But the true mark of the warrior was his ability to stun and capture his opponent alive. For this purpose warriors, especially the Jaguars and Eagles, wielded clubs. A vigorous attack could break bones and cause deep bruising, and the flimsy headgear provided little protection for the main target. Once incapacitated, the loser was pulled off the field by lower-level combatants as prisoners. The "flowery war" may seem humanitarian, except that the captives were subsequently sacrificed to the victors' god of war (Uitzilopochtli in the case of the city of Tenochtitlán). Well treated until the appropriate time, the drugged victims had their still-beating hearts removed with a surgical precision made possible by a highly skilled technician and an obsidian blade. The ultimate defeat of a rival city occurred when the victorious warriors invaded and destroyed the temple of its clearly inferior god of war.[3]

The Aztec ruler had a general duty to provide for the welfare of his people, and a special obligation to his fallen warriors. The wounded received treatment from shamans and healers who accompanied the army in the field. These latter could stanch bleeding wounds, splint broken bones, and apply herbal poultices. Those who were disabled by their wounds were provided light tasks with which to earn their keep. The Aztec state also provided veterans hospitals in the major cities of Tenochtitlán, Texcoco, Cholula, and Colhuacán.

The harming or enslavement of enemy noncombatants was taboo, and likewise the destruction of crops or other property. War was a highly ritualized activity, restrained by mutual understanding and acceptance of the rules. When Hernán Cortés and his 500 Spaniards, 14 cannon, and 16 horses went to war with Tenochtitlán in 1521, they allied themselves with the Tlaxcalans, resentful enemies of Moctezuma II and his Aztec warrior elite. But the Europeans also brought steel, horses, guns, and no respect for—or perhaps understanding—of Aztec warfare. The intention was not to defeat the Aztec god or gain captives for sacrifice but to terrorize, subjugate, and destroy. Men, women, children, old and young fell to the invaders' superior weapons and few were left to tend the wounded. The conquistadors' victory was made all the easier by the destruction of much of the populace by the diseases brought from Europe. Between June and August it was said that half the city died of smallpox, measles, and other scourges to which the natives had no immunity and little resistance. Thus arrived the European way of war.[4]

EUROPEANS AT WAR

During the Seven Years' War (1756–63), the kingdom of Prussia conscripted approximately 25 percent of its young men of military age.

Perhaps 180,000 men died while in service. Of those who were in uniform at the war's opening, only 1 of every 15 survived to its end.[5]

The Early Modern Army

Size of Armies

In 1494 Charles VIII of France, invaded Italy and the peninsula cowered in fear before his 18,000 men and 40 cannon. Early modern rulers bankrolled their armies and navies, and with the increasing reliance on firearms and cannon as well as the swelling size of field armies, the cost was huge. In the 1650s the English Commonwealth spent 90 percent of its budget on its naval war with the Dutch. Around 1700 Louis XIV of France wasted 75 percent of his royal revenues on seemingly endless wars, the upstart Peter the Great of Russia nearly 85 percent, and Frederick the Great of Prussia 90 percent.[6]

In 1632 Swedish King Gustavus Adolphus commanded an army of 183,000 men in Germany, and his was only one among several large armies in the field. By century's end Louis XIV's armed forces amounted to some 400,000 troops, and by 1710 Europe was filled with an estimated 1.3 million soldiers. Unlike the annual feudal levies of the Middle Ages, these were men whose lives were dedicated to serve continuously under military discipline. At any one time, however, the majority of European fighting men was in port or garrisoning fortresses or cities, and relatively few were on active campaign. In 1812 Napoleon invaded Russia along a 400-kilometer front with some 600,000 men and 1,500 cannon. In less than a year, an estimated 570,000, or 95 percent, died of wounds, disease, and environmental conditions.

Military Life

When Bernardino Ramazzini wrote his famed work on occupational health and safety in 1700, he included a chapter on the soldier's life. "One cannot imagine a more deplorable kind of existence than a soldier's," he wrote. They suffered from diseases shared in the crowded camps; "unwholesome food and impure water"; "lack of sleep, excessive toil, rain, heat, cold, and sudden alarms"; as well as "filth and neglect of personal cleanliness."[7] Of course he was far from the first to criticize camp life, but his analysis went deeper than previous observers'. He supported the era's acceptance of miasma, or poisoned air, as a major factor in diseases. Armies camped for too long in one place and human waste, corpses, and other "corruption" accumulated and tainted the air, causing fevers and other disease. To this simple fact he attributed headaches, delirium, convulsions, and diarrhea. The bad air, he believed, infected wounds, and the heat of late summers made all of this worse.

But Ramazzini also took into account the toll of military service on the human psyche. Having lived briefly among German soldiers in Italy, he noted that they often suffered from what they called *Heimweh* or "homesickness." He quoted their proverb, "Who seeks their Fatherland finds death." Not that homesickness itself kills, but it can become very depressive and distracting and lead to the kind of mistakes that endanger one's life. It can also lead to alcoholism or suicide. Of course the soldier also lives with the constant threat of violent death. Ramazzini records that his informants related how men might get a sense of imminent death: "They would foretell that they would die in the battle that followed," even making their farewells and giving their possessions away to their fellows.

Of course, Ramazzini only scratched the surface. The sex lives of soldiers spread venereal diseases; abuse of alcohol, tobacco, or opiates weakened men's stamina; and new recruits brought with them their own communicable diseases. Diets not only consisted of poor-quality food but often lacked important elements such as vitamins that are necessary for decent health. Careless garbage disposal and food storage invited rats that carried plague fleas. Arguments turned violent cost lives, as did dueling and corporal punishment for infractions of disciplinary rules.

One hero in the battle against senseless military deaths was the eighteenth-century Englishman John Pringle. As physician-general of the British army from 1742 to 1758, he published his *Observations on the Diseases of the Army* (1752). He and his book advocated a wide range of reforms in military living conditions, from frequent bathing to regular and vigorous exercise, and maintenance of environmental sanitation to avoidance of overcrowding.[8]

Weapons and Wounds

On the battlefields of Europe and around the world, men were subjected to an increasingly dangerous set of conditions. Crossbows were fading out as fired projectiles took their place. Older weapons, eventually carried by officers, included swords that stabbed and slashed, and pole weapons including pikes and halberds that stabbed, slashed, and crushed. The lacerations resulting from the stabbing and slashing were created only with the strength of the human arm and were fairly clear: in and out or across. These, of course, could penetrate vital organs, cause the contents of bowels or stomach to flow into the body cavities and create sepsis, spawn internal hemorrhaging or external bleeding, break bones, or sever tendons and muscles. As long as armies were relatively small, the fallen wounded covered a small area and would often be found and treated rather easily and quickly. Of course, the fewer men fighting the fewer wounded. Wounds could be sutured (sewn) or tourniquets applied; red-hot implements could be used to cauterize wounds; simple fractures could often be splinted. When fighting in the Americas or Asia, Europeans suffered other kinds of wounds, including those caused by war clubs, spears, and arrows. A curious but ineffective treatment for wounds was made popular by a seventeenth-century Paracelsian: weapon salve. One created the salve and applied it to the wounded person's blood left on the wounding weapon. Sympathetic action at a distance was supposed to make the wound heal. (It of course begs the question how one obtains the offending weapon.) Prominent physician J.-B. van Helmont thought it reasonable, though a Jesuit called it the "devil's deceit."

Beside the huge expansion in the size of armies, the so-called military revolution made gunpowder weapons at first rare, then common, then mandated. Both artillery and handheld firearms used the controlled chemical explosion of gunpowder to propel more or less spherical projectiles in the general direction of the enemy. After observing the power of massed Swiss and Spanish pikemen, seventeenth-century European generals began arranging their firearm-wielding troops in long, straight lines, standing as close together as possible. The inaccuracy of the weapons meant that no one could aim at an individual even 50 yards away and hope to hit him. But a hundred men standing close together and firing simultaneously could hurl a hundred lead balls at a similar mass and certainly hit something. Of course, the closely packed men were just as fine a target as they stood and spent precious seconds— as much as a minute—reloading their weapons. Men were placed several rows deep to allow those in the rear to fire after the front rows did. This created a murderous environment as one mass faced the other and fired away.

Archers could fire much more accurately and with little time between shots, but arrows were relatively clean weapons that penetrated and caused relatively little tissue damage. What Europeans discovered was that once the fired ball entered the body, it could create all kinds of havoc. It moved rather slowly and often lodged in the body. Being made of soft lead, it could change shape upon impact. It could ricochet off of bones, splintering them and scattering sharp fragments. It could tear up major organs and break bones. Dead tissue becomes fodder for bacteria, resulting in serious and continuing infections, tetanus, gas gangrene, and painful death. Compared to arrowheads or sharp weapons, musket balls themselves were relatively sterile, but they did carry bits of filthy, germ-laden uniform into the wound and setting infection. In a volley a man could be hit more than once, compounding the internal damage.

Because of the frequency of infection, doctors perceived that the projectiles were poisonous and the wounds needed to be treated accordingly. Pouring hot oil into the wound or cauterizing it with a hot iron was a typical treatment, especially after 1514 when Giovanni da Vigo came out with his *Compendious Practice of the Art of Surgery*. It was translated across Europe and saw 40 editions. An important figure who challenged this orthodoxy was the French surgeon Ambroise Paré. Over his career he served four French kings on 17 military campaigns in the mid-sixteenth century. At the siege of Turin in 1537, he ran out of boiling oil and replaced it with a mixture of turpentine, egg yolks, and rose oil. This far gentler approach worked much better and revolutionized gunshot treatment through its inclusion in his *Method of Treating Gunshot Wounds* of 1545. Paré pioneered numerous means of increasing battlefield victims' survival rates. He created new medical instruments; he used sour wine as a form of antiseptic; he performed amputation on the battlefield before infection set in and ligatured blood vessels afterward; and he created workable prosthetic devices for amputees.[9]

One of the major sources of leg wounds requiring amputation was the cannonball. This was usually a solid sphere of iron varying in size with the diameter of the cannon's barrel. Obviously, these did not explode but rather acted like low-flying, or even rolling, bowling balls, tearing through the massed infantry ranks, hitting not one man but potentially many before coming to a stop. These were also used against fortifications, making venerable medieval walls and towers obsolete. When striking masonry they sent an explosion of brick, stone, and mortar fragments that could lacerate and blind. Other types of ordnance were also developed, including several types of antipersonnel shrapnel designed to hurl a wave of small, metal projectiles at infantry at close range, and at sea chains that were fired into the enemy's rigging to shred sails and mangle masts. Early cannon suffered from poor metallurgy, poorly formulated or stored powder, ill-fitting projectiles, and a general lack of standardization among guns in a given unit. Over time industry provided weapons and ammunition that were more reliable, more accurate, more mobile, standardized into predictable and interchangeable sizes, and overall more deadly.

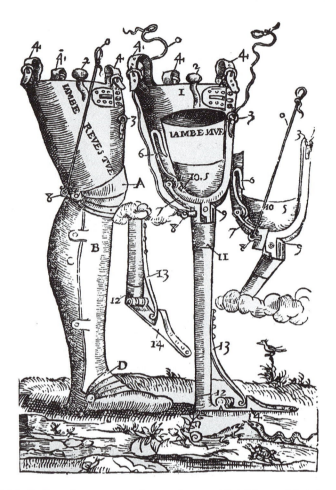

Figure 11.3 Full and cutaway views of an artificial leg with joints at the knee and ankle, invented by the French military surgeon Ambroise Paré; from a 1575 edition of his works. (National Library of Medicine)

Finally, this new battlefield paradigm meant many burns of different types. Poorly cast cannon overheated or even exploded; powder could be very unstable and either not work or do so unpredictably; gunners made errors in pouring powder into hot barrels and causing premature flashes; firing mechanisms misfired, especially a problem with early matchlock firearms that had to be lit with a burning fuse-like match. Faces, hands, and fingers were the most common victims. Deep burns could fester and become infected and even small explosions could blind and deafen. For such burns Paré suggested a folk remedy of salt and crushed onions.

War and Disease

In the midst of the Enlightenment, in the 1750s and 1760s during the Seven Years' War, European armies in Europe, Asia, and North America lost 88 men to death by disease for every 1 man who died of battle wounds.

Camp Diseases

As we have seen, camp life could hold many dangers, but the most immediate was disease. Thousands of men living densely together, in far from sanitary and hygienic conditions, eating and drinking whatever came their way: this was the perfect milieu for many diseases. Dysentery was caused by protozoa or bacteria consumed in tainted drinking water. Once passed out of the body in feces or urine, where there are poor hygiene and sanitation the cycle continues. While it might not kill one directly, it did dehydrate the victim and weaken his immune responses, making it easier for him to catch other illnesses. Very similar in spread was the bacterial disease typhoid fever, an intestinal disease that could reach epidemic levels if general food or water supplies were affected.

Typhus was caused by a bacterial organism that is carried by human body lice. These thrived where clothing was heavy and rarely laundered, and the body rarely bathed. Flu-like chills, fever, and nausea usually did not lead to prostration and death, but they can and did. Typhus's first appearance in history was among the Spanish besieging Granada, Spain, in 1489–90. Seventeen thousand died in their camps. Only a few years later perhaps 30,000 French soldiers succumbed during their siege of Spanish-held Naples. Mosquitoes carried and spread malaria, and local epidemics were known as far north as England. Since mosquitoes fed on humans, they simply passed the protozoa from infected carrier to new victim. Since the insects preferred marshy environments, it is not surprising to find outbreaks in low-lying ground where troops had landed or besieged port cities.

Overcrowding in camps allowed tuberculosis, scarlet fever, influenza, and measles to spread quickly among the nonimmune members of the army. Since the medical cultures of the day had no knowledge of the diseases' causes, means of spreading, and ways to control them, army officials had no medical reason for taking the steps that would have made military service much safer.

The Spread of Disease Due to War

The spread of disease due to war did not require that an army on the move be diseased from the beginning. As the men marched and countermarched across the countryside, they interacted with populations that harbored unfamiliar diseases—especially true outside of Europe—and like a saturated and dripping sponge developed the diseases themselves and spread them in their wake. Armies and local populations exchanged all manner of diseases, from plague to venereal diseases. Wounded soldiers were routinely left to suffer with local villagers or towns; stragglers and deserters could carry disease far and wide, as could refugees fleeing from approaching troops. Poor locals often stripped clothing from fallen soldiers, providing fresh meals for hungry lice, and troops often stole bedding and spare clothing from unlucky and disease-ridden villagers.

Men also passed through civilian populations as they gathered for war before an offensive or to defend the frontiers of a state. Fortified towns and cities were strongholds in which soldiers lived alongside residents, sharing food, water, insects, and even beds. After a loss or unsuccessful campaign, deserters multiplied and scattered across the countryside, living off of whatever came their way. Weakened by hunger, fatigue, and the shock of battle, with nothing in the way of medical aid or other resources, they were easy targets for many diseases even hundreds of miles from their camps.

War in the Tropics

European colonialism came at a tremendous military cost. Ever-larger ships whose sides were lined with an ever-larger number of cannon and manned by ever-larger skilled crews (650–950 men per ship of the line in the later eighteenth century) transported tens of thousands of infantry across rough seas to disease-ridden ports whose climates were like sauna baths. The British, French, and Spanish, and to a lesser extent the Dutch and Portuguese, wrestled for control of small islands in the Caribbean Sea and Indian Ocean with both elements of their national armies and battalions of mercenaries who worked for commercial organizations such as the Dutch East India Company and the English East India Company.[10] They fought with each other, with the natives, and with local competitors for bases, influence, and control of resources. Far more costly than any pitched battles or duels at sea were the losses due to tropical diseases, including yellow fever and malaria, and environmental illnesses such as heat stroke.

For example, in 1741 the British sent a force of 22,000 troops to seize Cartagena (Colombia); it was the largest known amphibious landing of troops until World War II. Already weakened by bad food shipboard and the other discomforts of the crossing, fully half of the force fell to yellow fever during the unsuccessful three-month campaign. In the same year half of a force sent to capture Santiago, Cuba, fell ill to malaria and yellow fever and the attack was aborted. The British captured Havana, Cuba, in 1762, but disease eliminated about 8,000 of their 15,000-man force. In 1782 the British sent 7,000 troops to Jamaica. As reported by physician John Hunter, soon after landing only 2,000 were fit for duty; fully 25 percent died of disease. During the wars of the French Revolution, the British tried unsuccessfully to seize French holdings in the Caribbean. They won victories on several islands in 1793, but they abandoned them all as disease destroyed their occupying armies. An estimated 80,000 British troops died on Martinique, St. Lucia, and Guadeloupe, with perhaps 50,000 killed on St. Domingue alone. On their part, the French sent 35,000 men, of whom only 6,000 lived to return to France.

Africa would soon become known as the white man's graveyard, and most colonial ventures date from after our period. Europeans did, of course, have slaving colonies along the west coast. Yellow fever was endemic among native populations in many regions, but in what is today Senegal the disease was unknown. When a ship brought slaves carrying the disease into the British fort of St. Louis, the result was what is considered Africa's first yellow fever epidemic, as mortality rates reached 60 percent.

The major problem was what the British called lack of "seasoning." Residents who had lived in tropical regions for some time often acquired immunity from light initial infections of certain diseases, especially yellow fever. When a large influx of "unseasoned" Europeans set up camp, the result was an epidemic and the weakening or destruction of the force. The British had the correct idea in creating 12 West Indian regiments of black soldiers to protect their Caribbean colonies.

Malaria and yellow fever were not alone in crippling colonial armies. Typhus took its toll, as did dysentery and other enteric (bowel) illnesses. These were accompanied by dehydration and fever, which could quickly weaken and kill sufferers. A study of the 1820s and 1830s in the British Caribbean indicated that these cases were second only to yellow and malarial fevers as causes for death, and 20 percent of cases were fatal. Other potentially fatal conditions that were common included venereal diseases, alcohol abuse, lung problems, vitamin deficiencies, skin conditions and abscesses, and wounds of various types. Britain's black soldiers may have been naturally protected from yellow fever and malaria, but they were subject to smallpox, respiratory problems, dysentery and other bowel conditions.[11]

CARE FOR THE WOUNDED AND VETERANS

Care in the Field

We noted above that the Aztec state provided care for those of their warriors who were wounded and disabled in battle. These facilities were the closest things to hospitals that their culture had, since most sick and injured people were treated in their homes. Though Europeans had had hospitals for centuries, they played virtually no role in medieval military health care. This changed during the early modern period. As the seventeenth-century French leader Cardinal Richelieu claimed: "2,000 men leaving hospital cured, and in some sense broken into the profession, are far more valuable than even 6,000 new recruits." A century earlier the English army surgeon Thomas Gale attacked the "cobblers, horse-gelders, and tinkers" who treated soldiers, and established six rules for the military surgeon: he should be paid decently; he should do no harm; he should work quickly lest the wound worsen; he should give a truthful prognosis; he should be aware of the pain he is inflicting; and he should accept no cash from the wounded.[12] Battlefield surgeons appeared first among the Swiss in the sixteenth century, and German armies borrowed the practice. The sixteenth-century Spanish armies quickly created the most responsive field facilities, but few advances followed. By 1600 standardized kits with instruments, bandages, and useful drugs were being issued to medics, and by 1700 barber-surgeons served at the company level. Books helped surgeons prepare for the terrible conditions they would face (but only 34 titles appeared across eighteenth-century Europe), while eighteenth-century France (1731), Saxony (1748), Austria (1784), and Prussia (1795) established military surgical schools.[13]

Hospitals for the Wounded

The Spanish commander the Duke of Alva in 1567 established the earliest recognized military hospital at Mechelen (Malines) in the Netherlands, though it had a rocky start. It was made a permanent facility in 1585 and given a staff of 49 and 330 beds. From 1596 fines on rowdy soldiers supported the hospital. For almost 100 years it was the only such permanent facility in Europe.[14] In 1629 French military authorities required every French fortress to provide an infirmary for the sick and injured, and a surgeon to attend them. The project took 80 years to complete. London provided wounded Englishmen with some 350 dedicated beds in two large hospitals, and from the early seventeenth century counties were expected to care for wounded soldiers, especially during the Civil War.[15]

Britain's naval authority was the Admiralty, and it formed a "Sick and Hurt Board" to see to medical facilities for the ill and injured. From the 1740s permanent hospitals were established in Portsmouth (Haslar) and Plymouth (Stonehouse), England's two busiest naval ports. Here one could get the oversight, care, and discipline lacking in inns or private houses. Staff were prepared to treat every type of condition from depression to serious wounds to venereal disease. A study of Haslar Hospital for 1753–57 indicates that of 14,418 patients, 9,862 were discharged as cured, a rate of 68 percent. The other third died, remained, or were moved to a longer-term care facility.[16]

Care for Veteran Soldiers

Facilities to provide long-term care for invalid veterans were rather later in coming. Since these were not men who were being recycled to the battlefield, there was less of an incentive for authorities to provide medical care or even a residence. Nonetheless, such provision was at least a sign of good faith on the part of governments. When founded in kingdoms they were also a form of royal charity. French king Henry IV built the House of Christian Charity in 1605 to house disabled veterans. Another of the earliest was "Our Lady of Hals," created as a charity for crippled Spanish veterans serving in the Netherlands. In 1640 it housed 346 residents. Nearby the Dutch established the Soldatengasthuis (lit. Soldier Guest House) in Amsterdam, which was set up in the 1640s near the end of the Thirty Years' War. In 1670 Louis XIV established the famous Hôtel des Invalides in Paris, where Napoleon is buried today; and in Dublin the English founded Kilmainham Royal Hospital a decade later. The Royal Hospital at Chelsea appeared in 1682 and that for ex-sailors at Greenwich near London in 1694, both designed by the great architect Christopher Wren. Most disabled veterans in England were cared for in county facilities, with quality of care differing widely across the island.[17]

Historian Geoffrey Hudson studied Greenwich Hospital and noted that these huge facilities were effective controlling the residents and their activities. They wanted their freedom to move about as much as they were able, come and go as they pleased, have sex, fight, use vulgar language, abuse alcohol, and otherwise live as military men did. Since the hospital staff were far more interested in maintaining a disciplined living environment than providing much in the way of medical help, confinement was the rule. This changed over time, however, as the institution became more medicalized, and practitioners replaced shipboard discipline with more therapeutic policies. This included better food and environmental conditions such as ventilation and light.[18]

Both the hospitals for the wounded and veterans' facilities proved to be the perfect places for medical training and for experimentation with untried techniques and drugs such as patent medicines. The military had a stake in quick and inexpensive answers to medical problems. With only a thin veil of ethics, doctors and surgeons could follow the courses of a wide variety of therapies to determine when and how well they worked. On the one hand, many new orthopedic and surgical methods emerged from such experimentation. On the other, eighteenth-century patent medicines saturated with opiates, alcohol, or both were given countless trials. An army or navy contract for providing some proprietary remedy could earn a man a fortune.

WAR WITHIN THE HOUSE OF ISLAM

Despite their nickname, the "gunpowder states" lagged behind Europeans in the adoption and development of firearms. Ottoman heavy artillery, most effective in sieges of walled fortifications, put the Turks ahead of their Safavid and Mughal rivals. But the Ottoman Empire fought on at least two fronts, in the east against India and Persia and in the Balkans and Central Europe against the Holy Roman Empire and its allies. Traditional weapons such as swords, polearms, and arrows continued in use alongside matchlocks and later muskets. Turkish armies were well organized and highly disciplined by comparison with those of European states. Training and punishment were brutal and effective. Camp life was far healthier for the Turks, whose leaders saw that ample food was supplied, provisions made for the sick and wounded, and a standard of sanitation established. Nonetheless, maintaining tens of thousands of men in the confines of an encampment or siege setting invited disease. The rule of thumb was when mustering troops to double the number of men needed to be battle-ready.

Turkish commanders limited campaign stops to 30 to 40 days, even when besieging a city or fortress. Their siege of Safavid Baghdad in 1638 lasted just 39 days. As in Europe, both besiegers and besieged suffered from crowded conditions, deteriorating sanitation, and dwindling supplies. Diseases that included dysentery, dropsy, influenza, and—perhaps most common—typhus (*huma-i muharrika*) took an enormous toll. In 1630 between 8,000 and 9,000 Ottoman soldiers died in battle at Hillah fighting the Safavids. During the previous two-year campaign, disease took an estimated 30,000 lives. When defeat was the order of the day, retreat could mean a trek of hundreds of desert miles with the scourges of wounds, heat, hunger, thirst, and disease. In 1626 an English observer with a retreating Ottoman army noted that in a single day some 12,000 men perished.

Soldiers who suffered serious battle wounds were provided stipends known as "wounded injury money" from imperial coffers; families of dead soldiers received pensions. Among the Turks, battlefield surgeons were at least as common as among early modern European forces, and sultans took pride in staffing mobile medical detachments.[19] Turkish commanders and the sultan himself were aware of European advances in dealing with the wounded, and many innovations were readily adopted. Safavid Persian surgeons also utilized both traditional and newly developed methods of dealing with battle wounds. An arrow was either left in place until pus provided a lubricant for its removal; or it was wiggled back and forth to loosen and remove it; or a special knife was employed to penetrate the wound to where the tip of the arrow was lodged. In the case of poisoned arrows, the surrounding flesh was cut away to halt the progress of the toxin. To remove bullets, during the rule of Shah Abbas (d. 1629) surgeons developed an extractor with a spoon-shaped tip.[20] As always, necessity was the mother of invention.

CONCLUSION

Impressed by the successes of the European way of waging war, the Islamic gunpowder states, the Chinese and Japanese empires, and even North American natives adopted some of its tools and methods. Yet the costs in lives and treasure of creating and maintaining huge and continuously serving armies were enormous. Newer weapons were expensive, complicated, and of questionable reliability but offered much greater killing and maiming power. Yet the calculus of the germ was every early modern army's greatest foe. Military health care developed around the need to recycle the wounded so they could fight and bleed another day.

NOTES

1. See James H. Sweet, *Domingos Álvares, African Healing, and the Intellectual History of the Atlantic World* (Chapel Hill: University of North Carolina Press, 2011).

2. Ole Peter Grell, "War, Medicine and the Military Revolution," in his *The Healing Arts: Health, Disease, and Society in Europe, 1500–1800* (Manchester, UK: Open University Press, 2004), 257–83; on smallpox see Ian Glynn and Jennifer Glynn, *The Life and Death of Smallpox* (New York: Cambridge University Press, 2004); on scurvy see David I. Harvie, *Limeys: The Conquest of Scurvy* (Stroud, UK: Sutton, 2002).

3. Jacques Soustelle, *Daily Life of the Aztecs* (London: Phoenix Press, 1961/2002), 203–15.

4. Gordon Schendel, *Medicine in Mexico: From Aztec Herbs to Betatrons* (Austin: University of Texas Press, 1968), 33.

5. Geoffrey Parker, *The Military Revolution: Military Innovation and the Rise of the West, 1500–1800* (New York: Cambridge University Press, 1989), 148.

6. Ibid., 62, 148.

7. Bernardino Ramazzini, *The Diseases of Workers* (Chicago: University of Chicago Press, 1940), 359–75; quotations on p. 359.

8. Virginia Smith, *Clean: A History of Personal Hygiene and Purity* (New York: Palgrave Macmillan, 2007), 248–50.

9. Harold Ellis, *The Cambridge Illustrated History of Surgery* (New York: Cambridge University Press, 2009), 125; Richard A. Gabriel and Karen Metz, *A History of Military Medicine*, vol. 2, *From the Renaissance through Modern Times* (Westport, CT: Greenwood Press, 1992), 59–60.

10. During the French Revolution the British East India Company controlled a force of between 115,000 and 155,000 mercenaries and sepoys, making it one of the largest armies in the world; Mark Harrison, "Disease and Medicine in the Armies of British India, 1750–1830," in *British Military and Naval Medicine, 1600–1830*, ed. Geoffrey L. Hudson (New York: Rodopi, 2007), 87–120; quotation pp. 87–88.

11. Richard Sheridan, *Doctors and Slaves: A Medical and Demographic History of Slavery in the British West Indies, 1680–1834* (New York: Cambridge University Press, 1985), 13–16.

12. Zachary B. Friedenberg, *Surgery over the Centuries* (London: Janus, 2009), 160.

13. See also John Wright, *A History of War Surgery* (Stroud, UK: Amberley, 2011).

14. Parker, *The Military Revolution*, 185–86, n.94; 72–73.

15. Mark Harrison, *Disease and the Modern World: 1500 to the Present* (Malden, MA: Polity Press, 2004), 66; Eric Gruber von Arni, *Hospital Care and the British Standing Army, 1660–1714* (Burlington, VT: Ashgate, 2006).

16. Harrison, *Disease and the Modern World*, 66; Patricia Crimmin, "British Naval Health, 1700–1800: Improvement over Time?," in Hudson, *British Military*, 183–200.

17. Christine Stevenson, "From Palace to Hut: The Architecture of Military and Naval Medicine," in Hudson, *British Military*, 227–52.

18. Geoffrey Hudson, "Internal Influences in the Making of the English Military Hospital: The Early-Eighteenth-Century Greenwich," in *British Military*, 253–72; see also his "Disabled Veterans and the State in Early Modern England," in *Disabled Veterans in History*, ed. D. A. Gerber (Ann Arbor: University of Michigan Press, 2000), 117–44.

19. Rhoades Murphey, *Ottoman Warfare: 1500–1700* (New Brunswick, NJ: Rutgers University Press, 1999), 130–31.

20. Cyril Elgood, *Safavid Medical Practice* (London: Luzac, 1970), 156–59.

CHAPTER 12

Medical Institutions

For most of human history, most people lived most of their lives within a few miles of where they had been born. The family has always been the primary institution of health care in every known society. As communities developed greater specialization, epidemics of infectious diseases became more common, and individuals traveled and relocated more, societies developed a wider and wider range of health-related authorities and facilities. The bulk of this chapter is taken up with Western institutions, since Western societies developed a very wide range of types and institutions, and transplanted many of these across the globe between 1500 and 1800. In the centuries that followed, most of the rest of the world borrowed and adapted them for themselves. Several important facilities, such as insane asylums and military hospitals, are dealt with in detail in other chapters.

THE CHINESE

Chinese Medical Authorities

China had a highly hierarchical society, with the emperor and his court in Peking (Beijing) at the apex of the pyramid. Though possessed of theoretically unlimited power, China's ancient religious culture mandated that imperial benevolence flow from the top down. Seeing that his people—especially the poor—had adequate provision for their health when needed was an important part of this mandate. For example, state storehouses had long supplied medicinal herbs and other necessities, and state infirmaries tended the acutely ill or injured. Medical education was both a part of and a specialty within the preparation for service in the state bureaus, and there was often a matter of preference as to whether one was a bureaucrat or physician. Medical specialists served to organize medical provision and practice at every level from prefecture to county, and formal medical bureaus dated back to the early fourteenth century. At times of extraordinary need, the state provided special medical bureaus with expanded duties and powers. The Chinese were no strangers to droughts, floods, famines, and epidemics, especially in the 1580s and 1640s. Were special bureaus motivated by benevolence? Perhaps in part, but the overriding factors were control of the people and maintenance of order.

Order was above all the responsibility of the Imperial Medical Bureau (*taiyiju*). Located in the imperial palace, it had responsibility for the health and well-being of the imperial family and household, and for overseeing all of the emperor's benevolence that flowed down to the towns and villages. The bureau was the principle repository and copying center for Chinese medical classics, and the national center for medical education and professional testing (as the Imperial Medical Institute [*taiyi yuan*] from the fifth century CE). It established the official curriculum and canon of recognized medical classics for the nation, and oversaw the provision of medical officers and bureaucrats throughout China.[1]

Chinese Medical Facilities

The multigenerational Chinese family remained the keystone of society, and whenever possible problems of health or illness were confined to its quarters. While Chinese culture provided for the local poor in donation-supported settlements called *yangji yuan*, and for travelers who became sick or injured, the old, infirm, insane, or diseased were their families' responsibility. In addition, since many diseases and conditions were thought to result from angry spiritual forces, there was an important element of avoiding shame or "keeping face" when a family member fell ill. Additionally, the belief in troublesome spirits or demons made Buddhist and Daoist monasteries and shrines natural places of reconciliation and healing. Monks were often very adept not only at spiritual healing but at herbal and manipulative therapies as well. State-supported infirmaries tended the needy as outpatients or by providing limited live-in arrangements, but these did not evolve into hospitals in the Western sense. Benevolence was also an individual's responsibility, and many wealthy Chinese supported charity dispensaries that distributed medicines and had salaried physicians on staff. In short, the Chinese provided a high level of health care for its people, but not by developing the kinds of institutions associated with the West. One exception would be the leper asylum.

Chinese Leper Houses

Hansen's disease, commonly called leprosy, takes a terrible toll on the human body. The bacteria attack the skin and nerves causing physical deformation, especially of the face. As the condition progresses the sufferer will reek from the disease, and is likely to lose bits of his or her body. Though it is only mildly contagious, the fearsomeness and unpleasantness of leprosy, and the belief that the cause was supernatural punishment, led the ancient Chinese to exclude lepers from society, forcing them to beg along the roads.

This policy shifted in the sixteenth century, and leprosy became the only chronic disease for which people were institutionalized in early modern China. In 1518 the first asylum for sufferers of *mafeng* appeared in Fujian Province. Many other *mafeng yuan* followed across Qing China. Local civil authorities established these as a matter of public order, funneling some financial support from the state. Usually these were small, walled villages of huts located well outside cities, yet close enough so that the lepers could beg for their subsistence. Supporting lepers was good charity, so donations provided some relief and may have kept begging lepers out of the public eye. But the *mafeng yuan* was not a religious establishment, and trustees of the asylum rather than monks or others kept order and tended the suffering. It was rather a place of isolation where the incurable went to die. Though there was no set imperial policy or central direction, the 1724 imperial edict to provide official communal facilities for the poor and the acutely insane included leper asylums.[2]

THE ISLAMIC WORLD

The Bimaristan

Like the Chinese, Muslims valued aid to the needy as a religious and cultural benefit. But "needy" had a broader context for Islam. Along with the physically and economically disadvantaged, scholars, some religious authorities, and people on the *hajj*, or pilgrimage to Mecca, were worthy of charitable support from individuals, including women

Figure 12.1 Engraving by 17th-century artist Abraham Bosse, "The Infirmary of the Sisters of Charity (La Charité) during a visit of [French Queen] Anne of Austria, ca. 1640." The Parisian hospital has high ceilings and tall windows that allow good light and ventilation, and the patients have beds in curtained-off cubicles. (Photo by Hulton Archive/Getty Images)

and society's political leaders. Since the Prophet Muhammad's time, such giving has been formalized as one of the four pillars of Islam. The characteristic Muslim institution for the provision of health care was the bimaristan. Scholars argue about the bimaristan's early history, but it is clear that Islam had adapted ancient Greek, Christian, and Persian hospitals to their own purposes in Baghdad by the ninth century CE, even earlier elsewhere. A city such as Baghdad, Cairo, Damascus, or Istanbul might have dozens of these facilities, built across generations by individual patrons—including caliphs and sultans—or donations from many. Bimaristans provided care for the poor, travelers, and those who needed special treatments such as cataract removals. In 1284 a magnificent example, the Mansuri, was constructed in Cairo. It admitted men and women, excluding no one (some places did exclude slaves and soldiers, for example), and is said to have had accommodations for 8,000. Certain cases were relegated to special wards to isolate them from others, and a wide variety of physicians and specialist healers were available. Teaching was carried out, often utilizing patients as examples, long before the practice appeared in Christian Europe. A pharmacy was on site, as were a dispensary, medical library, and prayer room. An ex-palace, the grounds were graced by restful gardens, streams, and fountains.[3] Provision of water was for both hygienic and therapeutic reasons. The sound of flowing water was good for the spirit, and bathing in water was a form of treatment for certain conditions.[4] It seems that the high quality of accommodations, food, and care of these places drew the lazy and shiftless, which led to careful screening for admissions.[5]

The Ottoman Empire

Muslim Turks had their own facilities for the poor, sick, and travelers, the *imareti*, which is often translated soup kitchen.[6] As they collected new territories, they constructed more of these, adopted the

Figure 12.2 The Ikinu Beyazit Kulliyesi (welfare complex) on the grounds of the Sultan Bayezid II Mosque in Edirne, Turkey. Dating from the 15th century, the institution included a medical school and a hospital. The complex now houses a museum dedicated to the history of medicine in Turkey. (Valery Shanin/Dreamstime)

bimaristan (*bimarhane* in Turkish), and continued supporting many of the existing hospitals from Istanbul to Mecca. The conquerors were making their mark in the tradition of the Muslim dynasties that preceded them. As with Christian charitable foundations, for Muslims the act of founding or supporting a bimaristan was spiritually beneficial, part of the benevolence expected of one on his way to paradise. These hospitals were usually named for the founder and supported with endowments of agricultural land that provided rents.[7] All classes could find treatment, foreigners included, and all services were rendered without any compensation or expectation of donations. The patient, however, had to be Muslim and in need of medical help. Non-Muslims were not welcome and in larger cities could usually find their own medical help. The standard endowment agreement stipulated that only "the sick, the wounded, and those who suffer injuries and aches" could be admitted. Ottoman hospitals even housed the mentally and emotionally ill, unlike most European hospitals. Like Londoners and Aztecs, Turks visited the grounds during spring to be entertained by the mad.[8] Women, on the other hand, might have their own quarters either within the *bimarhane* or in a separate facility, or they would be denied treatment. When possible, women healers rather than male physicians were employed to deal with female patients.[9]

Though within the hospital certain spaces were functionally separate, such as women's quarters and the prayer room, regardless of complaint pairs of patients randomly shared small rooms. The Galenic notion of miasma—poisoned air as the cause of disease—trumped physicians' recognition of contagion.[10] This differed from, for example, Cairo's Mansuri Hospital, in which patients were segregated by ailment into wards. Also, Ottoman hospitals were not so much themselves the all-purpose complexes that they had been earlier but rather one part of a site that contained a bathhouse, imaret, madresa (religious school), mosque, and other facilities that were typical objects of the charity of the wealthy.

Yet given the size of the major cities, the numbers of facilities and beds available were small. Istanbul, Cairo, and Aleppo each had only a half dozen major foundations in the sixteenth century. A few new major medical facilities graced the growing cities of the seventeenth century, but there were not many, and their traditional layout and patterns of use began to change.[11] As the sultans edged westward, adopting a wider and wider range of European medical ideas and practices during the eighteenth century, the hospitals that were founded reflected the latest in European medicine.

The Safavids

Next door to the Turks the picture was very different. In the vast region dominated from Persia, the bimaristan had been in decline since even before the Mongol destruction of the thirteenth century. Unlike the Ottoman sultans, the Safavid shahs spent virtually nothing on repairing medical facilities or building new ones. Both travelers' accounts and native records describe once proud structures reduced to holding a few madmen, serving as prisons, or being used as warehouses for food to be given to the poor. Those that still functioned were described as being overcrowded with the sick poor, and with none of the amenities traditionally associated with the venerable institution.[12]

THE EUROPEANS

As early modern states gained more authority over their citizens or subjects, they exercised more power over health care providers and facilities through public officials and boards. Royal and municipal hospitals replaced church hospitals in both Protestant and Catholic countries, though in Catholic lands they remained staffed by dedicated men and women religious. Over time, new and more specialized facilities emerged with new needs: general hospitals, veterans' and sailors' hospitals, lunatic asylums, pest (plague) houses, clinics, and teaching hospitals.

European Health Authorities

About the time of the Black Death (1347–52), most European urban areas had two types of health-related authorities. One was the guild or guilds that regulated the organization, qualifications, and practices of physicians, surgeons, and apothecaries. The second was various sets of local laws that set standards for those who sold food, for the location of loud or noxious businesses such as smiths, tanneries, or butcher shops, and for the cleanliness of public streets and byways. Central governments, such as the English or French monarchs, tended to have little to say outside of London or Paris. In large part this was due to the lack of any effective bureaucracy that would have been able to carry into effect the royal writ. During and in the wake of the plague, a few self-governing Italian city-states—Venice, Milan, Florence—experimented with special emergency boards consisting of a few important men (but not physicians) who created extraordinary rules for handling the epidemic or aftermath. In 1485 Venice established a permanent health magistracy; Milan followed quickly, and Florence did so in 1527. Being permanent, these magistracies expanded their oversight and legislative authority to include a very wide range of concerns, including prostitution, sanitation, medical care, trade during times of epidemic, and control of the poor and itinerant tramps. During plague time, these magistracies had extensive powers to round up plague victims who could or would not be cared for at home and compel them to enter pest houses, to restrict the movements of anyone suspected of having the plague, and even to enter the homes of victims and destroy all of their belongings in the name of public safety.[13]

In the sixteenth century the Spanish crown developed the office of *protomedicato*, a regional board of respected physicians (*protomédicos*), usually crown-appointed, that was given responsibility for health and medical matters. England relied on Parliament to make most public health decisions, with local jurisdictions reliant on parish officials and sheriffs. As epidemics swept through the islands in the sixteenth and seventeenth centuries, Parliament and local officials dusted off the regulations and plans from the past episodes and reinstated them. There was one clear evolutionary trend, though, and that was toward the ever-greater use of coercion, from forced closures of theaters and other meeting places, to quarantine of suspected people and goods, to mandatory isolation of victims in the local pest house or with one's entire family in one's own house. France followed Milan in developing health commissions across the country by 1600. These had broad powers in normal times and expansive ones during an emergency. In 1720–21 Western Europe's last major plague epidemic ravaged France's Mediterranean coast around Marseille. The royal government took control and utilized the army to create and man a cordon sanitaire, or health blockade, to keep potentially infected people from moving outside the stricken region. It was a tool used by the Habsburg government along its long border with the Turks, and in both cases it appears to have helped keep the plague at bay.[14] In 1772 Louis XVI established the Royal Society of Medicine whose real function was to investigate medical practitioners and medicinal suppliers to ensure that all were meeting the society-approved levels of quality.[15]

It seems clear that in 1500 only a few attempts at any sort of public health organization of policy were to be found in Europe, whereas by 1800 organizational infrastructures existed across much of the continent. Countermeasures against plague played a large, if not determining, role in developing these organizations and policies. But there were other considerations. Europe's authoritarian governments extended their tentacles of power down to the village levels with bureaucrats, commissioners, and health officers—in Prussia literally health police—to ensure that their greatest resource, people, was kept in reasonably sound health and the exploding populations in good order. In the long run, controlling health is the surest way to control a society.[16]

European Health Facilities

Before 1500 Europe's most advanced nations and city-states had developed only a handful of types of health care facilities. Monasteries and convents had infirmaries for sick religious and in rural areas for local folk and travelers who fell ill. Leprosaria were in decline as the dreadful Hansen's disease faded from Europe, but lazarettos or "houses" in which plague victims were placed were just being developed. Hospitals had evolved little from their medieval ancestors, housing the elderly, crippled, pregnant, sick, diseased, and exhausted. Unlike the Islamic bimaristan, the later medieval hospital was strictly for the economically needy. Larger cities might also have an orphans' home and one for foundlings (abandoned children), and perhaps a facility specifically for sick or pregnant prostitutes (often named after Saint Mary Magdalen, traditionally the prostitute Jesus converted). No one really expected cures to take place in hospitals, as they were essentially warehouses of the incapable. A babe might be born, a fracture knit, or a fever break, but these charitable institutions, almost always connected to the Catholic Church, were only secondarily places of healing.[17] For cures there were religious shrines, from local holy wells or churches with relics to major pilgrimage destinations, such as Rome, Compostela, or Canterbury. When, out of Christian love for God and one's neighbor, the wealthy provided hospices or any health-related facility, the act was considered an aid for one's eternal destination after death. Doing such a good deed helped balance the bad or evil actions in one's life and increased the odds of joining God in Paradise.

Between 1500 and 1800 a flurry of new types of care facilities changed the landscape of institutional health care. Even before the Reformation (from 1517), the Catholic king of France secularized hospitals, though nuns and religious brothers still provided much of the staffing. Protestant Henry VIII of England shut down the Catholic hospitals when he closed the kingdom's monasteries, and they revived only slowly under subsequent civil control. While a few major hospitals remained "general" hospitals, many more specialized centers emerged. Some of these were for infectious diseases, others for elder care or pregnant women. Kings, city governments, and wealthy patrons created smaller and arguably more effective places where healing of the body trumped that of the spirit. This trend toward creating specific spaces where medicine was practiced in the hope of healing is sometimes called the medicalization of health care institutions.

Continuing Problems

The Leprosarium

Medieval leprosaria were charitable houses located outside towns to house the sufferers from this terrible disease. By the thirteenth century perhaps 19,000 of these hospices were scattered from Russia to Ireland. By the early modern period, however, most of these had been closed as the disease all but disappeared from Europe south of Scandinavia. Still, even in the seventeenth century Dutch towns usually had a leper house. This may have been made necessary by the Dutch commercial contacts with areas of Scandinavia and the Indian Ocean where leprosy was still very active (see below).[18]

The Pest House or Lazaretto

The pest house or lazaretto for plague victims grew out of the leprosarium, and even the name lazaretto and its variations derive from Saint Lazarus, the patron of lepers. Formal medicine blamed bubonic plague on poisoned air, or miasma, yet there was a clear popular notion that plague was contagious. If indeed contagious, then victims needed to be isolated to prevent plague's spread, whether within or beyond a given community. Sometimes called a plague hospital, the pest house was normally a temporary feature on the landscape, since unlike leprosy the plague was acute—the patient either dying or recovering within a short time. Epidemics generally lasted four or five months, centering on August, and returned on average at 10- or 15-year intervals. Though some Dutch and northern French cities had permanent lazarettos, most accommodations were temporary collections of huts or requisitioned monasteries or hospitals. Major, permanent facilities were famously located in Venice from the later fifteenth century and in Milan from 1524. Milan's later facility had an enormous courtyard for temporary shelters as well as 288 surrounding rooms, and Venice's held an estimated 7,000 sufferers at one time in 1630. To the extent possible with such numbers, paid personnel nursed victims with the hope of their recovery. Smaller institutions had fairly high recovery rates, as high as 50 percent in seventeenth-century Tuscany. Quarantine facilities were related to pest houses, except that people were placed in

Figure 12.3 *Federico Borromeo Visiting the Infected at the Lazaretto* (1670) by Italian painter Luigi Pellegrino Scaramuccia depicts the Catholic archbishop paying a visit to the plague hospital in Milan during the horrific plague of 1630. The fresco is in the Accademia Ambrosiana in Milan, itself founded by Borromeo. (De Agostini/Getty Images)

quarantine for a set period—traditionally 40 (Italian *quaranta*) days—to see if they developed the illness. In the eighteenth century many of these permanent facilities found new life in the battle against such diseases as yellow fever, smallpox, and, later, cholera.[19]

Orphanages and Foundling Hospitals

In Catholic Europe female monasteries and convents and parish rectories were the dropping-off point for abandoned children and most unfostered orphans. In the wake of plague, there were inevitable spikes of both orphaning and abandonment, and these spurred the foundations of facilities dedicated to caring for and raising both types of unfortunate children. Foundlings differed somewhat in that they had been "thrown away" by a parent or parents, and there was the possibility that the mother might return to retrieve the child. In his 1410 will, the Tuscan merchant Francisco Datini founded two, a foundation for foundlings in Prato and the famous Ospedale degli Innocenti in Florence. Having been orphaned as a child and having fathered an illegitimate child, he understood the societal need.[20] With the Reformation, the need did not disappear in Protestant countries, but the monasteries and nuns did. New arrangements had to be made, as discussed in chapter 5.

General Hospitals and Hôtels Dieu

General hospitals and *hôtels dieu* were medieval institutions that served a wide variety of needs: hospice for the dying or sick travelers, orphanage, maternity hospital (usually for unwed mothers), and old folks' home. The great example was in Paris, but London's St. Thomas and St. Bartholomew, Granada's King's Hospital, and the Royal Hospital in Santiago di Compostela followed similar lines. In Catholic countries Augustinian and Franciscan women religious provided most of the caregiving staff, but the French began secularizing the administration of its *hôpitaux généraux* even before 1500. This was in part because the French crown did not trust the institutional Church, but also because of the perception that women's religious orders had decayed since the fourteenth century. Increasingly, these hospitals were medicalized by the emphasis on permanent medical staff (surgeons, physicians, apothecaries) and the exclusion of many long-term residents. During the late seventeenth and early eighteenth centuries, France boasted some 200 *new* general hospitals and 2,000 other medical foundations, many staffed by new Catholic nursing orders. Henry VIII closed London's hospitals but reinstated St. Thomas and St. Bart's, which remained London's only general hospitals until the mid-eighteenth century.

The 1700s witnessed a great growth in hospital numbers and sophistication. Patients now slept in separate beds, only the sick were admitted, wards for various conditions minimized cross-infection, and record keeping allowed for administrators and authorities to see patterns in illnesses and the effectiveness of treatments. Not only did educational anatomical dissections increase in line with Europe's Enlightenment, but pathology emerged as a branch of medicine. In London five new hospitals appeared between 1720 and 1745, each with a special emphasis, and by 1800 London hospitals could serve 20,000 patients annually. The remainder of Britain had no general hospitals before 1700, but by 1750 Edinburgh (1729), Winchester and Bristol (1737), York (1740), Exeter (1741), Bath (1742), and Northampton (1743) were supplied, as were all sizeable towns by 1800.[21] In the Netherlands, Scotland, London, Vienna, and elsewhere, medical teaching was increasingly linked to major hospitals. The Enlightened

Habsburgs in Austria adopted the idea of medical police and secularized much of their health care provision, including the creation of the Allgemeines Krankenhaus (General Hospital) in 1784. It had four surgical wards, and 86 beds for clinical teaching out of a total of 1,600 beds. The Habsburg Empire added new hospitals in Olmütz (1787), Linz (1788), and Prague (1789). By the outbreak of the French Revolution, the French could count 177 general hospitals, and Paris alone had 48 hospitals with 20,000 beds for the city of 700,000 people. Even Catherine the Great's Russia had a new (if backward by Western standards) facility in the Obukhov Hospital.[22]

New Needs Met

Syphilis or Pox Hospitals

Syphilis or pox hospitals emerged in the sixteenth century with the horrific spread of the new disease syphilis or the pox, which suddenly struck Europe in the mid-1490s. Hospital authorities across Europe were loath to mix these new patients, carrying the obvious blight of their sexual misconduct, with their other patients, and the troubling possibility of contagion led to isolation. First, separate wards appeared in some hospitals, and this led to separate structures when symptoms were found to be chronic. In Germany dozens of small, publicly funded facilities—usually about a dozen beds, though Augsburg had 122—sprang up. In Italy these were the Incurable Hospitals. Naples's held 600 patients in 1535; Rome's San Giacomo served 1,400 men and 330 women in 1569. Despite the Italian label, people were here to be cured by extreme sessions of sweating to purge the "humoral" poison. Mercury and/or a native American tree wood known as guaic were used to induce perspiration, a regimen that could last up to 30 days, making the "cure" almost as bad as the disease. In Germany, between 16 and 24 percent of patients died as a result of treatment. The need for treatment and care continued through the early modern period, though the religious or moral prejudice against the venereal component of venereal disease (sexual misconduct) tended to fade. Older hospitals expanded, and new ones, such as Lock Hospital in London (1746), were established to meet the ongoing need.[23]

Insane Asylums

Insane asylums also appeared in the sixteenth century for the first time. The insane had traditionally been allowed to wander at will, with the dangerously insane locked away in jails, cellars, attics, or prisons. As chapter 9 discusses, from the sixteenth through eighteenth century cities and individual patrons created new facilities called hospitals, asylums, or residences for those emotionally or mentally disturbed people who had no family to care for them. As with other illness and institutions, insanity and the asylum were gradually medicalized, so that by the later eighteenth century the asylum became a place of therapy as well as human storage.

Eighteenth-Century Innovations

The professionalization of medical practitioners, the Enlightened belief in science, progress, and humanity, and the growth of state self-interest in preserving its population in good health combined to make the eighteenth century a watershed in the institutionalization of medicine. Growing populations meant more of every type of illness, and medical specialization among practitioners led to even more specialized spaces for treatment. Between 1749 and 1765 London's pregnant poor got beds in four new lying-in or maternity hospitals. Originally only for married women, the administrators soon learned to ask no questions. These quickly became excellent training facilities for midwives, both male and female.

Londoners also pioneered dispensaries—what Americans might call walk-in clinics—for the poor. Physician George Armstrong set up the first in Red Lion Square in 1769 to help the mothers of sick infants with advice and medicine. A second was founded by the Quaker John Lettsom to serve any poor person. His General Dispensary became the model for another 11: set up in a rented space, offering neither beds nor surgery, just drugs and counsel. Subscribers who made regular contributions were called governors, and each was allowed to send one patient per guinea donated. In 1770 it had 100 governors; eight years later it had 1,400.[24]

The nearly constant drumbeat of war in Europe and its colonies led to the fielding of armies of unprecedented size. Training was time consuming, and the veteran soldier or sailor was not easily replaced. As discussed in chapter 11, the Enlightened self-interest of rulers and their military advisers led to the foundation of dozens of military hospitals that cared for the wounded and ill, and to veterans' hospitals in which those permanently damaged by service might be cared for. The experimentally inclined of the age found that these facilities were perfect forums for testing new methods of treatment and drugs, for clinical teaching and training of military surgeons, and for conducting autopsies and the study of pathology.

EUROPEAN INSTITUTIONS ABROAD

An eighteenth-century scholar remarked that by the mid-seventeenth century, Europe and its colonies "around the world" could boast of some 563 medical facilities.[25] Some of these in "colonies" served the merchants, soldiers, sailors, and other resident whites, while some served the natives with European medicine or a mix of European and local medical traditions. In many cases, European medicine abroad both influenced local healing and was in turn influenced by it.

Mexico

The Aztecs provided a few hints of their pre-Columbian institutions. The importance of the warrior in society was underlined by the existence of institutions for both the recuperating wounded and the permanently disabled. They were provided by the ruler and were located in Tenochtitlán, Cholula, Colhuacán, and Texcoco. The Aztec state also used these places as centers for the distribution of food to the poor. In Tenochtitlán the state also provided for people with disfiguring characteristics that kept them from being considered normal members of Aztec society. These unfortunates with withered limbs, clubfeet, harelips, skin diseases, or other deformities were housed near the royal zoo and gawked at by visitors, much as Londoners visited the insane asylum at Bedlam for amusement. Those with serious diseases had long been sacrificed to the gods, their maladies understood as signs of divine displeasure. Under the later kings, however, they were isolated away from society and treated with a salve known as *teocotl* in Nahuatl. One final health-related institution was the royal botanical garden established by Moctezuma I. Sources claimed it was five miles in circumference and contained medical specimens from throughout southern North and Central America. It allowed Aztec healers to study the growth and healing properties of plants but also supplied the needed materia medica for the court.[26]

The Spanish brought the institutions of European medicine with both colonists and natives in mind. Every mission was a medical station that sought to heal the native body as well as spirit. As many Mexicans discovered, however, the robed and bearded men brought death—by contagion—at least as often as health. San Nicolás in Santo Domingo, the first hospital for poor Spaniards, was founded in the New World (1503). In 1517 the *protomedicato*, with oversight on all aspects of formal health care provision, was appointed to Santo Domingo.

The city government rather than the crown appointed the first *proto-medicato* for Mexico City, in 1525. The first order of business was regulation of all practitioners who were neither physicians nor surgeons, including both natives and colonists. The year before, Hernán Cortés founded the first general hospital in the New World, the Hospital de la Concepción de Nuestra Señora. Known simply as the Hospital de Jesús, it was the headquarters for the *protomedicato*. Cortés provided estates to support his foundation, which welcomed poor Spaniards and Indians. He also set up the hemisphere's first leprosarium, in 1526/28 at Tlaxplana on his estate near Mexico City.[27] Shortly after, Vasco Quiroga set up a series of Christian missionary pueblos with hospitals in the province of Michoacán. In the early 1530s Pedro de Gante founded the Hospital Real de Indios exclusively for natives in Mexico City. After expansion it had eight wards and beds for 200 patients. In 1534 the Royal Hospital of St. Joseph for Natives was set up by the Franciscans with the patronage of King Charles I. In the mid-1530s the first Archbishop of Mexico City created the Hospital of St. John the Divine for syphilitic Spaniards. A second appeared in the 1539, the Hospital del Amor di Dios, also with episcopal support and a staff of 18. A second leprosarium was also founded in sixteenth-century Mexico City: San Lazaro by Dr. Pedro Lopéz in 1572. In 1541 Charles decreed that every town have at least one hospital for poor Spaniards and natives. These would be staffed by both Spanish and Indian physicians, surgeons, and apothecaries.

In Mexico City one might say that the earliest medical education institution was the barber-surgeon Francisco Soto, who was licensed to take both Spanish and native apprentices to learn his craft. The National University of Mexico was founded in 1551, and the faculty of medicine was in place by 1575. In 1628 the *protomedicato* was formalized, reorganized, and became the ex officio head of the medical faculty, which operated until 1832. Its members were appointed by the crown and absorbed all remaining health care authority in New Spain. The office of the *protomedicato* now licensed all practitioners, prosecuted malpractice cases, and oversaw medical education, midwives, public sanitation, apothecaries, and the sales of food.[28] Since many missionaries were practitioners, and the Catholic Church ran so many Mexican hospitals (128 by the early 1600s), this was also a power play by the government against the Church.[29]

Colonial Mexico's needs for health care facilities remained great because the shocks of the initial importation of new germs and diseases by colonists continued to reverberate, and the Spanish invaders suffered from native diseases and from the conditions of the transatlantic voyage. Epidemics swept Mexico through the eighteenth century, and in 1770 King Charles III of Spain even established the Mexican National Lottery to help fund treatment for sufferers from smallpox and syphilis.[30]

Caribbean Slaves

Institutional care for slaves, who were considered little more than chattel property, was no matter of benevolence or even humanistic obligation but of the maintenance of human tools. To its owner, keeping a slave well enough to function was the equivalent of maintaining a plow horse in good health. Provision of health care was a matter of self-interest, and the humanity of the slave was at best a second thought. As property, the slave was expected to remain on the master's property even when desperately ill, so public or church-run facilities had no place. The typical plantation did have some accommodation for the sick and injured, but these differed radically from one to the next. "Infirmaries," "hothouses," "hospitals," or "sick houses" were often permanent but simple one-room buildings, sometimes segregating the sexes by a wall. A trustee caregiver oversaw the place, which would have been supplied with simple instruments and drugs characteristic for the environment and season. If a slave needed a white physician or surgeon, the practitioner would meet the patient in these quarters, so practitioners saw their conditions firsthand. But these facilities were as much prisons as hospitals, and the overseer had to ensure that no one was taking advantage of the rest they afforded. Even critics accepted the need for barred windows, locked doors, and shackles inside.[31]

One might think these dated back to the earliest slave presence, but until the Enlightenment and abolition movement of the eighteenth century, many owners paid little attention to slave health since they could be so cheaply replaced. Now, wars and laws threatened the traffic in enslaved Africans, and both slave health and reproduction became matters of concern. In the British West Indies, the earliest mention of a slave hospital is from about 1750, and Cuban records postdate 1800. Visiting and resident physicians wrote recommending hospitals for slaves, and Dr. James Grainger in 1769 urged they be well ventilated and provided with a fireplace, toilet, bathing facility, and an herb garden for medicinal plants. As slave hospitals appeared the owners defended them, but both slaves and medical practitioners decried the awful conditions. Critics pointed to the minimal concern for hygiene and resulting infection, the food that was poor even by standards of slavery, and the lack of adequate personnel. The slave caregivers were untrained and unmotivated, and white practitioners made all too rare an appearance. Slaves themselves resented the facilities, as they separated them from their families and friends; they stunk and their people, even if black, forced nasty medicines and painful treatments on them; and they were houses of death from which too many never returned.

From 1784 French authorities in Haiti required plantation hospitals built well on good, well-drained ground, with good ventilation and paved floors. The *hôpitalière* was to run the facility and live in a room in it, alongside male and female wards.[32] In 1798 the Leeward Islands mandated the provision of plantation hospitals, and two years later the governor of Trinidad required access to each plantation's facilities and personnel and an annual summary of activity.

Asia and the Indian Ocean

Provision of European-style health care in Asian and Indian Ocean colonies, trading colonies, and open ports was not a matter of sharing European medicine with the natives, except where Roman Catholic missions established the Church's presence. Most infirmaries, clinics, hospitals, and other institutions arose from the need to treat white sailors, merchants, colonists, soldiers, and emissaries who were far from their Portuguese, Spanish, Dutch, French, or English homes. These varied in size from small infirmaries to the 1,500-patient Portuguese Royal Hospital of the Holy Spirit in Goa. In 1569 the hospital of Saint Raphael was founded in Macao and quickly became a major Jesuit establishment. Unusually, its staff used both Western Galenic medicine and Chinese healing techniques, such as acupuncture and moxibustion. It was also unusual in that it had a ward for sufferers from Hansen's disease (leprosy).[33]

Traditional leper hospitals were often founded by Europeans, ostensibly to serve (or incarcerate) native victims. In Goa, the Portuguese established Saint Lazarus hospital as early as 1529. In 1578 the Franciscan friars were operating a leprosarium at Naga in Japan and later the Spanish invited them to establish one in Manila.[34] Dutch Calvinists also founded leper hospitals, as at Batavia, where two were situated onshore and a third at Purmevend. The ideal was to have lepers cared for at home under mandatory isolation, but when doctors found them without supervision they were locked up. In 1690, 171 inmates were resident, of whom 164 were natives and 7 were European or mixed ancestry.[35]

NOTES

1. Zhenguo Wang, *History and Development of Traditional Chinese Medicine* (Beijing: Science Press, 1999), 162–67.

2. Angela Ki Che Leung, *Leprosy in China: A History* (New York: Columbia University Press, 2009), 96–109.

3. Miri Shefer-Mossensohn, *Ottoman Medicine: Healing and Medical Institution, 1500–1700* (Albany: State University of New York Press, 2009), 160–65.

4. Ibid., 83–84, 152–55.

5. Peter E. Pormann and Emilie Savage-Smith, *Medieval Islamic Medicine* (Washington, DC: Georgetown University Press, 2007), 99–100; Shefer-Mossensohn, *Ottoman Medicine*, 99.

6. Shefer-Mossensohn, *Ottoman Medicine*, 20.

7. Ibid.; see chapter 3 on the Muslim endowment—*waqf* in Arabic or *vakif* in Turkish.

8. Ibid., 135, 169–70; in Cairo, however, it seems that lunatics were drawn to the newly popular coffee houses, where they were described as "spitting saliva" (p. 157). In general see Michael W. Dols, *Majnun: The Madman in Medieval Islamic Society* (Oxford: Clarendon Press, 1992).

9. Shefer-Mossensohn, *Ottoman Medicine*, 117–37.

10. Ibid., 172–79; see also Justin Stearns, *Infectious Ideas: Contagion in Premodern Islamic and Christian Thought in the Western Mediterranean* (Baltimore: Johns Hopkins University Press, 2011).

11. Shefer-Mossensohn, *Ottoman Medicine*, 115, 198.

12. Cyril Elgood, *Safavid Medical Practice: The Practice of Medicine, Surgery, and Gynecology in Persia between 1500 and 1750* (London: Luzac, 1970), 27, 107.

13. Joseph P. Byrne, *Daily Life during the Black Death* (Westport, CT: Greenwood Press, 2006), chap. 7.

14. Paul Slack, "Responses to Plague in Early Modern Europe: The Implications of Public Health," *Social Research* 55 (1988): 433–53; Alexandra Parma Cook and Noble David Cook, *The Plague Files: Crisis Management in Sixteenth-Century Seville* (Baton Rouge: University of Louisiana Press, 2009).

15. Dorothy Porter, ed., *The History of Public Health and the Modern State* (Amsterdam: Rodopi, 1996), 7, 47.

16. On "mercantilism and medical police" see ibid., 5–8.

17. Colin Jones, "The Construction of the Hospital Patient in Early Modern France," in *Institutions of Confinement: Hospitals, Asylums, and Prisons in Western Europe and North America*, ed. Norbert Finzsch and Robert Jütte (New York: Cambridge University Press, 1996), 57–59.

18. Iris Bruijn, *Ship's Surgeons of the Dutch East India Company: Commerce and the Progress of Medicine in the Eighteenth Century* (Leiden, Netherlands: Leiden University Press, 2009), 108; Paul Zumthor, *Daily Life in Rembrandt's Holland* (Stanford, CA: Stanford University Press, 1994), 155.

19. Byrne, *Daily Life*, chap. 6.

20. See Philip Gavitt, *Charity and Children in Renaissance Florence: The Ospedale degli Innocenti, 1410–1536* (Ann Arbor: University of Michigan Press, 1991).

21. Roy Porter, ed., *Cambridge History of Medicine* (New York: Cambridge University Press, 2006), 184–85.

22. Jones, "The Construction," 55–74; Gunter B. Risse, "Before the Clinic Was 'Born': Methodological Perspectives in Hospital History," in Finzsch and Jütte, *Institutions of Confinement*, 75–96.

23. Robert Jütte, "Syphilis and Confinement: Hospitals in Early Modern Germany," in Finzsch and Jütte, *Institutions of Confinement*, 97–115.

24. Robert Kilpatrick, " 'Living in the Light': Dispensaries, Philanthropy, and Medical Reform in Late Eighteenth-Century London," in *The Medical Enlightenment of the Eighteenth Century*, ed. Andrew Cunningham and Roger French (New York: Cambridge University Press, 1990), 254–80.

25. Quoted in Rolande Graves, *Born to Procreate: Women and Childbirth in France from the Middle Ages to the Eighteenth Century* (New York: Peter Lang, 2001), 152.

26. Bernard R. Ortiz de Montellano, *Aztec Medicine, Health and Nutrition* (New Brunswick, NJ: Rutgers University Press, 1990).

27. On Cortés see Gordon Schendel, *Medicine in Mexico: From Aztec Herbs to Betatrons* (Austin: University of Texas Press, 1968), 89, 90, 92, 105.

28. Ibid., 99–100.

29. Sherry Fields, *Pestilence and Headcolds: Encountering Illness in Colonial Mexico* (New York: Columbia University Press, 2008), 76–80. Schendel, Medicine in Mexico, Chapter 7.

30. See Noble David Cook and W. George Lovell, *"Secret Judgments of God": Old World Disease in Colonial Spanish America* (Norman: University of Oklahoma Press, 1992); Donald B. Cooper, *Epidemic Disease in Mexico City, 1761–1813* (Austin: University of Texas Press, 1965); on the lottery, Schendel, *Medicine in Mexico*, 119–20.

31. Richard Sheridan, *Doctors and Slaves: A Medical and Demographic History of Slavery in the British West Indies, 1680–1834* (New York: Cambridge University Press, 1985), 268–290.

32. Karol K. Weaver, *Medical Revolutionaries: The Enslaved Healers of Eighteenth-Century Saint Domingue* (Chicago: University of Illinois Press, 2006).

33. Linda L. Barnes, *Needles, Herbs, Gods, and Ghosts: China, Healing, and the West to 1848* (Cambridge, MA: Harvard University Press, 2005), 46.

34. See Linda Newson, *Conquest and Pestilence in the Early Spanish Philippines* (Honolulu: University of Hawaii Press, 2009).

35. Harold J. Cook, *Matters of Exchange: Commerce, Medicine, and Science in the Dutch Golden Age* (New Haven, CT: Yale University Press, 2007), 375; Bruijn, *Ship's Surgeons*, 108–9.

CHAPTER 13

Healing and the Arts

The various literary, visual, and performance arts are means by which a culture expresses its shared hopes and fears, likes and dislikes, joys and frustrations. They may be a matter of pure entertainment or contain important messages. They can be used to teach, warn, celebrate, vent, mock, or merely record. During the early modern period poets, painters, playwrights, physicians, satirists, illustrators, historians, and other creative folk produced works of art, literature, and drama that did all of these. What follows is a sampling of some of these cultural responses to human health, illness, drugs, and healing.

THE VISUAL ARTS

The Physician Portrayed

In matters of health and wellness, there was no more typical icon than the physician. In the visual art of China, Europe, and the Islamic world, he stands out quite literally from his sick patients: teacher, healer, philosopher. In later medieval European illustrations, he stands taking a pulse or holding up a urine flask, or lecturing from a podium over a cadaver. His fine robes and headgear set him apart from those around him. Pulse taking was an iconic activity when depicting a physician, since all of the learned traditions of medicine utilized it. Chinese and Muslim artists used the image in paintings and illustrations ranging from books of

Figure 13.1 Illustration after a Dutch painting by Franz van Mieries of Leyden depicting a doctor feeling a woman's pulse, an activity that is an iconic representation of the physician. (National Library of Medicine)

occupations to medical classics. Among Europeans it was the Dutch genre artists of the seventeenth century who present us well-dressed doctors gently holding the wrist of their—usually female—patient.[1] Doctors also appeared at hospital bedsides and deathbeds. While European artists generally stayed away from depicting doctors engaged in much beyond consulting with a patient or diagnostic pulse taking, Ottoman, Safavid, Mughal, and Chinese artists often depicted other medical procedures. This may have been due to the fact that European physicians were very jealous of their social role as the practitioners who diagnosed and prescribed, while surgeons or others performed the messy tasks.

While most of these pictures were meant to be merely illustrative and their doctors generic, the Renaissance also developed the personal portrait. Throughout the early modern period, many European physicians

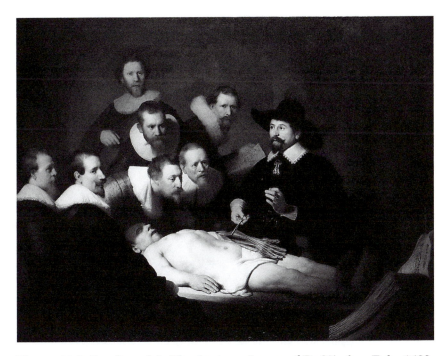

Figure 13.2 Rembrandt's *The Anatomy Lesson of Dr Nicolaes Tulp*, 1632. Today the work is in the Mauritshuis museum in The Hague. (National Library of Medicine)

had themselves painted as members of their society's elite. Most European physician portraits depict the subject in an intellectual setting, surrounded by books, art, and other symbols of good taste and learning. Perhaps the most famous painting of a physician, however, is that by Rembrandt of the Amsterdam doctor Nicolas Tulp. Surrounded by eager and well-dressed students, he sits over a cadaver dissecting it and explaining what they all see. He is shown as expert and teacher, not only a healer but also one who hands his experience and knowledge to others.[2]

Not all portraits of medical men were flattering, however. A well-documented type was the quack hawking his wares from a stage. Another was the physician's caricature. The artists sought to demean traits of certain doctors or of generic members in a variety of ways. Some were shown as animals such as blood-sucking leeches or ignorant donkeys; others had distorted physical features or carried moneybags or terrifying medical instruments. The doctor often appeared as greedy, as killer no less than curer, as one thankful for the outbreak of disease, as fawning sycophant, or as incompetent boob.[3]

Vesalius and Anatomical Illustration

Andreas Vesalius of Brussels studied and taught medicine in Padua, Italy. Trained as a Galenist, he found by conducting his own dissections that the old Greek was wrong on many counts. He produced a massive and beautifully illustrated guide to anatomy titled *On the Fabric of the*

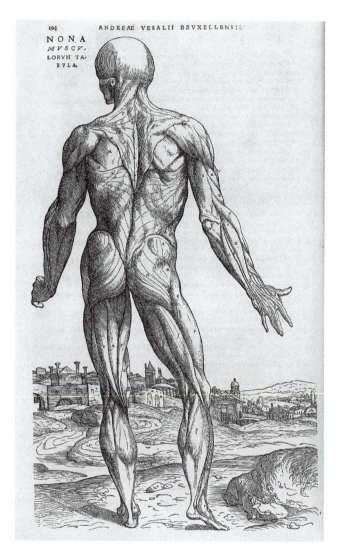

Figure 13.3 Image of the musculature of the human body from Andreas Vesalius' *De corporis humani fabrica libri septem* (*Seven Books on the Fabric of the Human Body*), 1543. (National Library of Medicine)

Human Body (1543) that revolutionized anatomical depiction. Though he wrote the text, a true artist working in Venice, perhaps with Titian, produced the many masterful engravings. The frontispiece shows Vesalius in a dissection theater in direct contact with the cadaver while a great crowd swirls in an arc around him. He is in charge because he is the expert, and according to Vesalius the expert gets his hands dirty.

The illustrations are of the human body variously posed from bare skeleton to fully covered in skin. Their naturalism was right in step with the tastes of the age and the attention to detail made them very useful as tools for medical training. Both his criticisms of Galen and the extraordinary quality of the images were the gold standard for those who would produce books of anatomy.[4]

Hogarth and the Ills of London Society

William Hogarth was a painter and engraver who worked in eighteenth-century London. He is most noted for his several series of engraved scenes that depict the downfall of contemporary unfortunates. They are at the same time tragic, amusing, and serious social commentary. The earliest was a series of five scenes called the *Harlot's*

Figure 13.4 In this plate from William Hogarth's "A Harlot's Progress" (1732), Moll sits in a chair dying while two doctors argue over their cures. (National Library of Medicine)

Progress of 1732. Instead of taking an honest job, young Moll Hackabout enters a brothel and dedicates her life to the sex trade. At first a comfortable mistress, she declines into becoming a streetwalker who contracts venereal disease. In the fifth and final scene, she lays dying as two identifiable physicians with their backs to her argue over which remedy will save her. A year later the very popular *Rake's Progress* featured a young man-about-town who lives a life of dissolute self-indulgence. In the eighth and last panel, we find the antihero ruined and a patient in Bedlam, London's notorious madhouse. In *Marriage A-la Mode* (1745) Hogarth depicted the rise and fall of another young woman. She married a nobleman, then found a lover, who killed her husband and was in turn hanged for the crime. In the last scene her child is held up to her as she sinks into eternal slumber, empty by her side the bottle of laudanum that she drained to kill herself.

Hogarth's undated "Damn the Doctor" features a miserable man with a bandaged head sitting on the side of his bed vomiting into a basin. Above him on the bed curtains is the phrase Damn the Doctor, which is no doubt a commentary on the labeled bottle of physician-provided "Gargle" sitting on the nearby shelf. In 1726 he visually commented on a contemporary news item: a woman gave birth to a score of rabbits! In *Cuniculari or The Wise Men of Godliman in Consultation*, three physicians from London stand by the birth bed seriously considering the phenomenon as rabbits frolic about the room. Here Hogarth lampoons the gullibility of the doctors (and society in general) for taking the hoax at face value. Finally, one might point to the famous "Beer Lane and Gin Alley" in which Hogarth attacks the contemporary lower-class love of high-proof distilled gin over the less intoxicating beer preferred by the middling classes. Beer Lane is a place of order, peace, and prosperity, while the poverty-stricken drunkards of Gin Alley loll about inebriated, a mother letting fall a baby from her ample lap as she reels in laughter.[5] As the Chinese used to say: a picture is worth a thousand words.

DOCTORS IN DRAMAS AND NOVELS

Among progressive later eighteenth-century Hebrew and Yiddish-speaking European Jews, the *maskil* was an heroic figure. He was the man of science and medicine, icon of the Haskalah, the Jewish Enlightenment. He was rational and thus effective. As a healer he sought to reform the older approaches to healing that were embedded in Jewish communities. He was secular and European and stood in contrast to rabbinical and traditional Jewish folk healers. His popularity as a figure was expressed in such comedies as Isaac Euchel's 1793 "Rabbi Henekh or What One Does with It."[6]

Tobias Smollett and the Royal Navy

In 1748 English novelist Tobias Smollett published *The Adventures of Roderick Random*. He had been trained as a surgeon in Glasgow and became a ship's surgeon on one of the ships that sailed British troops to Cartagena in the ill-fated 1740 invasion. Thousands died as yellow fever swept the soldiers and sailors, and commanding officers did little to save the expedition. Smollett constructed a portion of his novel around a second surgeon's mate who had to deal with the fruitless orders he was given and the utter chaos of the doomed effort. The picture of both naval and medical incompetence that cost the lives of so many shocked contemporary society.[7] His description of his own first posting to the sick bay on *The Thunderer* reflects his horror and revulsion at conditions of the ill at sea:

> Here I saw about 50 miserable distempered wretches suspended [in hammocks] in rows, so huddled upon one another that not more than 14 inches of space was allotted for each with his bed and bedding; and deprived of the light of the day, as well as of fresh air; breathing nothing but a noisome atmosphere of the morbid steams exhaling from their own excrements and diseased bodies, devoured with vermin hatched in the filth that surrounded them.

In *Roderick* the captain is an unreasonable disciplinarian who states that there should be no sick men on his ship and that all 60 of those on sick call were faking to avoid duty. The ship's doctor is no more than a toady who confirms in turn that each is indeed a fraud. As all undergo discipline rather than rest and care, many of the 60 die of their medical conditions and the floggings. *Roderick* was fiction, but it revealed to the English reading public the dark underside of the famed naval service that was building and protecting the British Empire.[8]

Chinese Dramas

Theater was a rather new art form in China during the Ming period. Most playwrights were scholars who would have studied medicine to some extent and may have practiced as physicians. Revered historical or divine physicians sometimes appear as characters, and they are dressed in priests' robes and treated very respectfully. Various sorts of medical practitioners also appear in many period plays or operas. As a stock type, these figures were usually either "painted face characters" played as "humorous, proud and exaggerative" or as outright jesters in the guise of country hicks with very ugly faces. The characters' Chinese names often reflect their clown-like status: Dr. Sending People to Their Death-Bed or Dr. Stupid Worm. Often appearing in romantic comedies, they are called on to "heal a broken heart" or advance some scheme on the lovers' parts. They bumble through diagnoses and confuse medical terms, prescribe ridiculous treatments, or otherwise display a total lack of common sense. Some are quite open about their incompetence. In the play *Tan Kuei's Bracelet Box*, the title character's mother hires the doctor Si Chuan, who came from three generations of doctors and introduces himself as follows:

> I know well how to feel people's pulse and remember well the character-istics of medicine. How can I guess what disease that people get? Spells are my only prescriptions. I don't know what's cold or fever, leprosy or insane. To the consumptive [lung] cases, I give purgative drugs and to the digestive disturbances, I give cardiatonics [heart medicine]. I tell the adult he gets children's disease, and the gentleman that he gets woman's ailment. I make people cry and weep all around me. Yesterday I was compelled to attend a funeral service in which I offered my apology, and this morning I was beaten like hell for having made a wrong treatment. I am the messenger of the king of Hades as well as the assistant of the coffin shops. Several times I've decided to give up my job, but then I've nothing to make a living.[9]

Not exactly confidence inspiring, but then it is farce.

Often the plays have fun with cultural norms, such as the unwilling-ness of women to be examined by a male doctor, and specific diagnostic techniques such as pulse taking. In the work *Lung Kao Chi*, a sick girl's father has his servants hire a doctor. The man of medicine mocks the practice of diagnosis: "Your excellency! What do the doctors know about pulse feeling in this day? A good doctor is a doctor who guesses right." He goes on to explain that he plans to experiment on the girl: "Sir, is there a doctor who does not treat his patient as an experimental object?" Finally, the father calls out: "Attendants, I have told you to get a good doctor, and why do you get a fellow like him? Get him out of here!"[10] Like the father, the playwright knows that there are both good and poor physicians. Chinese theatrical pieces did not take aim at the medical pro-fession itself as much as mock and perhaps criticize the practitioners who had little to offer and yet were allowed to peddle their services.

Not all stage doctors were clowns, however. In tragic operas they could be anything from mischievous to evil, depending on the librettist's needs. Since doctors determined life and death for their patients, if gain were to be had from killing a patient, it took little motivation to tip the scale. Doctors knew drugs that healed and those that killed, and often the most helpless were in their care. Poisoned medicine was a favorite means. But doctors could also be heroic, though they were usually in stories of the gods of medicine or appeared in contemporary stories in the guise of good, knowledgeable physicians.[11]

Molière's French Doctors

The great sixteenth-century French playwright known as Molière wrote his comedies for the royal court. His audiences were not common folk but the age's aristocracy, including King Louis XIV himself. Above all else the playwright hated hypocrisy and mercilessly lampooned the false and self-righteous. He also had little use for physicians and featured them in several of his plays: *The Flying Doctor*, *Love Is the Doctor*, *The Doctor in Spite of Himself*, and *The Imaginary Invalid*.

The Doctor in Spite of Himself is Sganarelle the woodcutter (originally played by Molière himself) mistaken for a physician. Despite having neither knowledge nor skills, he decides to play the role to the hilt and adopts the costume, behaviors, and even vocabulary of a man of medicine. His cynical side comes out in lines such as "payment comes whether we kill or cure," and "dead men, of all people the most discreet, tell no tales of the doctor who has sent them to their long account." Sganarelle's fraudulence is that of many stock characters in European fiction, but like many others Molière harbored and displayed a true disgust with the pretensions of the medical professionals. Where the Chinese playwright might recognize that there were honorable physicians, one senses that everyone in Molière's world was a Sganarelle.

In act 2 of *Love Is the Doctor*, no fewer than five physicians are called upon to cure the depressed female lead. The result is a cacophony of theories and recommendations meant by the playwright to undermine any faith that there is a science behind medicine. Though Dr. Filerin counsels getting along, it is only for the sake of not making the profession look bad, not to reassure or aid the patient. In the end her lover, feigning to be a doctor, reveals her disease to be love sickness and himself to be the cure. The *Flying Doctor* has no wings but is in fact the lead's valet who jumps in and out of a window pretending to be both the physician and the physician's twin brother. He introduces himself thusly:

> No common doctor am I, if you please.
> All other doctors are, in my opinion,

Pretenders not approaching my dominion.
My talents are unique and most peculiar
With Insights with which I could school
Dull doctors who by barely trammel dreck,
Who know selamalec, selamalec.[12]

The *Imaginary Invalid* (1673) was Molière's final work and is a complicated farce in three acts. The title character was the hypochondriac
Argan, whose daughter he hoped to marry off to the spindly son of
his physician Dr. Purgeon. The daughter, of course, loves another. The
faithful and feisty maid Toinette pretends to be a second doctor who
undermines Argan's faith in all doctors by prescribing that his eye
and arm be removed since they are sucking up all his body's nutrients.
After ridding himself of Purgeon and the son, Argan himself is made a
physician in a ritual performed by gypsies. Molière played Argan the
hypochondriac during a performance of which he died of a very real
hemorrhage brought on by his tuberculosis.[13]

MEDICINE IN POETRY

In antiquity poets were believed to possess special gifts from the gods,
their creative spirits touched by the divine. By the early modern period
that notion had faded, though poets continued to thrive through the rel-
evance and beauty of their works. Printing was revivified in China and
introduced into Europe, stimulating demand for new and popular works
and supplying a relatively inexpensive way to fill demand. Matters medical, from printed acupuncture charts to treatises on childhood diseases to
multivolume studies of tropical medicinal plants, enjoyed a steady
demand. Poetic literature offered everything medical from nutritional
advice to deep social criticism clothed in biological terms.

Syphilus

Girolamo Fracastoro was an early-sixteenth-century Italian physician
and poet. He was born in Verona and trained in medicine at Padua.
He is noted as a scientist for his study *On Contagion* (1546), a pioneering
work on infectious diseases that imagined them as caused by tiny
seeds. In 1530 Fracastoro published his Latin poem *Syphilus, or Three
Books on the French Disease*. He had begun the work 20 years earlier
during a retreat to the countryside during a plague epidemic. The ravages of the new venereal scourge were at the center of the medical
world's attention. Poetic treatment of diseases and other medical problems was neither new nor rare. Book 1 follows the standard model in

describing the symptoms of the French disease (or Neapolitan if you were French). In book 2 Fracastoro poetically lays out the current treatments, concentrating on the use of mercury, both poison and healing agent. Book 3 is the popularization of the newly discovered South American natural remedy called guaiacum. He wraps this in a fable about a South American shepherd boy named Syphilus. One day the youngster inadvertently cursed the sun, and the sun god responded by inflicting the lad with a horrible disease. After repenting for his blasphemy, Syphilus discovered the remedy guaiacum and was cured in body and spirit. The poem presents a medical message promoting guaiacum wrapped in a typical Renaissance pastoral form, with a deeper message of the connections between immorality and disease, and repentance and cure.[14]

Medical Illness and Societal Illness

As the Chinese Ming dynasty came to an end in its failing struggle with the Manchu in 1637, poet Zhang Dai compared the Ming defeat to an epidemic:

> Dead soldiers, dead bandits, death spread everywhere.
> The defeat of Liaodong is like a piece of rotting flesh.
> The poison spread by hostile spears more powerful than the plague.[15]

Poets in Europe as well as China saw their societies as metaphorical human bodies writ large. Like the body, society could be healthy or unhealthy, harming itself or under attack by external forces. It was an old theme that found favor in early modern times. The sick society needed to be strengthened and healed, lest it die. But who was the doctor? And what was the proper treatment?

During epidemics the trope of the sick society became most evident. When plague struck literally the entire population was affected. Like a plague political corruption and incompetence, immorality, poverty and shiftlessness, toleration of the wrong religion, and a host of other ills undermined the health of societies. Poet-critics such as Englishman Thomas Dekker called out for change. In Dekker's eyes the plague was God's way of punishing the many sins of human—and especially London—society. When Queen Elizabeth died and James I came to the throne (1603), the plague raged in London. Dekker claimed that God was punishing England for glorifying Elizabeth and called on the new ruler (personified as the healing god Apollo) to make England well again. The idea that illness is a divine punishment for immoral behavior was quite ancient, but writers like Dekker used the moralizing in a particularly effective way: repent and stop sinning or we will all be punished with plague again and again. The sins Dekker denounced were not individual failings as much as social ones: the harming of the poor and disadvantaged; the flight of political leaders, doctors, priests, and the rich from London during epidemics; shutting the plague-stricken poor in their houses; and placing faith in medicine rather than God.[16] In the mid-seventeenth century Thomas Hobbes also wrote of the sick English political body of his day. For him, the disease was the antiroyalist radicalism of many members of Parliament and those who supported them; the cure was the surrender to royal absolutism.

In eighteenth-century France the sickness poets tried to cure was the absolutist royal court with all of its indolence, corruption, wars, and lack of concern for the people. The aristocrats that populated it were "tapeworms" who sucked the life from the rest of the body politic. Revolution would serve as a purgative, ridding the social body of the worm and return the body to health. In another metaphor the king himself was the gangrenous limb infecting the rest of the body. Execution of the king was merely amputation of the infected limb. Critics of Caribbean slavery varied the theme: slavery was a sickness that infected the island societies. Every act of violence against the workers was a wound. Abolition was the cure, and the physician was either the mother countries' leaders or the islands' own revolutionaries.[17]

Medical Poetry among the Safavids

From its Near Eastern roots Islam developed two particularly indigenous art forms, calligraphy and poetry. In the Safavid Empire, poised between the Mughals to the east in India and the Ottoman Turks to the West, there continued a form of "common person's medical guide," or what we might call a medical self-help literature. This is interesting more for its form than its content, as it was composed in verse not prose. The huge infusion of Greek prose scientific literature during the Middle Ages, and its translation into Arabic, set the tone for Islamic medical writing throughout our period. When writing for the commoner, however, some physicians utilized easily memorized poetry to convey fundamentals of health and healing when a physician or surgeon was not at hand. Best known was *The Poem on Medicine* by the eleventh-century Persian philosopher and physician Avicenna (Ibn Sina). The qasida is a poem of undetermined length that maintains a consistent rhyme pattern, and a rubi'a consists of four lines, the first, second, and fourth of which rhyme. A rubayat is a set of many four-line poems that are related.

The best and most prolific of these medical poets was Yusuf of Herat, a physician and son of a physician, writing in the sixteenth century. He wrote only in Persian verse and usually on medical subjects. Perhaps his earliest work in qasida is a 128-line poem on drugs ("Selected Benefits") penned in 1507. By 1530 he had entered the service of the first Mughal emperor in India, for whom he wrote his qasida "Elegy on the Protection of Health." Two short works of qasida, "Evidence from the Urine" and "Evidence from the Pulse," appeared in 1535. His most famous rubayat were "The Medicine of Yusuf" and "Collection of Benefits," the latter of which remained a popular guide down to the twentieth century. Advice for good health includes the lines,

> To keep your brain clear each day eat some meat,
> But avoid all foods which increase body heat.
> Stay not awake in the hours of the night
> And to sleep much by day is also not mete.

His advice for the corpulent rings true today:

> If you are obese, I mean covered with fat,
> I will tell you a cure that will remedy that.
> Avoid foods that give pleasure, shun comfort and sloth,
> And you'll soon have a shape that you like to look at.

On the other hand, we do have better remedies for venereal diseases today:

> Oh you who suffer from Foreigners' Pox,
> This treatment, I am sure, health's door soon unlocks.
> First an ointment of mercury wisely prepare,
> For daily applied paths of spreading it blocks.[18]

Shorter poetic medical fragments appear in other Safavid works across the period. In the eighteenth century there was a revival among Arab speakers of poetic works that discuss the same themes of self-help, diet, and herbal remedies.[19] Though embedded in a centuries-old tradition, these may have been influenced by seventeenth-century popular medical literature in English and other vernaculars, though these were rarely versified.

Laudanum and Romanticism

In the 1960s American Dr. Timothy Leary personally experimented with and advocated the recreational use of LSD. It was a drug that supposedly "expanded the mind" and increased the vision and creativity of artists and musicians. The medicine laudanum played something of the same role among poets and writers of the later eighteenth century. Laudanum was a blend of opium derivative and strong alcohol. Medically used to curb pain, it was addictive and when used in moderation induced a pleasant high that released one from inhibitions. Romanticism was a European cultural movement that abandoned the emphasis on rationality and intellect that shaped the Enlightenment and its Age of Reason. For the Romantic poet or painter, the natural world was not something to dominate and harness but to experience and to which one should succumb. An emphasis on subjective feelings replaced the search for objective knowledge among these artists. The pharmacy provided the drug that seemed to induce artificially the introspection and spontaneity of the poet; it was believed to loosen the bonds people had on their passions, releasing them to explore the world, intensify their feelings, and express themselves on the page.

The list of notable Romantic poets who experimented with or became addicted to laudanum is long and impressive. In France it included the creative circle around Chateaubriand. Among German Romantics who used laudanum were Johann Wolfgang Goethe, Friedrich Schiller, and Friedrich Schlegel; and English poets included Samuel Taylor Coleridge, Sir Walter Scott, William Wordsworth, Percy Bysshe Shelley, John Keats, and Lord Byron. For his part Coleridge had suffered several diseases when young, was given laudanum, and early on became addicted to opiates. Shelley on the other hand took the drug as a means of calming his nerves. He became dependent and was rarely without a bottle. He admitted the negative side effects of using laudanum, including uncontrollable muscle spasms, memory lapses, and bizarre dreams. Knowing it to be a poison, he came close to killing himself with the drug that supposedly enhanced poetic genius.[20]

NOTES

1. Julie Anderson, Emm Barnes, and Emma Shackleton, *The Art of Medicine: Over 2000 Years of Images and Imagination* (Chicago: University of Chicago Press, 2011), 100–101.

2. Irvine Loudon, ed., *Western Medicine: An Illustrated History* (New York: Oxford University Press, 1997), 18–22.

3. Anderson, Barnes, and Shackleton, *Art of Medicine*, 109–10, 113–18.

4. Jonathan Sawday, *The Body Emblazoned: Dissection and the Human Body in Renaissance Culture* (New York: Routledge, 1996); Benjamin A. Rifkin, Michael J. Ackerman, and Judith Folkenberg, eds., *Human Anatomy: A Visual from the Renaissance to the Digital Age* (New York: Abrams, 2006), 68–81 on Vesalius, 83–227 on other early modern illustrators; Anderson, Barnes, and Shackleton, *Art of Medicine*, 34–35.

5. For some of the images and descriptions see Anderson, Barnes, and Shackleton, *Art of Medicine*, 118–19.

6. John M. Efron, *Medicine and the German Jews: A History* (New Haven, CT: Yale University Press, 2001), 66.

7. Tobias Smollett, *The Adventures of Roderick Random* (Athens: University of Georgia Press, 2012).

8. Quotations from Paul Harper, "Tobias Smollett and the Practice of Medicine," *Yale Journal of Biology and Medicine* 2 (1930): 409–16.

9. T'ao Lee, "The Doctor in Chinese Drama," *Chinese Medical Journal* 68 (1950): 36-7.

10. Lee, "The Doctor," 38–9.

11. Lee, "The Doctor," 34–48.

12. Translation by Timothy Moody at http://moliere-in-english.com/flying_doctor.html. "Dreck" is slang for feces and "selamalec" is a parody of the Muslim Arabic greeting, a reference to the Islamic medical tradition.

13. Laurence Brockliss and Colin Jones, *The Medical World of Early Modern France* (New York: Oxford University Press, 1997), 336–44.

14. Girolamo Fracastoro, *The Sinister Shepherd: A Translation of Girolamo Fracastoro's Syphilidis sive de morbo libri tre*, trans. William van Wyck (Whitefish, MT: Kessinger, 2007); Jon Arrizabalaga, John Henderson, and Roger French, *The Great Pox: The French Disease in Renaissance Europe* (New Haven, CT: Yale University Press, 1997), 245–51.

15. Jonathan D. Spence, *Return to Dragon Mountain: Memories of a Late Ming Man* (New York: Viking, 2007), 187–88.

16. Margaret Healy, *Fictions of Disease in Early Modern England: Bodies, Plagues and Politics* (New York: Palgrave, 2002).

17. See Karol K. Weaver, *Medical Revolutionaries: The Enslaved Healers of Eighteenth-Century Saint Domingue* (Chicago: University of Illinois Press, 2006).

18. Cyril Elgood, *Safavid Medical Practice: The Practice of Medicine, Surgery, and Gynecology in Persia between 1500 and 1750* (London: Luzac, 1979), 106–15; the translations were by "Dr. Lichtward of the American Medical Mission in Meshed" and are in Elgood, *Safavid Medical Practice*, 114–15.

19. Peter E. Pormann and Emilie Savage-Smith, *Medieval Islamic Medicine* (Washington, DC: Georgetown University Press, 2007), 68, 171.

20. Thomas Dormandy, *Opium: Reality's Dark Dream* (New Haven, CT: Yale University Press, 2012), 76–84; and his *The Worst of Evils: The Fight against Pain* (New Haven, CT: Yale University Press, 2006), 134–36.

Glossary

Alembic—a setup for distilling liquids.

Amulet—an object worn by a person that is believed to protect him or her from harm.

Aseptic—free of disease-causing germs.

Asymptomatic—not displaying symptoms.

Cachexy—general physical weakness caused by malnutrition.

Chrysome—cloth in which a newborn is wrapped.

Clyster—enema.

Cupping—Western medical technique of heating a cup whose mouth was pressed against the skin creating suction and supposedly drawing out illness-causing substances in the body.

Decoct—to extract by boiling.

Emetic—substance that induces vomiting.

Endemic—disease or condition that is continually present among a population.

Enteric—related to the intestines.

Feral—usually of an animal: undomesticated or wild.

Guild—European civic organization of masters in a single occupation or profession; included physicians, surgeons, and apothecaries.

Invasive—a medical procedure that affects internal organs or structures by breaking through the skin or entering through an orifice.

Jinn—in Islam a spirit, often troublesome or malevolent.

Lithotomy—surgical procedure to remove kidney, gall bladder, or bladder stones.

Lochia—postpartum vaginal discharge of blood, mucus, and placental material.

Miasma—poisoned air that causes disease.

Motile—able to move by its own power.

Nahuatl—the language of the Aztecs.

Natalism—set of attitudes or policies that promote high rates of birth in a population.

Opiate—derivative of opium poppies.

Panacea—substance that is claimed to cure all ills.

Pandemic—outbreak of a disease across a large geographic area and for a long time.

Pathogen—disease-causing agent.

Phlebotomy (also bloodletting, bleeding)—medical procedure that opens a blood vessel to release what a practitioner considered excess blood.

Podagra—gout or inflammation of the big toe.

Poultice—a soft mixture of ingredients smeared on the body to induce healing.

Purgative—substance that causes the body to evacuate or purge a particular substance; laxative is an example.

Sepsis—blood poisoning.

Souk—Middle Eastern market.

Sudorific—drug that induces perspiration.

Suppurate—to produce and discharge pus.

Talisman—object handled or worn to bring good luck, heal, or protect one from sickness or evil.

Thoracic—related to the human chest area.

Bibliography

Aberth, John, ed. *The Black Death: The Great Mortality of 1348–1350: A Brief History with Documents*. Boston: Bedford/St. Martin's, 2005.

Alchon, Suzanne Austin. *A Pest in the Land: New World Epidemics in a Global Perspective*. Albuquerque: University of New Mexico Press, 2003.

Allen, Robert C., Tommy Bengtsson, and Martin Dribe, eds. *Living Standards in the Past: New Perspectives on Well-Being in Asia and Europe*. New York: Oxford University Press, 2005.

Anderson, Julie, Emm Barnes, and Emma Shackleton. *The Art of Medicine: Over 2000 Years of Images and Imagination*. Chicago: University of Chicago Press, 2011.

Anderson, Stuart. *Making Medicines: A Brief History of Pharmacy and Pharmaceuticals*. London: Pharmaceutical Press, 2005.

Andrews, Jonathan, and Andrew Scull. *Customers and Patrons of the Mad-Trade: The Management of Lunacy in Eighteenth-Century London, with the Complete Text of John Monro's 1766 Case Book*. Berkeley: University of California Press, 2002.

Andrews, Jonathan, and Andrew Scull. *Undertaker of the Mind: John Monro and Mad-Doctoring in Eighteenth-Century England*. Berkeley: University of California Press, 2001.

Arnold, Catharine. *Bedlam: London and Its Mad*. New York: Pocket Books, 2008.

Arnold, David. *Warm Climates and Western Medicine: The Emergence of Tropical Medicine, 1500–1900*. Atlanta, GA: Rodopi, 1996.

Arrizabalaga, Jon, John Henderson, and Roger French, eds. *The Great Pox: The French Disease in Renaissance Europe*. New Haven, CT: Yale University Press, 1997.

Ballard, Martha. *A Midwife's Tale: The Life of Martha Ballard Based on Her Diary, 1785–1812*. Edited by Laurel Ulrich. New York: Knopf, 1990.

Barnes, Linda L. *Needles, Herbs, Gods, and Ghosts: China, Healing, and the West to 1848*. Cambridge, MA: Harvard University Press, 2005.

Bell, Rudolph. *How to Do It: Guides to Good Living for Renaissance Italians*. Chicago: University of Chicago Press, 1999.

Bengtsson, Tommy, Cameron Campbell, and James Lee, eds. *Life under Pressure: Mortality and Living Standards in Europe and Asia, 1700–1900*. Cambridge, MA: MIT Press, 2004.

Berinstain, Valerie. *India and the Mughal Dynasty*. Translated by Paul G. Bahn. New York: Abrams, 2001.

Bollet, Alfred Jay. *Plagues and Poxes: The Impact of Human History on Epidemic Disease*. New York: Demos, 2004.

Borsch, Stuart J. *The Black Death in Egypt and England: A Comparative Study*. Austin: University of Texas Press, 2005.

Brandon, David. *Life in a 17th Century Coffee Shop*. Stroud, UK: Sutton, 2007.

Brentjes, Sonja. *Travelers from Europe in the Ottoman and Safavid Empires, 16th–17th Centuries: Seeking, Transforming, Discarding Knowledge*. Aldershot, UK: Ashgate, 2010.

Brockliss, Laurence, and Colin Jones. *The Medical World of Early Modern France*. New York: Oxford University Press, 1997.

Brockliss, Laurence, and Heather Montgomery, eds. *Childhood and Violence in the Western Tradition*. Woodbridge, CT: Oxbow Books, 2010.

Broman, Thomas H. *The Transformation of German Academic Medicine, 1750–1820*. New York: Cambridge University Press, 1996.

Brook, Timothy. *Vermeer's Hat: The Seventeenth Century and the Dawn of the Global World*. London: Bloomsbury Press, 2008.

Broomhall, Susan. *Women's Medical Work in Early Modern France*. New York: Manchester University Press, 2004.

Bruijn, Iris. *Ship's Surgeons of the Dutch East India Company: Commerce and the Progress of Medicine in the Eighteenth Century*. Leiden, Netherlands: Leiden University Press, 2009.

Burke, Michael E. *The Royal College of San Carlos: Surgery and Spanish Medical Reform in the Late Eighteenth Century*. Durham, NC: Duke University Press, 1977.

Burton, Robert. *Some Anatomies of Melancholy* (1621). New York: Penguin Books, 2008.

Byrne, Joseph P. *Daily Life during the Black Death*. Westport, CT: Greenwood Press, 2006.

Byrne, Joseph P. *Encyclopedia of Pestilence, Pandemics, and Plagues*. Westport, CT: Greenwood Press, 2008.

Carlin, Claire L. *Imagining Contagion in Early Modern Europe*. New York: Palgrave, 2005.

Carrell, Jennifer Lee. *The Speckled Monster: A Historical Tale of Battling Smallpox.* New York: Dutton, 2003.

Chakravarti, Paromita. "Natural Fools and the Historiography of Renaissance Folly." *Renaissance Studies* 25 (2011): 208–27.

Charlton, A. "Medical Uses of Tobacco in History." *Journal of the Royal Society of Medicine* 97 (2004): 292–96.

Chipman, Leigh. *The World of Pharmacy and Pharmacists in Mamluk Cairo.* Boston: Brill, 2010.

Coe, Sophie D., and Michael D. Coe. *The True History of Chocolate.* New York: Thames and Hudson, 1996.

Cook, Alexandra Parma, and Noble David Cook. *The Plague Files: Crisis Management in Sixteenth-Century Seville.* Baton Rouge: University of Louisiana Press, 2009.

Cook, Harold J. *Matters of Exchange: Commerce, Medicine, and Science in the Dutch Golden Age.* New Haven, CT: Yale University Press, 2007.

Cook, Noble David. *Born to Die: Disease and New World Conquest, 1492–1650.* New York: Cambridge University Press, 1998.

Cook, Noble David, and W. George Lovell, eds. *"Secret Judgments of God": Old World Disease in Colonial Spanish America.* Norman: University of Oklahoma Press, 1992.

Cooper, Donald B. *Epidemic Disease in Mexico City, 1761–1813.* Austin: University of Texas Press, 1965.

Crimmin, Patricia. "British Naval Health, 1700–1800: Improvement over Time?" In *British Military British Military and Naval Medicine, 1600–1830,* edited by Geoffrey L. Hudson, 183–200. New York: Rodopi, 2007.

Crosby, Alfred W. *The Columbian Exchange: Biological Consequences of 1492.* Westport, CT: Greenwood Press, 1972.

Crosby, Alfred W. *Ecological Imperialism: The Biological Expansion of Europe, 900–1900.* New York: Cambridge University Press, 1986.

Cunningham, Andrew, and Ole Peter Grell. *The Four Horsemen of the Apocalypse: Religion, War, Famine and Death in Reformation Europe.* New York: Cambridge University Press, 2000.

Dean, Carolyn. "Sketches of Childhood." In *Minor Omissions: Children in Latin American History and Society,* edited by Tobias Hecht, 21–51. Madison: University of Wisconsin Press, 2002.

Dikötter, Frank, Lars Laamann, and Zhou Xun. *Narcotic Culture: A History of Drugs in China.* Chicago: University of Chicago Press, 2004.

DiMarco, Vincent. *It Has Helped to Admiration: Eighteenth-Century Medical Cures from the Kitchen Book of Bridget Lane, 1737.* New York: iUniverse, 2010.

Dols, Michael W. *The Black Death in the Middle East.* Princeton, NJ: Princeton University Press, 1977.

Dols, Michael W. *Majnun: The Madman in Medieval Islamic Society.* Oxford: Clarendon Press, 1992.

Dormandy, Thomas. *Opium: Reality's Dark Dream.* New Haven, CT: Yale University Press, 2012.

Dormandy, Thomas. *The Worst of Evils: The Fight against Pain*. New Haven, CT: Yale University Press, 2006.

Duffin, Jacalyn. *Medical Miracles: Doctors, Saints and Healing in the Modern World*. New York: Cambridge University Press, 2009.

Dunlap, Barbara. "The Problems of Syphilitic Children in Eighteenth-Century France and England." In *The Secret Malady: Venereal Disease in Eighteenth-Century Britain and France*, edited by Linda Evi Meriens, 114–27. Lexington: University Press of Kentucky, 1997.

Eckman, Peter. *In the Footsteps of the Yellow Emperor: Tracing the History of Traditional Acupuncture*. San Francisco: Long River Press, 2007.

Efron, John M. *Medicine and the German Jews: A History*. New Haven, CT: Yale University Press, 2001.

Elgood, Cyril. *Safavid Medical Practice: The Practice of Medicine, Surgery, and Gynecology in Persia between 1500 and 1750*. London: Luzac, 1970.

Ellis, Harold. *The Cambridge Illustrated History of Surgery*. New York: Cambridge University Press, 2009.

Ellis, Markman. *The Coffee House: A Cultural History*. London: Orion, 2005.

Equiano, Olaudah. *The Life of Olaudah Equiano*. Mineola: Dover Books, 1995.

Evenden, Doreen. *The Midwives of Seventeenth-Century London*. New York: Cambridge University Press, 2006.

Fabbri, Christiane Nockels. "Treating Medieval Plague: The Wonderful Virtues of Theriac." *Early Science and Medicine* 12 (2007): 247–83.

Ficino, Marsilio. *Three Books on Life*. Translated by Carol Kaske and John Clark. Tempe, AZ: Medieval and Renaissance Texts and Studies, 1998.

Fields, Sherry. *Pestilence and Headcolds: Encountering Illness in Colonial Mexico*. New York: Columbia University Press, 2008.

Finucci, Valeria. " 'There's the Rub': Searching for Sexual Remedies in the New World." *Journal of Medieval and Early Modern Studies* 38 (2008): 523–57.

Finzsch, Norbert, and Robert Jütte, eds. *Institutions of Confinement: Hospitals, Asylums, and Prisons in Western Europe and North America: 1500–1950*. New York: Cambridge University Press, 1996.

Fissell, Mary E. *Vernacular Bodies: The Politics of Reproduction in Early Modern England*. New York: Oxford University Press, 2004.

Foucault, Michel. *Discipline and Punish: The Birth of the Prison*. Translated by Alan Sheridan. New York: Pantheon, 1977.

Foucault, Michel. *Madness and Civilization: A History of Insanity during the Age of Reason*. Translated by Richard Howard. New York: Pantheon, 1965.

Fracastoro, Girolamo. *The Sinister Shepherd: A Translation of Girolamo Fracastoro's Syphilidis sive de morbo libri tres*. Translated by William van Wyck. Whitefish, MT: Kessinger, 2007.

Franco, G., F. Franco, and L. Paita. "Focusing Bernardino Ramazzini's Preventive View in Health Protection." In *Contributions to the History of Occupational and Environmental Prevention*, edited by Antonio Grieco, Sergio Iavicoli, and Giovanni Berlinguer, 31–41. New York: Elsevier, 1999.

Freedman, Paul. *Out of the East: Spices and the Medieval Imagination.* New Haven, CT: Yale University Press, 2008.

French, Roger. *Dissection and Vivisection in the European Renaissance.* Burlington, VT: Ashgate, 1999.

Friedenberg, Zachary B. *Surgery over the Centuries.* London: Janus, 2009.

Furst, Lillian R., ed. *Women Healers and Physicians: Climbing a Long Hill.* Lexington: University Press of Kentucky, 1997.

Furth, Charlotte. *A Flourishing Yin: Gender in China's Medical History, 960–1665.* Berkeley: University of California Press, 1999.

Gabriel, Richard A., and Karen Metz. *A History of Military Medicine.* Vol. 2, *From the Renaissance through Modern Times.* Westport, CT: Greenwood Press, 1992.

Gately, Iain. *Drink: A Cultural History of Alcohol.* New York: Gotham Books, 2009.

Gates, William. *An Aztec Herbal: The Classic Codex of 1552.* Mineola, NY: Dover, 1939/2000.

Gavitt, Philip. *Charity and Children in Renaissance Florence: The Ospedale degli Innocenti, 1410–1536.* Ann Arbor: University of Michigan Press, 1991.

Gavitt, Philip. *Gender, Honor, and Charity in Late Renaissance Florence.* New York: Cambridge University Press, 2011.

Gelfand, Toby. *Professionalizing Modern Medicine: Paris Surgeons and Medical Science and Institutions in the Eighteenth Century.* Westport, CT: Greenwood Press, 1980.

Gélis, Jacques. *History of Childbirth: Fertility, Pregnancy, and Birth in Early Modern Europe.* Translated by Rosemary Morris. Cambridge: Polity Press, 1991.

Gentilcore, David. *Medical Charlatanism in Early Modern Italy.* New York: Oxford University Press, 2006.

Gilman, Sander, and Zhou Xun. *Smoke: A Global History of Smoking.* London: Reaktion Books, 2004.

Glynn, Ian, and Jenifer Glynn. *The Life and Death of Smallpox.* New York: Cambridge University Press, 2004.

González, Ondina E. "Down and Out in Havana: Foundlings in Eighteenth-Century Cuba." In *Minor Omissions: Children in Latin American History and Society,* edited by Tobias Hecht, 102–113. Madison: University of Wisconsin Press, 2002.

González, Ondina, and Bianca Premo, eds. *Raising an Empire: Children in Early Modern Iberia and Colonial Latin America.* Albuquerque: University of New Mexico Press, 2007.

Gorbach, Sherwood L., John G. Bartlett, and Neil R. Blacklow, eds. *Infectious Diseases.* Philadelphia: Lippincott, 2003.

Graves, Rolande. *Born to Procreate: Women and Childbirth in France from the Middle Ages to the Eighteenth Century.* New York: Peter Lang, 2001.

Green, Monica. *Making Women's Medicine Masculine: The Rise of Male Authority in Pre-modern Gynaecology.* New York: Oxford University Press, 2008.

Grehan, James. "Smoking and 'Early Modern' Sociability: The Great Tobacco Debate in the Ottoman Middle East." *American Historical Review* 111 (2006): 152–77.

Grell, Ole Peter. *Paracelsus: The Man and His Reputation, His Ideas and Their Transformation*. Leiden, Netherlands: Brill, 1998.

Grell, Ole Peter. "War, Medicine and the Military Revolution." In *The Healing Arts: Health, Disease, and Society in Europe, 1500–1800*, 257–83. Manchester, UK: Open University Press, 2004.

Griffin, J. P. "Venetian Treacle and the Foundation of Medicines Regulation." *British Journal of Clinical Pharmacology* 58 (2004): 317–25.

Gruber von Arni, Eric. *Hospital Care and the British Standing Army, 1660–1714*. Burlington, VT: Ashgate, 2006.

Hanson, Marta. *Speaking of Epidemics in Chinese Medicine: Disease and the Geographic Imagination in Late Imperial China*. New York: Routledge, 2011.

Hargreaves, A. S. "Toothdrawers in English Popular Literature." *Bulletin of the History of Dentistry* 41 (1993): 51–57.

Hargreaves, A. S. *White as Whales Bone: Dental Services in Early Modern England*. Leeds, UK: Northern Universities Press, 1998.

Harper, Paul. "Tobias Smollett and the Practice of Medicine." *Yale Journal of Biology and Medicine* 2 (1930): 409–16.

Harrison, Mark. "Disease and Medicine in the Armies of British India, 1750–1830." In *British Military and Naval Medicine, 1600–1830*, edited by Geoffrey L. Hudson, 87–120. New York: Rodopi, 2007.

Harrison, Mark. *Disease and the Modern World: 1500 to the Present*. Malden, MA: Polity Press, 2004.

Harrison, Mark. *Medicine in an Age of Commerce and Empire: Britain and Its Tropical Colonies, 1660–1830*. New York: Oxford University Press, 2010.

Harvie, David I. *Limeys: The Conquest of Scurvy*. Stroud, UK: Sutton, 2002.

Hayden, Deborah. *Pox: Genius, Madness, and the Mysteries of Syphilis*. New York: Basic Books, 2004.

Haydock, David Boyd, and Patrick Wallis. *Quackery and Commerce in Seventeenth-Century London: The Proprietary Medicine Business of Anthony Daffy*. London: Wellcome Trust, 2005.

Healy, Margaret. *Fictions of Disease in Early Modern England: Bodies, Plagues and Politics*. New York: Palgrave, 2002.

Hecht, Tobias. *Minor Omissions: Children in Latin American History and Society*. Madison: University of Wisconsin Press, 2002.

Heinrichs, Erik Anton. "The Plague Cures of Caspar Kegler: Print, Alchemy, and Medical Marketing in Sixteenth-Century Germany." *Sixteenth Century Journal* 43 (2012): 417–40.

Hopkins, Donald R. *The Greatest Killer: Smallpox in History*. Chicago: University of Chicago, 2002.

Hudson, Geoffrey. "Disabled Veterans and the State in Early Modern England." In *Disabled Veterans in History*, edited by D. A. Gerber, 117–44. Ann Arbor: University of Michigan Press, 2000.

Hudson, Geoffrey. "Internal Influences in the Making of the English Military Hospital: The Early-Eighteenth-Century Greenwich." In *British Military and Naval Medicine, 1600–1830*, edited by Geoffrey L. Hudson, 253–72. New York: Rodopi, 2007.

Hunter, Paul. *Waterborne Disease: Epidemiology and Ecology*. New York: Wiley, 1997.

Issac, Peter. "Pills and Print." In *Medicine, Morality and the Book Trade*, edited by Robin Myers and Michael Harris, 25–48. New Castle, DE: Oak Knoll Press, 1998.

Jannetta, Ann Bowman. *Epidemics and Mortality in Early Modern Japan*. Princeton, NJ: Princeton University Press, 1987.

Jenner, Edward. *Vaccination against Smallpox*. Amherst, MA: Prometheus, 1996.

Jones, Colin. "The Construction of the Hospital Patient in Early Modern France." In *Institutions of Confinement: Hospitals, Asylums, and Prisons in Western Europe and North America*, edited by Norbert Finzsch and Robert Jütte, 55–74. New York: Cambridge University Press, 1996.

Jones, Colin. "Pulling Teeth in Eighteenth-Century Paris." *Past and Present* 166 (2000): 100–45.

Jones, Susan D. *Death in a Small Package: A Short History of Anthrax*. Baltimore: Johns Hopkins University Press, 2010.

Jütte, Robert. "Syphilis and Confinement: Hospitals in Early Modern Germany." In *Institutions of Confinement: Hospitals, Asylums, and Prisons in Western Europe and North America*, edited by Norbert Finzsch and Robert Jütte, 97–115. New York: Cambridge University Press, 1996.

Kidwell, Clara Sue. "Aztec and European Medicine in the New World, 1521–1600." In *The Anthropology of Medicine: From Culture to Method*, edited by Lola Romanacci-Ross, Daniel E. Moerman, and Laurence R. Tancredi, 19–30. Westport, CT: Bergin and Garvey, 1997.

Kilpatrick, Robert. " 'Living in the Light': Dispensaries, Philanthropy, and Medical Reform in Late Eighteenth-Century London." In *The Medical Enlightenment of the Eighteenth Century*, edited by Andrew Cunningham and Roger French, 254–80. New York: Cambridge University Press, 1990.

King, Helen. *Midwifery, Obstetrics and the Rise of Gynaecology: The Uses of the Sixteenth-Century Compendium*. Burlington, VT: Ashgate, 2007.

King, Roger. *The Making of the "Dentiste," c. 1650–1760*. Aldershot, UK: Ashgate, 1998.

Kiple, Kenneth F., ed. *Cambridge Historical Dictionary of Disease*. New York: Cambridge University Press, 2003.

Kiple, Kenneth F., and Stephen Beck. *Biological Consequences of the European Expansion, 1450–1800*. Aldershot, UK: Ashgate, 1997.

Klairmont-Lingo, A. "Women Healers and the Medical Marketplace of Sixteenth-Century Lyon." *Dynamis* 19 (1999): 79–94.

Knight, Katherine. *How Shakespeare Cleaned His Teeth and Cromwell Treated His Warts: Secrets of the Seventeenth-Century Medicine Cabinet*. Stroud, UK: Tempus, 2006.

Kusukawa, Sachiko. "The Medical Renaissance of the Sixteenth Century: Vesalius, Medical Humanism, and Bloodletting." In *The Healing Arts, 1500–1800*, edited by Peter Elmer, 58–83. Manchester, UK: Manchester University Press, 2004.

Laroche, Rebecca. *Medical Authority and Englishwomen's Herbal Texts, 1550–1650*. Burlington, VT: Ashgate, 2009.

Lawlor, Clark. *From Melancholia to Prozac: A History of Depression*. New York: Oxford University Press, 2012.

Laws, Bill. *Spade, Skirret, and Parsnip: The Curious History of Vegetables*. Stroud, UK: Sutton, 2004.

Lee, T'ao. "The Doctor in Chinese Drama." *Chinese Medical Journal* 68 (1950): 34–48.

Leiby, John S. "San Hipólito's Treatment of the Mentally Ill in Mexico City, 1589–1650." *The Historian* 54 (1992): 491–98.

Leti, Geneviève. *Santé et société esclavagiste à la Martinique*. Paris: Editions L'Harmattan, 1998.

Leung, Angela Ki Che. *Leprosy in China: A History*. New York: Columbia University Press, 2009.

Lindemann, Mary. *Medicine and Society in Early Modern Europe*. New York: Cambridge University Press, 1996.

Lipsett-Rivera, Sonya. "Model Children and Models for Children in Early Mexico." In *Minor Omissions: Children in Latin American History and Society*, edited by Tobias Hecht, 52–71. Madison: University of Wisconsin Press, 2002.

Li Shih-chen. *Chinese Medical Herbs: A Modern Edition of a Classic Sixteenth-Century Manual*. Mineola, NY: Dover, 1973.

Liu, Xinru. *The Silk Road in World History*. New York: Oxford University Press, 2010.

Loudon, Irvine, ed. *Western Medicine: An Illustrated History*. New York: Oxford University Press, 1997.

Maehle, Andreas-Holger. *Drugs on Trial: Experimental Pharmacology and Therapeutic Innovation in the Eighteenth Century*. Atlanta, GA: Rodopi, 1999.

Mantovani, A., et al. "A Historical Overview of Occupational Diseases Connected with Animals." In *Contributions to the History of Occupational and Environmental Prevention*, edited by Antonio Grieco, Sergio Iavicoli, and Giovanni Berlinguer, 239–46. New York: Elsevier, 1999.

Marland, Hilary, ed. *The Art of Midwifery: Early Modern Midwives in Europe*. New York: Routledge, 1993.

Marland, Hilary, and Margaret Pelling. *The Task of Healing: Medicine, Religion, and Gender in England and the Netherlands, 1450–1800*. Rotterdam: Erasmus, 1996.

Martensen, R. L. *The Brain Takes Shape: An Early History*. New York: Oxford University Press, 2004.

Martin, A. Lynn. *Alcohol, Violence, and Disorder in Traditional Europe*. Kirksville, MO: Truman State University Press, 2009.

Matossian, Mary K. *Poisons of the Past: Molds, Epidemics, and History*. New Haven, CT: Yale University Press, 1989.

Matthee, Rudi. *The Pursuit of Pleasure: Drugs and Stimulants in Iranian History, 1500–1900*. Princeton, NJ: Princeton University Press, 2005.

McCaa, Robert. "Spanish and Nahuatl Views on Smallpox and Demographic Catastrophe in Mexico." *Journal of Interdisciplinary History* 25 (1995): 397–431.

McClure, Margaret. *Coram's Children: The London Foundling Hospital in the Eighteenth Century*. New Haven, CT: Yale University Press, 1981.

McNeill, J. R. *Mosquito Empires: Ecology and War in the Greater Caribbean, 1620–1914*. New York: Cambridge University Press, 2010.

Meriens, Linda Evi. *The Secret Malady: Venereal Disease in Eighteenth-Century Britain and France*. Lexington: University Press of Kentucky, 1997.

Monahan, W. Gregory. *Year of Sorrows: The Great Famine of 1709 in Lyon*. Columbus: Ohio State University Press, 1993.

Moran, Bruce T. *Distilling Knowledge: Alchemy, Chemistry, and the Scientific Revolution*. Cambridge, MA: Harvard University Press, 2005.

Morens, David. "Characterizing a 'New' Disease: Epizootic and Epidemic Anthrax, 1769–1780." *Journal of Public Health* 93 (2003): 886–93.

Murphey, Rhoades. *Ottoman Warfare, 1500–1700*. New Brunswick, NJ: Rutgers University Press, 1999.

Nappi, Carla. *The Monkey and the Inkpot: Natural History and Its Transformation in Early Modern China*. Cambridge, MA: Harvard University Press, 2009.

Needham, Joseph. *Science and Civilisation in China*. Vol. 6, *Biology and Biological Technology*, Part 6, *Medicine*. Edited by Nathan Sivin. New York: Cambridge University Press, 2000.

Newson, Linda. *Conquest and Pestilence in the Early Spanish Philippines*. Honolulu: University of Hawaii Press, 2009.

Ng, Vivian W. *Madness in Late Imperial China: From Illness to Deviance*. Norman: University of Oklahoma Press, 1990.

Numbers, Ronald, ed. *Medicine in the New World: New Spain, New France, and New England*. Knoxville: University of Tennessee Press, 1987.

Nutton, Vivian. "The Fortunes of Galen." In *The Cambridge Companion to Galen*, edited by R. J. Hankinson, 355–90. New York: Cambridge University Press, 2008.

Ortiz de Montellano, Bernard R. *Aztec Medicine, Health, and Nutrition*. New Brunswick, NJ: Rutgers University Press, 1990.

Osterfeld, Richard S., Felicia Keesing, and Valerie T. Eviner, eds. *Infectious Disease Ecology*. Princeton, NJ: Princeton University Press, 2008.

Osterhammel, Jürgen, and Niels Petersson. *Globalization: A Short History*. Princeton, NJ: Princeton University Press, 2005.

Packard, Randall M. *The Making of a Tropical Disease: A Short History of Malaria*. Baltimore: Johns Hopkins University Press, 2007.

Paice, Edward. *Wrath of God: The Great Lisbon Earthquake of 1755*. Waltham, MA: Quercus, 2010.

Palmer, Richard. "Pharmacy in the Republic of Venice in the Sixteenth Century." In *The Medical Renaissance of the Sixteenth Century*, edited by Andrew Wear, R. K. French, and I. M. Lonie, 100–117. New York: Cambridge University Press, 1985.

Paré, Ambroise. *The Apologie and Treatise of Ambroise Paré Containing the Voyages Made into Divers Places with Many of His Writings upon Surgery*. Edited by G. Keynes. Mineola: Dover Books, 1968.

Parker, Geoffrey. *The Military Revolution: Military Innovation and the Rise of the West, 1500–1800*. New York: Cambridge University Press, 1989.

Patterson, K. David. *Pandemic Influenza, 1700–1900*. Totowa, NJ: Rowman and Littlefield, 1986.

Pelling, Margaret. *The Common Lot: Sickness, Medical Occupations and the Urban Poor in Early Modern England*. New York: Longman, 1998.

Perkins, Wendy. *Midwifery and Medicine in Early Modern France: Louise Bourgeois*. Exeter, UK: University of Exeter Press, 1996.

Peterson, Kaara L. *Popular Medicine, Hysterical Disease, and Social Controversy in Shakespeare's England*. Burlington, VT: Ashgate, 2010.

Phillips, Derek. *Well-Being in Amsterdam's Golden Age*. Amsterdam: Pallas, 2008.

Piekarski, C. "Some Aspects of Early Developments in Occupational Health Care in the German Mining Industry." In *Contributions to the History of Occupational and Environmental Prevention*, edited by Antonio Grieco, Sergio Iavicoli, and Giovanni Berlinguer, 187–93. New York: Elsevier, 1999.

Pierce, John R., and Jim Writer. *Yellow Jack*. Hoboken, NJ: Wiley, 2005.

Ping, Chen, ed. *History and Development of Traditional Medicine*. Beijing: Science Press, 1999.

Pollock, Linda. *With Faith and Physic: The Life of a Tudor Gentlewoman, Lady Grace Mildmay, 1552–1620*. London: Collins and Brown, 1993.

Pormann, Peter E., and Emilie Savage-Smith. *Medieval Islamic Medicine*. Washington, DC: Georgetown University Press, 2007.

Porter, Dorothy, ed. *The History of Public Health and the Modern State*. Amsterdam: Rodopi, 1996.

Porter, Roy, ed. *Cambridge History of Medicine*. New York: Cambridge University Press, 2006.

Porter, Roy. *Quacks: Fakers and Charlatans in Medicine*. Stroud, UK: Tempus, 2001.

Porter, Roy, and Mikulas Teich. *Drugs and Narcotics in History*. New York: Cambridge University Press, 1997.

Pretel, A., and M. Ruiz Bremón. "Social and Medical Protection for the Working Population in the Age of Philip II." In *Contributions to the History of Occupational and Environmental Prevention*, edited by Antonio Grieco, Sergio Iavicoli, and Giovanni Berlinguer, 159–70. New York: Elsevier, 1999.

Quinn, Tom. *Flu: A Social History of Influenza*. London: New Holland, 2008.

Radden, Jennifer, ed. *The Nature of Melancholy: From Aristotle to Kristeva*. New York: Oxford University Press, 2000.

Ramazzini, Bernardino. *The Diseases of Workers*. Translated by Wilmer C. Wright. Chicago: University of Chicago Press, 1940.

Ransford, Oliver. *Bid the Sickness Cease: Disease in the History of Black Africa*. London: John Murray, 1983.

Rawcliffe, Carole. *Leprosy in Medieval England*. Rochester, NY: Boydell, 2006.

Read, Kirk D. *Birthing Bodies in Early Modern France*. Burlington, VT: Ashgate, 2011.

Riddle, John. *Dioscorides on Pharmacy and Medicine*. Austin: University of Texas Press,1985.

Riddle, John. *Eve's Herbs: A History of Contraception and Abortion in the West*. Cambridge, MA: Harvard University Press, 1997.

Rifkin, Benjamin A., Michael J. Ackerman, and Judith Folkenberg, eds. *Human Anatomy: A Visual History from the Renaissance to the Digital Age*. New York: Abrams, 2006.

Risse, Gunter B. "Before the Clinic Was 'Born': Methodological Perspectives in Hospital History." In *Institutions of Confinement: Hospitals, Asylums, and Prisons in Western Europe and North America*, edited by Norbert Finzsch and Robert Jütte, 75–96. New York: Cambridge University Press, 1996.

Rocco, Fiammetta. *Quinine, Malaria and the Quest for a Cure That Changed the World*. New York: HarperCollins, 2003.

Ruff, Julius R. *Violence in Early Modern Europe, 1500–1800*. New York: Cambridge University Press, 2001.

Saif, Liana. "The Arabic Theory of Astral Influence in Early Modern Medicine." *Renaissance Studies* 25 (2011): 609–26.

Sawday, Jonathan. *The Body Emblazoned: Dissection and the Human Body in Renaissance Culture*. New York: Routledge, 1996.

Scheid, Volker. *Currents of Tradition in Chinese Medicine, 1626–2006*. Seattle, WA: Eastland Press, 2007.

Schendel, Gordon. *Medicine in Mexico: From Aztec Herbs to Betatrons*. Austin: University of Texas Press, 1968.

Schiebinger, Londa. *Plants and Empire: Colonial Bioprospecting in the Atlantic World*. Cambridge, MA: Harvard University Press, 2004.

Schiebinger, Londa, and Claudia Swan, eds. *Colonial Botany: Science, Commerce, and Politics in the Early Modern World*. Philadelphia: University of Pennsylvania Press, 2005.

Schmidt, Jeremy. *Melancholy and the Care of the Soul: Religion, Moral Philosophy and Madness in Early Modern England*. Burlington, VT: Ashgate, 2007.

Schrader, Catharina. *"Mother and Child Were Saved": The Memoirs (1693–1740) of the Frisian Midwife Catharina Schrader*. Translated by Hilary Marland. Amsterdam: Rodopi, 1987.

Scull, Andrew. *The Disturbing History of Hysteria*. New York: Oxford University Press, 2009.

Shah, Saria. *The Fever: How Malaria Has Ruled Mankind for 500,000 Years*. New York: Farrar, Straus, Giroux, 2010.

Shahar, Shulamith. *Childhood in the Middle Ages*. New York: Routledge, 1992.

Sharp, Jane. *The Midwives' Book: Or The Whole Art of Midwifery Discovered* (1621). New York: Garland, 1985.

Shearing, Colin R. *Opium: A Journey through Time*. London: Mercury Books, 2004.

Shefer-Mossensohn, Miri. *Ottoman Medicine: Healing and Medical Institutions, 1500–1700*. Albany: State University of New York Press, 2009.

Sheridan, Richard. *Doctors and Slaves: A Medical and Demographic History of Slavery in the British West Indies, 1680–1834*. New York: Cambridge University Press, 1985.

Sherman, Irwin W. *The Power of Plague*. Washington, DC: American Society for Microbiology, 2006.

Shorter, Edward. *A History of Psychiatry: From the Era of the Asylum*. New York: Wiley, 1998.

Shoshan, Boaz. "The State and Madness in Medieval Islam." *International Journal of Middle East Studies* 35 (2003): 329–40.

Shrady, Nicholas. *The Last Day: Wrath, Ruin, and Reason in the Great Lisbon Earthquake of 1755*. New York: Viking, 2008.

Slack, Paul. "Responses to Plague in Early Modern Europe: The Implications of Public Health." *Social Research* 55 (1988): 433–53.

Smith, Leonard. *Lunatic Hospitals in Georgian England, 1750–1830*. London: Routledge, 2007.

Smith, Virginia. *Clean: A History of Personal Hygiene and Purity*. New York: Palgrave Macmillan, 2007.

Smollett, Tobias. *The Adventures of Roderick Random*. Athens: University of Georgia Press, 2012.

Soustelle, Jacques. *Daily Life of the Aztecs*. London: Phoenix Press, 1961/2002.

Spence, Jonathan D. *Return to Dragon Mountain: Memories of a Late Ming Man*. New York: Viking, 2007.

Stannard, Jerry. *Herbs and Herbalism in the Middle Ages and Renaissance*. Edited by Richard Kay and Katherine E. Stannard. Burlington, VT: Ashgate Variorum, 1999.

Stearns, Justin. *Infectious Ideas: Contagion in Premodern Islamic and Christian Thought in the Western Mediterranean*. Baltimore: Johns Hopkins University Press, 2011.

Stein, Claudia. *Negotiating the French Pox in Early Modern Germany*. Burlington, VT: Ashgate, 2009.

Stevenson, Christine. "From Palace to Hut: The Architecture of Military and Naval Medicine." In *British Military and Naval Medicine, 1600–1830*, edited by Geoffrey L. Hudson, 27–52. New York: Rodopi, 2007.

Strocchia, Sharon. "The Nun Apothecaries of Renaissance Florence: Marketing Medicines in the Convent." *Renaissance Studies* 25 (2011): 627–47.

Sweet, James H. *Domingos Álvares, African Healing, and the Intellectual History of the Atlantic World*. Chapel Hill: University of North Carolina Press, 2011.

Swiderski, Richard. *Anthrax: A History*. Jefferson, NC: McFarland, 2004.

Terpstra, Nicholas. *Lost Girls: Sex and Death in Renaissance Florence*. Baltimore: Johns Hopkins University Press, 2010.

Unschuld, Paul U. *Forgotten Treasures of Ancient Chinese Medicine: The I-hsüeh Yüan Liu Lun of 1757, by Hsü Ta-ch'un*. Brookline, MA: Paradigm, 1998.

Unschuld, Paul U. *Medical Ethics in Imperial China: A Study in Historical Anthropology*. Berkeley: University of California Press, 1979.

Unschuld, Paul U. *Medicine in China: A History of Ideas*. 2nd ed. Berkeley: University of California Press, 2010.

Unschuld, Paul U. *Medicine in China: A History of Pharmaceutics*. Berkeley: University of California Press, 1986.

Unschuld, Paul U. *What Is Medicine? Western and Eastern Approaches to Healing*. Translated by Karen Reimers. Berkeley: University of California Press, 2009.

van de Pol, Lotte. *The Burgher and the Whore: Prostitution in Early Modern Amsterdam*. New York: Oxford University Press, 2011.

Vanja, Christina. "Madhouses, Children's Wards, and Clinics: The Development of Insane Asylums in Germany." In *Institutions of Confinement: Hospitals, Asylums, and Prisons in Western Europe and North America*, edited by Norbert Finzsch and Robert Jütte, 117–32. New York: Cambridge University Press, 1996.

Veith, Ilza, trans. *The Yellow Emperor's Classic of Internal Medicine*. Berkeley: University of California Press, 2002.

Vesalius, Andreas. *On the Fabric of the Human Body (1543)*. 5 vols. Translated by William Frank Richardson. Novato, CA: Norman, 2003–9.

Vila, Anne C. *Enlightenment and Pathology: Sensibility in the Literature and Medicine of Eighteenth-Century France*. Baltimore: Johns Hopkins University Press, 1998.

Voeks, Robert. "African Medicine and Magic." *Geographical Reviews* 83 (1993): 66–79.

Waite, Gloria M. *A History of Traditional Medicine and Health Care in Pre-colonial East-Central Africa*. Lewiston, NY: Edwin Mellen, 1993.

Wallis, Patrick. "Consumption, Retailing, and Medicine in Early Modern London." *Economic History Review* 61 (2008): 26–53.

Wang, Zhenguo. *History and Development of Traditional Chinese Medicine*. Beijing: Science Press, 1999.

Watts, Sheldon. *Disease and Medicine in World History*. New York: Routledge, 2003.

Weaver, Karol K. *Medical Revolutionaries: The Enslaved Healers of Eighteenth-Century Saint Domingue*. Chicago: University of Illinois Press, 2006.

Webb, James L. A., Jr. *Humanity's Burden: A Global History of Malaria*. New York: Cambridge University Press, 2009.

Webster, Charles. *Paracelsus: Medicine, Magic, and Mission at the End of Time.* New Haven, CT: Yale University Press, 2008.

Whaley, Leigh. *Women and the Practice of Medical Care in Early Modern Europe, 1400–1800.* New York: Palgrave Macmillan, 2011.

Wilbert, Johannes. *Tobacco and Shamanism in South America.* New Haven, CT: Yale University Press, 1987.

Will, Pierre-Etienne. *Bureaucracy and Famine in Eighteenth-Century China.* Stanford, CA: Stanford University Press, 1990.

Will, Pierre-Etienne, and R. Bin Wong, eds. *Nourish the People: The State Civilian Granary System in China, 1650–1850.* Ann Arbor: University of Michigan, 1991.

Wilson, Lindsay. *Women and Medicine in the French Enlightenment: The Debate over Maladies des Femmes.* Baltimore: Johns Hopkins University Press, 1993.

Withey, Alun. " 'Persons That Live Remote from London': Apothecaries and the Medical Marketplace in Seventeenth- and Eighteenth-Century Wales." *Bulletin of the History of Medicine* 85 (2011): 222–47.

Woods, Robert. *Death before Birth: Fetal Health and Mortality in Historical Perspective.* New York: Oxford University Press, 2009.

Wooley, Benjamin. *Heal Thyself: Nicholas Culpeper and the Seventeenth-Century Struggle to Bring Medicine to the People.* New York: HarperCollins, 2004.

Woolley, Hannah. *The Gentlewoman's Companion; or, A Guide to the Female Sex: The Complete Text of 1675.* Totnes, UK: Prospect Books, 2001.

Wright, John. *A History of War Surgery.* Stroud, UK: Amberley, 2011.

Wu, Yi-Li. *Reproducing Women: Medicine, Metaphor, and Childbirth in Late Imperial China.* Berkeley: University of California Press, 2010.

Yangwen, Zheng. *The Social Life of Opium in China.* New York: Cambridge University Press, 2005.

Yuan-Ling, Chao. *Medicine and Society in Late Imperial China.* New York: Peter Lang, 2009.

Zinsser, Hans. *Fleas, Rats and History.* Boston: Little, Brown, 1963.

Zumthor, Paul. *Daily Life in Rembrandt's Holland.* Stanford, CA: Stanford University Press,1994.

Index

About the Author

JOSEPH P. BYRNE is a historian and professor of humanities in the Honors Program at Belmont University in Nashville, Tennessee. He has written *The Black Death* (Greenwood, 2004), *Daily Life during the Black Death* (Greenwood, 2006), and *Encyclopedia of the Black Death* (ABC-CLIO, 2012), and edited the *Encyclopedia of Pestilence, Pandemics, and Plagues* (Greenwood, 2008). He serves as series editor of Health and Wellness in Daily Life.